Helion & Company Limited
Unit 8 Amherst Business Centre
Budbrooke Road
Warwick
CV34 5WE
England
Tel. 01926 499 619
Email: info@helion.co.uk
Website: www.helion.co.uk
Twitter: @helionbooks
Visit our blog http://blog.helion.co.uk/



Designed & typeset by Farr out Publications, Wokingham, Berkshire
Cover design by Paul Hewitt, Battlefield Design (www.battlefield-design.co.uk)
Printed by Henry Ling Limited, Dorchester, Dorset



ISBN 978-1-913118-65-5

British Library Cataloguing-in-Publication Data
A catalogue record for this book is available from the British Library



We always welcome receiving book proposals from prospective authors.

# CONTENTS

Abbreviations 2

Introduction 3

1 Indian and Pakistan Armies of 1999 8
2 Rival Air Forces 19
3 Nuclear Factor 28
4 War Plans 34
5 Intelligence Failure 41
6 Orders of Battle in Kargil 45
7 Operation Vijay 51
8 Gunner's War 67
9 Operation Safed-Sagar – The IAF's Campaign 69
10 Diplomatic Endgame 76

Bibliography 77

Notes 78

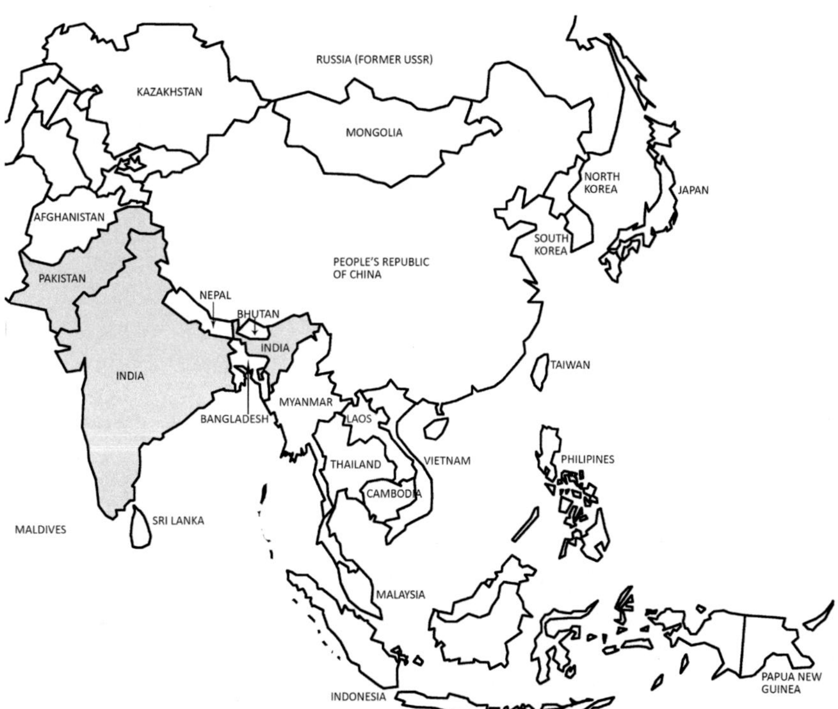


Note: In order to simplify the use of this book, all names, locations and geographic designations are as provided in *The Times World Atlas*, or other traditionally accepted major sources of reference, as of the time of described events.

**Dedicated to the late Brigadier Gurmeet Kanwal, whose encouragement and assistance were invaluable.**

# ABBREVIATIONS

| | |
|---|---|
| **AAA** | anti-aircraft artillery |
| **AAC** | Army Aviation Corps (India) |
| **AAD** | Army Air Defence (India) |
| **AB** | air base |
| **ADC** | Air Defence Command (India) |
| **ADCC** | Air Defence Command Centre (India) |
| **ADGES** | Air Defence Ground Environment System (India) |
| **AGPL** | Actual Ground Position Line |
| **AIADMK** | *All-India Anna Dravida Munnetra Kazhagam* (All India Anna Dravidan Progressive Federation) |
| **AM** | Air Marshal (military commissioned officer rank, equivalent to Lieutenant General) |
| **An** | Antonov (the design bureau led by Oleg Antonov) |
| **APC** | armoured personnel carrier |
| **ARC** | Aviation Research Centre (India) |
| **ARDE** | Armament Research and Development Establishment (India) |
| **ARN/S** | Army Reserve North/South (Pakistan) |
| **ASC** | Army Service Corps (India) |
| **ASCC** | Air Standardisation Coordinating Committee |
| **ATGM** | Anti-Tank Guided Missile |
| **BADZ** | Base Air Defence Zone |
| **BARC** | Bhabha Atomic Research Centre |
| **BIT** | Brigade Intelligence Team |
| **BJP** | Bharatiya Janata Party (India) |
| **BSF** | Border Security Force (India) |
| **CADA** | Corps of Air Defence Artillery (India) |
| **CBRN** | chemical, biological, radiological, nuclear |
| **CCRP** | continuously controlled release point |
| **CEP** | circular error probable |
| **CO** | commanding officer |
| **COIN** | counterinsurgency |
| **CRC** | control and reporting centre |
| **DGMI** | Director General Military Intelligence (India) |
| **DRDO** | Defence Research and Development Organization (India) |
| **ELINT** | electronic intelligence |
| **EME** | Electrical and Mechanical Engineers |
| **FAA** | forward assembly area |
| **FCNA** | Force Command Northern Areas (Pakistan) |
| **FF** | Frontier Force (Pakistan) |
| **GBP** | British Pounds Sterling |
| **GOC** | general officer commanding |
| **GPS** | Global Positioning System |
| **GR** | Gurkha Rifles |
| **HAWS** | High Altitude Warfare School (India) |
| **HEER** | high explosive extended-range |
| **HMG** | heavy machinegun |
| **HU** | Helicopter Unit (Indian Air Force) |
| **IAF** | Indian Air Force |
| **IAK** | Indian Administered Kashmir |
| **IAP** | international airport |
| **IB** | Intelligence Bureau (India) |
| **ICV** | infantry combat vehicle |
| **IFV** | infantry fighting vehicle |
| **IFG** | Indian Field Gun |
| **IFSU** | Intelligence and Field Surveillance Unit |
| **INC** | Indian National Congress |
| **INSAS** | Indian Small Arms System |
| **IRBM** | intermediate-range ballistic missile |
| **ISI** | Inter-Services Intelligence (Pakistan) |
| **JAK LI** | Jammu and Kashmir Light Infantry |
| **JCO** | Junior Commissioned Officer |
| **JIC** | Joint Intelligence Committee |
| **LAC** | Line of Actual Control |
| **LDP** | laser designation pod |
| **LFG** | Light Field Gun (India) |
| **LGB** | laser guided bomb |
| **LoC** | Line of Control |
| **MANPADs** | man-portable air defence system |
| **MBRL** | multi-barrel rocket launcher |
| **MBT** | main battle tank |
| **MiG** | Mikoyan i Gurevich (the design bureau led by Artyom Ivanovich Mikoyan and Mikhail Iosifovich Gurevich, also known as OKB-155 or MMZ 'Zenit') |
| **MI** | Military Intelligence (India) |
| **MMG** | medium machinegun (FN-MAG on a tripod mount) |
| **MOF** | Mobile Observation Flight |
| **MOP** | Mobile Observation Post |
| **MRBM** | medium range ballistic missile |
| **NLI** | Northern Light Infantry (Pakistan) |
| **OC** | officer in command |
| **OCU** | Operational Conversion Unit |
| **OCU** | Operational Training Unit |
| **PAF** | Pakistan Air Force |
| **PAK** | Pakistan Administered Kashmir |
| **Para SF** | Paratroop Regiment (Special Forces [Capable]) |
| **PML-N** | Pakistan Muslim League (Nawaz) |
| **POK** | Pakistan Occupied Kashmir |
| **Raj Rif** | Rajputana Rifles (India) |
| **RAPID** | Reorganized Army Plains Infantry Division (India) |
| **RAF** | Royal Air Force (of the United Kingdom) |
| **RAW** | Research and Analysis Wing (India) |
| **RR** | Rasthtriya Rifles (India) |
| **SAM** | surface-to-air missile |
| **SFF** | Special Frontier Force (India) |
| **SIGINT** | signals intelligence |
| **SLR** | Self Loading Rifle |
| **Sqn** | squadron |
| **SRBM** | short range ballistic missile |
| **SSG** | Special Services Group (Pakistan) |
| **SSM** | Surface to Surface Missile |
| **SU** | signals unit |
| **TBRL** | Terminal Ballistic Research Laboratory (India) |
| **TEL** | transporter erector launcher |
| **TNW** | tactical nuclear weapon |
| **TRU** | transportable radar unit |
| **UAV** | unmanned aerial vehicle |
| **WASO** | Winter Air Support Operations |
| **WSO** | Weapons System Officer |

# INTRODUCTION

The Kargil War between the Republic of India and the Islamic Republic of Pakistan might be deemed to have started on 3 May 1999 and ended on 26 July 1999, making it a relatively long conflict by the standards of the Indian subcontinent. What began with an infiltration by the troops of the Northern Light Infantry Brigade of the Pakistani Army, supported by separatist 'Mujahidden' combatants into Indian controlled territory, saw the first use of air power by India since the 1971 India-Pakistan War and marked a turning point in relations between the two nations, increasing India's distrust of Pakistan and placing little faith in that country's civilian leadership, which, as fate would have it, was soon toppled.

The war was the subcontinent's media war, with Indian journalists from the dynamic and diverse Indian print media, as well as a new generation of young and competent television correspondents, flocking to the Kargil region to give first-hand accounts of the conflict. This helped to cement support for the war among the Indian public, which was treated to the spectacle of coffins draped in the Indian tricolour coming back from the battlefield. Correspondents to the Kargil theatre of operations also brought home to the Indian public the effort of the Indian Army and the conditions under which operations were conducted.

From an Indian perspective, the Kargil conflict brought out serious shortcomings in India's national security apparatus, caused much internal debate and ultimately led to an expert panel review of the Kargil conflict and the failures which allowed the Pakistani incursion to occur. The report produced by the Kargil Review Committee, was released and published in a redacted form and forms an important body of work on the subject of the war, being unsparing in criticism, recommending major changes to the existing system as well as crediting the ability of even the flawed Indian system to respond effectively to a threat.

From a Pakistani perspective, it is rather unfortunate that even to date there is a degree of reticence to acknowledge the extent of Pakistan's role in the conflict, the units of its armed forces involved, as well as the extent of their losses. It was only after a gap of thirteen years that the names of some of the soldiers of the NLI were acknowledged to have fallen in combat during the Kargil conflict. Even to date, despite a few books on the subject, Pakistan has not taken full ownership of its responsibility for the conflict.

The Kargil War was South Asia's first post-nuclear conflict, coming as it did roughly a year after both countries conducted nuclear tests. The war showed the limits of nuclear deterrence and demonstrated that limited conventional armed conflict was still possible despite the wider prospect of nuclear escalation. To this end, escalation management proved to be important.

Finally, the Kargil War also demonstrated that tactically brilliant operations could be strategically disastrous. Pakistan's execution of the incursions was nothing short of brilliant. However, it failed miserably to gauge its adversary's response, capacity, resolve, professionalism and determination – a trend which continues even today.

## Political Background

In early 1999, less than a year after both countries detonated nuclear weapons, there were genuine rays of hope for a degree of peaceful coexistence between the two rival countries. This was no mean feat as the two countries had a long post-independence history of tension and conflict. What follows is by no means a comprehensive account of the India-Pakistan conflicts prior to 1999 but is a rather brief overview of a rocky relationship between two closely related countries.

## A Rivalry based on Partition

In 1947, the entity that was British India gained independence, accompanied by a brutal and bloody partition.

The former British Indian Empire was divided in 1947 and two countries now existed. Pakistan, created at the behest of some elements from the Muslim community and in particular its leadership under Muhammad Ali Jinnah, was itself divided into East and West Pakistan, separated by over 1,000 miles of India in between.

Partition was accompanied by bloody communal riots which saw roughly 1 million persons killed and massive migrations as some Muslims moved to Pakistan while the overwhelming majority of Hindus and Sikhs located in territory allocated to Pakistan moved to India.

States ruled by royal families were given an option to join India or Pakistan, though some tried to become independent. The princely states of Hyderabad and Jundagh were absorbed into India in 1948 after some armed confrontation. However, the biggest problem came with respect to the princely state of Jammu and Kashmir where a majority Muslim population lived under a Hindu ruler. In this state, the territories of Gilgit and Baltistan fell without a shot being fired when a garrison of Kashmiri troops, under British officers, unilaterally declared allegiance to Pakistan and presented the Maharaja with a fait accompli.

## The 1948 Kashmir War[1]

A carefully orchestrated military operation, which saw Pakistani supported tribesmen stage an invasion of the state, led to the collapse of the Kashmiri State forces and several instances where Muslim soldiers mutinied and killed their Hindu comrades. Faced with this situation, Maharaja Hari Singh signed an instrument of accession to India. In 1948, the first Kashmir War was fought between the Indian troops and Pakistani Pathans invading from the northwest of the Kashmir region. The conflict ended with an Indian appeal to the UN which led to a ceasefire. India held some two thirds of the state with the rest in Pakistani hands. There was also a mutual agreement to a formation of a Line of Control (LOC), the Cease Fire Line that the troops of both nations were withdrawn behind. However, while the LOC was quite viable, the plans for a plebiscite fell apart. The plebiscite had a number of preconditions which formed part of UN resolution 47 of 1948, dated 21 April 1948.[2] This recommended a non-binding formula aimed at resolving the dispute. Noteworthy in the aforesaid resolution is that the Government of Pakistan should undertake to use its best endeavours:[3]

> (a) To secure the withdrawal from the State of Jammu and Kashmir of tribesmen and Pakistani Nationals not normally resident therein, who have entered the State for the purposes of fighting and to prevent any intrusion into the State of such elements and any furnishing of material aid to those fighting in the State.

The presence of Indian troops was to be reduced to a minimum – but they were not to be completely withdrawn. Pakistan has not withdrawn any troops or citizens from the area concerned. Moreover,

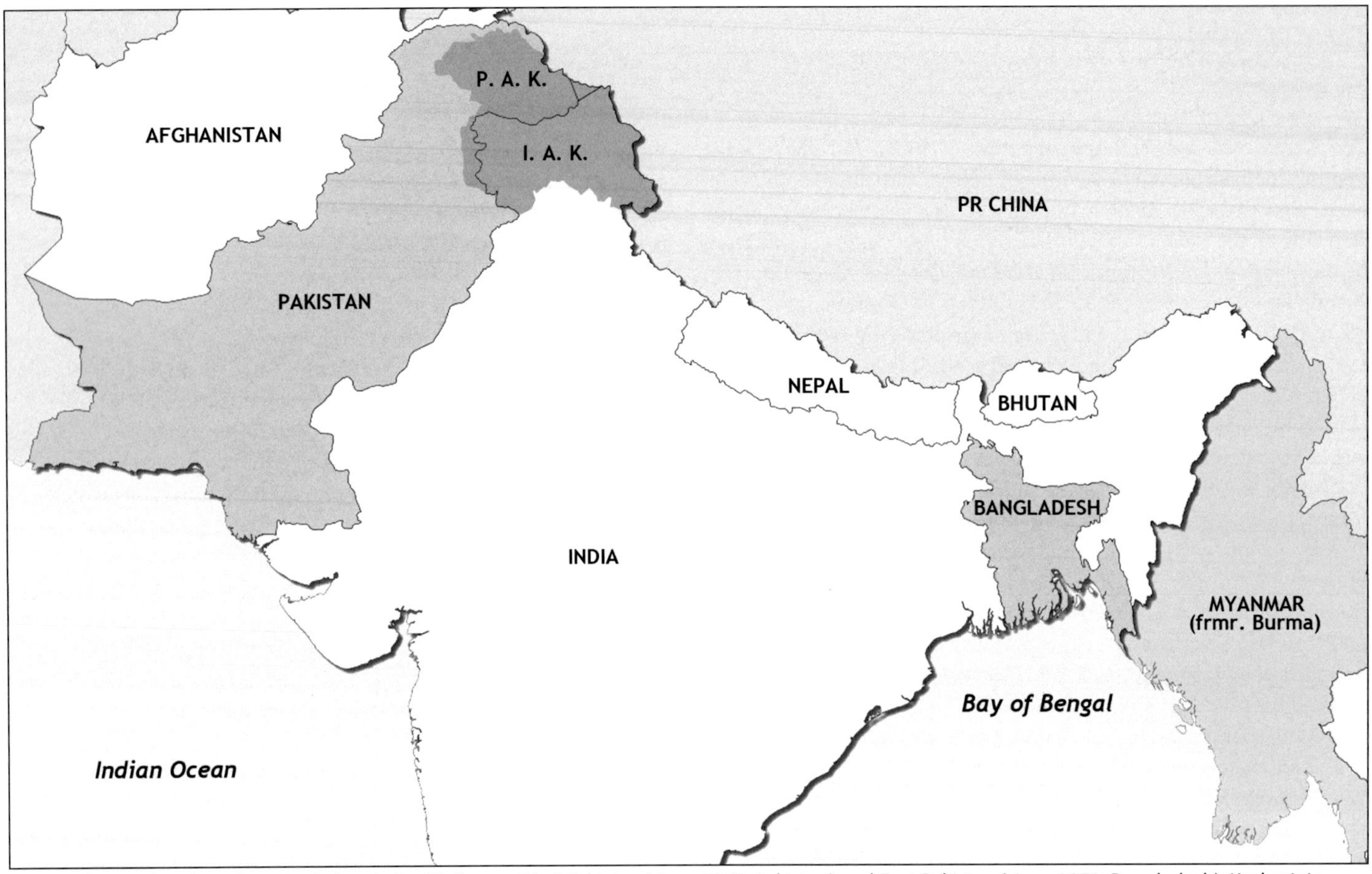


A map of central and northern India (centre), with former West Pakistan (since 1971: Pakistan) and East Pakistan (since 1971: Bangladesh). Kashmir is shown as 'integrated' by India and Pakistan since the war of 1948-1949. (Map by Tom Cooper)

the original territorial entity of Jammu and Kashmir no longer exists because:

(1) Pakistan had ceded land to China in the Shaksgam Valley in the state per the 1963 Sino-Pakistan Boundary Agreement; while
(2) The Askai Chin region has been occupied by China since the 1950s and following the 1962 war between India and China, this territory has remained under Chinese control.

While India subsequently followed a non-aligned foreign policy, Pakistan became allied to the United States of America, and thus joined the Baghdad Pact, the Central Treaty Organisation (CENTO), and the South-East Asia Treaty Organisation (SEATO), and signed a mutual defence agreement with the USA in 1954. This led to a rise in Pakistan's military and diplomatic influence in Washington as well as to an influx of US arms. Over the following years, India and Pakistan fought two major wars: in August 1965, Pakistan infiltrated close to 30,000 troops into the State of Kashmir. This effort was met with an Indian military counteroffensive and escalated into a general war. This conflict saw the first large-scale use of air power and armour in the subcontinent, and though it ended in a strategic stalemate, the experience gained by both militaries was used to effect in subsequent conflicts. The Kashmir War of 1965 was the last occasion on which Pakistan attempted to use force to wrest the control of Kashmir from India and, coming as it did after India's defeat in the war with China of 1962, probably represented Pakistan's best chance of doing so.[4]

The UN brokered a ceasefire and in 1966, India and Pakistan signed an agreement in Tashkent in the USSR, to resolve their issues in peaceful manner. However, the Indian Prime Minister Lal Bahadur Shastri died shortly after and thus the Tashkent Declaration proved ill-fated: it was to have virtually no long-term effect. The only of its points that was realised was the insistence on the observance of the 1948 Cease Fire Line (now the 'Line of Control'):

> The Prime Minister of India and the President of Pakistan have agreed that all armed personnel of the two countries shall be withdrawn not later than 25 February, 1966 to the positions they held prior to 5 August, 1965, and both sides shall observe the cease-fire terms on the cease-fire line.[5]

## 1971 India-Pakistan War[6]

Tensions between the two countries continued to flare up, and – following internal tensions that degenerated into the systematic repression and mass killings of people in what used to be East Pakistan – the two countries went to war with each other once again. After India supported an armed insurrection in East Pakistan, on 22 November 1971 an armoured clash provoked an air battle. In turn, West Pakistan then launched a pre-emptive strike on Indian air bases in the west.[7] In the course of the general war, the Indian armed forces defeated the Pakistani Army and Air Force in the East, enabling the creation of the independent country of Bangladesh. Simultaneously, Pakistan's attempts to relieve the pressure by attacking India in the West were thwarted and sizeable parts of the country occupied by the Indian Army. However, and despite numerous suggestions to the contrary, India had no intention of destroying Pakistan in that conflict. Instead, it sought to deliver only enough blows to the Pakistani armed forces, which had cultivated a myth of their invincibility. The 1971 India-Pakistan war thus marked an important psychological blow to the psyche and prestige of Pakistan and its armed forces.

The resulting dismemberment of the country and the armed forces' abject failure to prevent it, led to a deep resolve among many in Pakistan's military and intelligence elites to repay India in kind. That they have not been successful to date, despite making huge efforts to that end, has not caused any rethink in an ultimately self-destructive approach to relations with India.

The conflict led directly to the Shimla Declaration of 1972 which aimed at settling all disputes bilaterally. This agreement, signed between Prime Minister Indira Gandhi of India and Zulfikar Ali Bhutto of Pakistan had three particularly noteworthy elements:[8]

- A mutual commitment to the peaceful resolution of all issues through direct bilateral approaches.
- To build the foundations of a cooperative relationship with special focus on people to people contacts.
- To uphold the inviolability of the Line of Control in Jammu and Kashmir, which is a most important CBM between India and Pakistan, and a key to durable peace.

This latter point has been critical to India's approach to the Kashmir dispute. India believes that the Line of Control is to be respected while, as Kargil 1999 showed, Pakistan has a rather different approach.

## The 1972-1999 Period

Another result of the 1971 India-Pakistan War was that no major conflict between the two occurred until 1999. This is not to say there were no tensions: quite the contrary, Pakistan merely began applying different methods to destabilise India.[9] As first, it established links to the violent Sikh secessionist movement in the Indian Federal State of Punjab, thus resulting in a ten-year long insurgency that saw the deaths of thousands of people in terrorist attacks and subsequent vicious counterterrorist (COIN) operations, spearheaded by the Punjab Police. The conflict culminated in the storming of the Golden Temple in Amritsar, and the assassination of Indian Prime Minister Indira Gandhi, in 1984, followed by horrendous pogroms of the Sikhs.[10]

Yet, despite the intensity of this conflict, the Punjab Police – overwhelmingly Sikh in composition – supported by the army and paramilitary forces, was eventually able to contain, nullify and destroy the Sikh insurgents. Certainly enough, an irredentist Sikh ethnic movement remains active in Western countries, even if being a 'non-issue' in India. After 1987, an opportunity for Pakistani involvement was provided in Kashmir where rigged State assembly elections fuelled local resentment. Pakistani support for insurgents in Kashmir led to India adopting an increasingly harsh line against Pakistan and resulted in a relentless COIN campaign. Insurgent attacks in Kashmir – alongside operations in certain other areas – have all shown clear traces back to Pakistan: indeed, it soon became clear that the government in Islamabad was deploying religious extremists (so-called 'Jihadists') to infiltrate the country. The situation did not become better when several foreign powers – foremost the USA and Great Britain – then attempted to mediate, and equate India with Pakistan: on the contrary, they galled the government in New Delhi, prompting it to reject these overtures outright. Indeed, India's response to separatist violence, terrorist attacks, and jihadist infiltration in the period 1987-1993 became intense, then brutal, and – at times – excessive. However, in the grand picture, and despite (acknowledged) human rights violations by all of the parties involved, the status quo between India and Pakistan remained unchanged: New Delhi remained completely unmoved by criticism of its position on Kashmir, while Pakistan relentlessly supported the insurgents. This is how the situation remains at the time of writing.[11]

That all said, Pakistan's proxy-war in Kashmir continues to date – at the cost of thousands of lives. Despite its vociferous and well-oiled propaganda machine, Pakistan has come no closer to "internationalising" the Kashmir dispute in 2020 than it did in the period of 1987 to 1993. Pakistan, and all too often, the Western powers, underestimate the determination of India never to be divided along religious lines or partitioned ever again. Indeed, India is prepared to use coercion along with inducements to preserve its territorial integrity – at all costs and regardless of which political party governs in New Delhi. This has enabled the country and its society to withstand sustained pressure from Pakistan, sympathetic foreign governments, and an international media that have not been favourable to India.

## The War at the Top of the World and the War that Never Was

While India and Pakistan did not fight another major war between 1972 and 1997, they did become involved in several major confrontations. The first of these took place on 13 April 1984, when the Indian Army launched Operation Meghdoot to seize the Siachen Glacier.[12] Successfully concluded, this led to an ongoing confrontation between India and Pakistan where brigade-sized-formations – with ample artillery support and sustained by helicopters – were deployed against each other along the Line of Control. While the seizure of the Siachen Glacier represented a major setback for the Pakistani army – because Pakistan views the glacier as its territory – the scope of this conflict remained limited due to the high altitude and freezing local temperatures. However, the importance of the glacier is such that it is speculated that Pakistan launched its Kargil operation with a view to forcing an Indian withdrawal from the Siachen Glacier in exchange for a Pakistani withdrawal from Kargil. The Siachen conflict has blooded parts of the Indian and Pakistani armies like no other environment ever could and has turned many of their units into highly capable and experienced mountain and cold-weather troops. While neither side has made use of offensive air power – the Indian Air Force (IAF) did considered the use of its Hawker Hunter fighter jets – both have made much use of heliborne logistics, with the Indians gradually fine-tuning their air support into a sort of art. While tensions have meanwhile lessened, both armies remain deployed in the field in this theatre of operations.

A potentially much more serious event took place between 1986 and 1987. In late 1986, India conducted a table-top exercise to explore new integrated mechanized warfare tactics. These evolved into a full scale exercise – Operation Brasstacks – involving 150,000 men and thousands of tanks, armoured vehicles, artillery pieces and aircraft.[13] However, a series of miscommunications over this exercise led to a

Indian Army troops with a HAL Cheetah helicopter in the Himalayas. (Albert Grandolini Collection)

massing of forces along the Pakistani border, because Islamabad was worried that New Delhi actually planned a major strike to bifurcate the country with rapidly advancing mechanised units. This apprehension did not result in a war, but Pakistan was rattled by the new Indian strategy and inexorably moved towards nuclearization.

Pakistan's support for Kashmiri insurgents also led to a confrontation in 1990 but this was on a smaller scale. Instead, between 1987 and 1990 both countries began the process of weaponizing their hitherto nascent nuclear capability. Indeed, the year 1990 perhaps marked the point where Pakistan deployed its first weapons. This entire process culminated in the nuclear tests of 1998 when both nations demonstrated their nuclear weapons capability in the most dramatic fashion.

Prime Minister Atal Bihari Vajpayee of India. (Government of India Photo)

## Political Situation in 1999

In 1998, general elections were held in India after the government elected in 1996 collapsed and the 12th Lok Sabha (House of the People, the lower house of India's bicameral Parliament) was convened. New elections were called when Indian National Congress (INC) left the United Front government led by I.K. Gujral. The Bharatiya Janata Party's (BJP) Atal Bihari Vajpayee regained his position of Prime Minister getting support from 286 (out of 543) members of the parliament to form a majority government. The Vajpayee government was less than one year old when, in April 1999 it decided to brake the status quo through testing Indian nuclear weapons a month later, and then by launching work on improving systems for their deployment against targets in both Pakistan and the People's Republic of China (PRC).

International sanctions imposed upon New Delhi after the nuclear tests had an impact on the Indian economy but, this was relatively lessened by the internal growth dynamic of the Indian economy, which continued to progress. Indeed, while causing some initial difficulties in respect of financing specific large infrastructure projects, the sanctions petered out into more of a nuisance than an outright blow to the Indian economy. The rise of the BJP under Vajpayee's leadership also marked the end of the earlier domination of the INC of the political landscape. India had, since 1988 been ruled by a series of coalition governments of varying stability but were remarkably steady in their foreign policies. While economic reforms started in 1991 began freeing up the hitherto over-regulated and bureaucratised economy, changes of ruling dispensation in 1996 and then 1998, continued these policies of economic liberalisation and broader economic reform.

There was also, however, a rise in nationalistic sentiment which indirectly helped India to deal with economic sanctions. Many Indians who did not support Vajpayee, and despite having reservations about both the BJP and the nuclear tests, viewed the sanctions imposed – and some of the rhetoric emanating from Western countries – as being hypocritical given the US nuclear umbrella afforded to NATO countries and its Asia-Pacific allies. Following the 1998 nuclear tests, this rhetoric led to a hardening of attitudes towards some Western countries and a slight shift in foreign policy thinking, where it effectively divided foreign powers between those that supported India, and those that took punitive measures against it. This had implications in the short and medium term with respect to arms sales, infrastructure project awards, and even in basic economic ties: favour was given to supportive countries and a hard line taken against others who were not.

The Vajpayee government was dependent on its coalition partners for political support and while Vajpayee was popular, there was always a potential instability in his government. Indeed, a series of disputes among coalition partners – in which the BJP was neither party to nor responsible for – caused a great deal of friction in the government. In turn, this led to a significant degree of discord in governance and hindered the Vajpayee government's moves towards broad-based economic reforms that aimed to further bolster an economy that was showing signs of substantial improvement.

As discord mounted, Vajpayee's government collapsed on 17 April 1999, when the All India Anna Dravida Munnetra Kazhagam (AIADMK), with its 18 seats, withdrew its support. This led to a vote-of-confidence motion in the parliament, which the government lost 272 to 273, leading to a fresh general election in 1999. The election process was still ongoing with no voting having yet taken place when the Kargil crisis erupted.

## Loss of Time

For unexplained reasons, the Indian Election Commission scheduled the new elections for September 1999. This represented an incredible time lag of nearly five months: it resulted in a situation where the government was constrained in its ability to run everyday affairs of state and its agencies, and would find itself sanctioned by the election commission for any major new expenditure. This potentially could stymie any necessary government expenditure during a conflict and create a major dilemma. Precisely this factor was to have an overwhelming impact during the initial stages of the Kargil War, because the Election Commission sought to stop the Vajpayee

A Havildar (Sergeant) of the Indian Army, checking papers of a civilian in Kashmir. (Albert Grandolini Collection)

government from enacting certain policies and restrained it from signing contracts for arms and spare parts for available weapons systems. This eventually attracted the attention of the Indian Supreme Court: only its intervention lent a degree of rationality to the project and permitted the government to perform its duties largely unfettered by the diktats of the Election Commission. This assisted India during the Kargil war as spares and munitions were purchased as required.

### Sharif Administration in Pakistan

In contrast, as of 1999 Pakistan was run by a relatively stable government, but this was marred by massive problems of almost diametrically opposite nature to those of India. By 1996, large-scale corruption by the government of Benazir Bhutto had deteriorated the country's economy. During the parliamentary elections of 1997, the Pakistan Muslim League (Nawaz), led by Nawaz Sharif, won an overwhelming mandate and forged strong alliances with regional parties to bolster both his government's stability and to extend the reach of his government into hitherto alienated regions. Moreover, Sharif forged strong alliances with the powerful leadership of the Pakistani armed forces – the ultimate powerbroker in the country – and carefully cultivated his relationship with key military officers. This is what enabled him to, in response to India's nuclear tests, run a series of Pakistani nuclear tests in late May 1998, thus increasing his public standing. However, in reaction to these tests Sharif's government found itself facing massive difficulties because international sanctions were then imposed against Pakistan too, and they virtually crippled the country's weak economy.

When Western countries suspended their aid, Sharif reacted by freezing the country's foreign currency reserves. However, regardless of how small these reserves were, this only resulted in further worsening of the economic conditions. Thanks to infusions of assistance from the PRC and the Kingdom of Saudi Arabia, there was no economic collapse. On the contrary, Pakistan's economic resilience proved to be quite impressive. The government managed to maintain a degree of economic stability and, thanks to the importance given to the Pakistani armed forces in terms of budgetary priority, their overall capabilities remained – largely – unaffected.

### 21 February 1999: Lahore Declaration

Despite the tragedy of war that was to befall India and Pakistan later in the year, 1999 started with some of the brightest hopes for peace that the subcontinent had ever seen. In a move that was courageous and which marked a great leap of faith, Indian Prime Minister Vajpayee embarked upon a bus trip to Lahore for a summit with Prime Minister Sharif: this visit was to inaugurate a bus service between the two countries in the hope that citizen-to-citizen contact could lower tensions between the two countries. Vajpayee and Sharif then signed the Lahore Declaration, a bilateral agreement and governance treaty about the further development of nuclear arsenals, foremost aiming to avoid their accidental or unauthorised operational use. Ratified by the parliaments of India and Pakistan, the Lahore Declaration came into force the same year and was widely considered as a sign of a brighter future for both countries.

It is hard to overstate the possible importance of this treaty: without doubt, it was one of the most-important documents of this kind in the contemporary history of the subcontinent. The Declaration provided a mechanism to normalise the relations between the two countries with a view to easing the ever-present military tension. This mechanism perhaps offered the first occasion that in peacetime, when neither country was in the aftermath of armed inter-state conflict, where India and Pakistan decided to put forward a framework aimed at resolving their disputes peacefully and bilaterally.[14]

Prime Minister Nawaz Shair of Pakistan. (State Department Photo)

### Contents of the Lahore Declaration

The Lahore Declaration was signed on 21 February 1999, along with a memorandum of understanding (MoU). According to it, both governments, *inter alia*:

- Asserted their commitment to the vision of peace, stability and mutual progress;
- Asserted their full commitment to the Shimla Agreement and the UN Charter;
- Recognised that the development of nuclear weapons increased the responsibility of both nations towards avoiding an armed conflict; and
- Recognised the importance of confidence-building measures, aimed at avoiding accidental and unauthorised use of nuclear weapons.

Moreover, the two governments agreed to give each other an advance notification of ballistic missile flight tests and, if necessary, accidental or unexplained use of nuclear weapons to avoid the outbreak of a nuclear conflict.

In respect of the long-standing dispute over Kashmir, the Lahore Declaration and the MoU incorporated a joint commitment by both India and Pakistan, whereby they would seek to intensify efforts to resolve the Kashmir conflict and other areas of dispute. The two countries would further seek to enhance bilateral dialogue and to implement nuclear safeguards and enact such measures as were feasible in order to prevent conflict.

From India's standpoint, a major breakthrough was the fact that both governments condemned terrorism. They also committed themselves to non-interference in each other's internal affairs and reaffirmed the objectives of the South Asia Association for Regional Cooperation (SAARC). Finally, they also committed themselves to promoting the upholding of basic human rights. While these were rather generalised statements, nonetheless they were significant considering the age-old distrust between the two nations.

In the joint statement issued after the conclusion of the summit which led to the Lahore Declaration, both governments indicated that their foreign ministers would meet on a regular basis. This would allow them to consult each other on issues relating to the World Trade Organization (WTO) and information technology. Furthermore, a long-standing issue dealing with human-rights, civilian detainees, and soldiers deemed missing in action and possibly still held as prisoners of war was to be dealt with by a two-member ministerial committee. The summit ended with a reciprocal invitation to Prime Minister Sharif to visit India.

The euphoria over the Lahore Declaration, the apparent progress made and the atmosphere of goodwill that seemed to be pervasive proved to be short-lived. Both countries found themselves embroiled in their respective domestic political issues and there was no time to implement any of the provisions or measures envisaged. Unfortunately, a sinister parallel plan was at work in Pakistan which would end the hopes raised by the Lahore Declaration. This plan would culminate in the Kargil War of 1999.

# 1
# INDIAN AND PAKISTAN ARMIES OF 1999

Some of the basic formations that exist in both armed forces are virtually identical in India and Pakistan; indeed, they are identical to most of the Western-influenced armies, and as such some generalisations can be made. Nevertheless, the following chapter provides a detailed explanation for the purpose of the reader's easier orientation.[1]

## Organisational Structure

The basic infantry fighting formation in both the Indian and the Pakistani Army is the battalion. It is composed of four rifle companies and headquarters and support companies. Its heaviest weapons are generally mortars and machineguns, though some may also have anti-tank and surface-to-air missiles. In addition to basic infantry battalions, mechanized, parachute and commando battalions also exist, each created, trained and equipped for a special role. An average infantry battalion has the structure depicted in Table 1.[2]

Artillery and armoured formations have battalion-sized equivalents called regiments. These are organized in a similar manner – armoured regiments have four tank squadrons while artillery regiments have between three and four artillery batteries. All of these formations are of similar size, about 1,000 men. Battalion sized formations are amalgamated with other formations to form brigades.

In the India-Pakistan context, the most important formation is the brigade. Like the battalion, there are armour and artillery equivalents, but all share a basic similarity of structure. A brigade consists of three battalions or regiments and is usually provided with some supporting equipment – artillery and heavy mortars in the case of armour and infantry units. Some brigades, however, are designed to operate independently and these are given more supporting elements, including engineering and signals as well as additional artillery.

A typical brigade would have the structure depicted in the Table 2, whether operating as part of a division or independently.[3]

Brigades are usually grouped together, with additional artillery, engineering, signals and other support elements to form a division. India and Pakistan operate two basic types of division: infantry and armoured. India's infantry divisions are divided into plains and mountains formations which, as their names suggest are trained and equipped to fight in different geographic environments. The mountain divisions are primarily earmarked for use against China, though they could be converted for use on the plains after reequipment.

A typical infantry division comprises three infantry brigades, an artillery brigade and an armoured regiment. Support elements include an engineer regiment (as described in Table 3), a signal regiment and an air observation post flight, in addition to medical, transport, supply and repair units. Mountain divisions lack the armoured regiment and tend to have smaller calibre artillery. They also have more engineering and support/logistics elements than plains formations.

The largest formation of both the Indian- and the Pakistani Army is the corps. This formation, pioneered by Napoleon, consists of three divisions and their supporting arms. In the South-Asian context, there are two types of corps: Holding Corps and Strike Corps. The former are designed

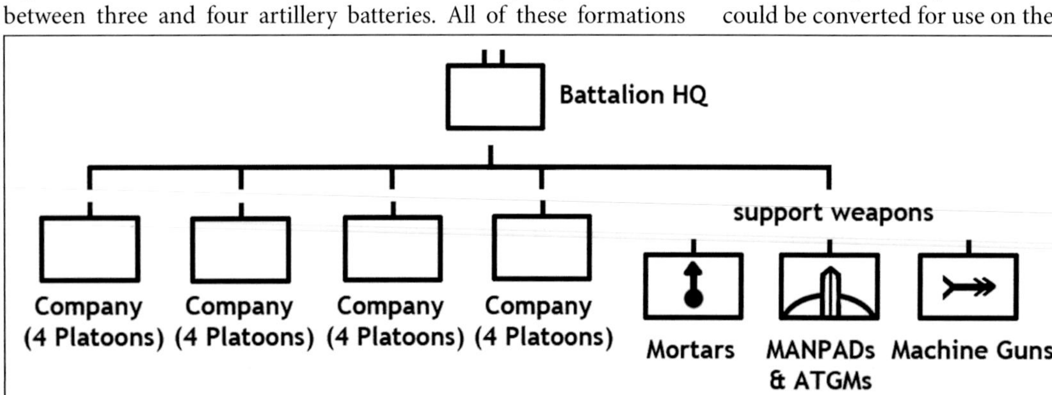


**Table 1: Typical Battalion Structure of the Indian Army**

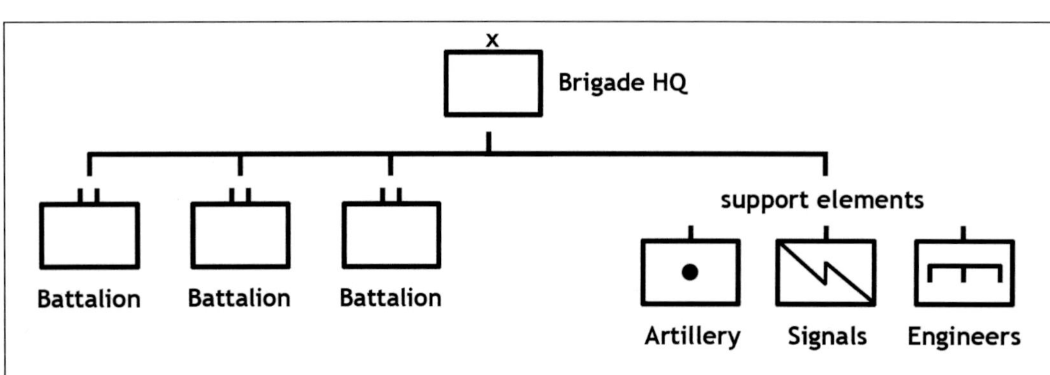


**Table 2: Typical Brigade Structure of the Indian Army**

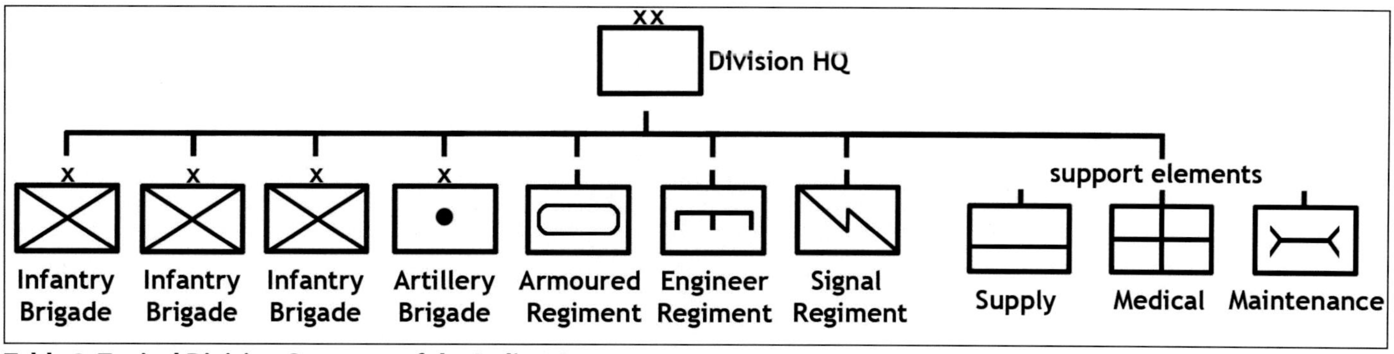


**Table 3: Typical Division Structure of the Indian Army**

| Command | Headquarters | Subordinate Units (Base) |
|---|---|---|
| **HQ Indian Army** | New Delhi | 50th Independent Parachute Brigade (Agra) |
| **Central Command** | Lucknow | I Corps (currently assigned to South Western Command) |
| **Eastern Command** | Kolkata | 23rd Infantry Division (Ranchi) |
| | | III Corps (Dimapur) |
| | | IV Corps (Tezpur) |
| | | XXXIII Corps (Siliguri) |
| **Northern Command** | Udhampur | XIV Corps (Leh) |
| | | XV Corps (Srinagar) |
| | | XVI Corps (Nagrota) |
| **Southern Command** | Pune | 41st Artillery Division (Raising) |
| | | XII Corps (Jodhpur) |
| | | XXI Corps (Bhopal) |
| **South Western Command** | Jaipur | 42nd Artillery Division (Raising) |
| | | I Corps (Mathura) |
| | | X Corps (Bhatinda) |
| **Western Command** | Chandimandir | 40th Artillery Division (Ambala) |
| | | II Corps (Ambala) |
| | | IX Corps (Yol) |
| | | XI Corps (Jalandhar) |
| **Army Training Command** | Shimla | |

**Table 4: Nominal Structure of the Indian Army**

for defensive operations while the latter is the principal offensive formation of both armies.

The Indian Army consists of 11 corps-sized formations with a total of 36 divisions and a number of independent brigades. The cutting edge of the Indian Army is centred around three powerful Strike Corps – each built around one armoured division. The other eight corps are defined as Holding Corps, though they may have significant offensive potential. There may be some minor changes to the order of battle (ORBAT), but no significant changes are expected in the foreseeable future. There are some differences between the ORBAT outlined in the Table 4, below and that listed in published sources, but this ORBAT is more representative of the current Indian Army than other sources.[4]

This translates into the overall order of battle as described in Table 5 on page 10.

In addition to these combat formations, the Indian Army has four engineer brigades and 14 Army Aviation Corps Helicopter Units. A separate Corps of Air Defence Artillery operates six air defence brigades and two surface-to-air missile groups. These elements were assigned to formations on a need basis, though – with units of the Corps of Air Defence Artillery (CADA) in particular – many of which were earmarked for deployment and operations with specific formations.

It should be noted that India's ten Mountain Divisions were largely earmarked for operations against China. These formations are not quite the same as standard infantry divisions and, as of 1999, tended to have a lighter artillery complement, centred around 105mm guns and 120mm mortars. In addition, assets such as transport, anti-tank missile units, and air defences were designed to operate in mountainous terrain without much by way of road or rail infrastructure. These mountain divisions were therefore not as heavily equipped as the standard infantry divisions and converting one into any other type of a formation would have been a difficult task.

Of note also is the single Indian parachute brigade, which was largely allocated the task of a rapid response reserve. In 1999, this unit – 50th Parachute Brigade – was seven battalions-strong: before long, it was reduced to four battalions and possessed artillery support in the form of a single artillery regiment equipped with either 75mm or 105mm guns.[5]

As previously mentioned, the principal offensive formations of the Indian Army are the three Strike Corps – 1 Corps, 2 Corps & 21 Corps. These are each built around a nucleus of a single armoured division and two infantry divisions – probably with a larger number of mechanised brigades than basic infantry formations. The typical Strike Corps has the structure described in the Table 6 on page 10.[6]

Contrary to the three Strike Corps, the Holding Corps were not as well supplied with support elements – such as CADA or engineers – and did not possess armoured formations larger than brigades or the armoured regiments attached to the infantry regiments. While

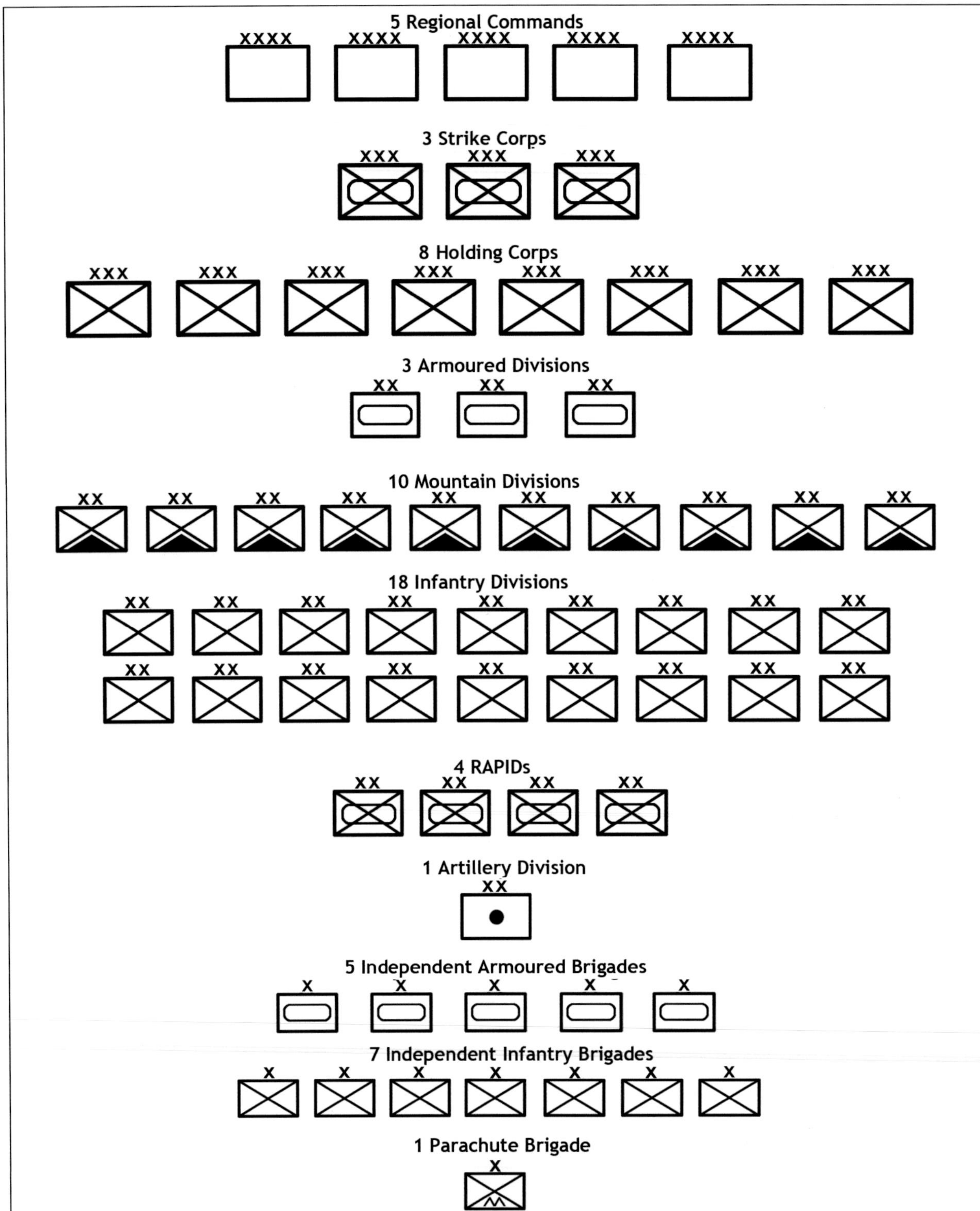


**Table 5: Indian Army ORBAT**

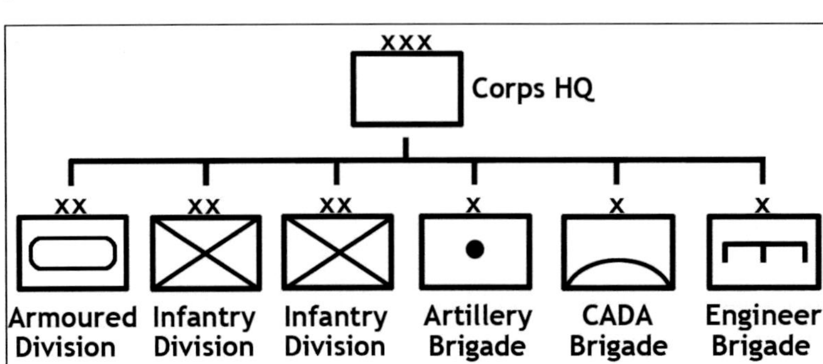


**Table 6: Typical Strike Corps Structure of the Indian Army**

Since the mid-1980s, the T-72M1 formed the backbone of the Indian armoured forces: by 1999, over 1,900 of them were in service with 35 regiments. (Albert Grandolini Collection)

About 900 T-55s were still available to the Indian Army as of 1999, about 200 of them were stored, while the rest served with 13 armoured regiments, and were in the process of being replaced by T-72s and Arjuns. (Albert Grandolini Collection)

they did possess significant offensive capability, these formations were largely designed to operate in a defensive role.

The Indian Army possessed a fairly varied arsenal of reasonably advanced weapons. Each combat arm – armour, artillery and infantry – was in the process of a massive modernization program. While this was slowed down by budgetary constraints in the early 1990s, it was resumed by the middle of the decade and had started to show clear results by 1999.

## Indian Combined Arms: Armour

Indian armour was divided into three basic formations:

- armoured divisions;
- independent armoured brigades; and
- armoured regiments assigned to infantry divisions

Depending on their type, these formations were equipped with three types of main battle tanks (MBTs): the Soviet-made T-72M1, modified T-55s of very diverse origins, and the Indian-made (though British-designed) Vijayanta. The T-72M1 was already the principal tank of the army, while the new Arjun MBT was in the process of entering service, but at an extremely slow rate.

As of the 1990s, the Indian Army planned to establish 65 armoured regiments by the year 2000, each with between 55 and 72 MBTs: as of 1999, 62 were already operational, equipped with more than 3,500 tanks. These were equipped as follows:[7]

- T-72M1: 35 regiments (over 1,900 MBTs)
- T-55: 13 regiments (700 in service, 200 stored)
- Vijayanta: 14 regiments (over 1,000 in service, 1,000 stored)

As of 1999, the T-72M1s were already in the process of being considered for a major upgrade program, focused on the provision of thermal sights, additional armour, better ammunition and fire-protection.[8]

## Artillery

As of 1999, India's regiment of artillery had undergone a reorganization programme which had resulted in the field branch of artillery being separated from the Corps of Air Defence Artillery and the Army Aviation Corps. It possessed close to 200 regiments with approximately 4,000 pieces of artillery of various types.

The vast bulk of India's artillery was towed – which was rather surprising considering the increased mechanization of the Indian Army. The 130mm Catapult and 105mm Abbot self-propelled guns were now being phased out of active service due to age and mechanical problems.

India's tube artillery regiments each possessed eighteen guns, each divided into three six-gun batteries. These were classed as mountain, field, medium, heavy, para and light and heavy mortar units. The sole heavy regiment was nominally equipped with 7.2-inch howitzers but effectively the regiment had morphed into 333 Missile Group with Prithvi missiles.

The mountain regiments were – in the past – equipped with either 76mm Yugoslav-made M48 guns, OTO Melara M56 105mm howitzers, or with an Indian-designed 75/24mm howitzer. By the time of the Kargil War, however, all mountain and field regiments were equipped with the Indian designed and manufactured 105mm Indian Field Gun (IFG), or its lighter counterpart, the Indian Light Field gun (LFG). The latter two weapons equipped a substantial proportion of the Indian artillery regiments.

Perhaps outnumbering the IFG and LFG in service in 1999 was the 130mm M-46 field gun. This weapon was extraordinarily popular in Indian service though deemed to be more suited to the plains as opposed to the mountains. However, even with mobility limitations it was widely employed to great effect. The 122mm D-30 howitzer was a less popular weapon in Indian service and these were largely relegated to the infantry formations deployed on the plains, where their traverse and decent range made them quite useful. That said, they were viewed as delivering too light a shell and as such the type was not popular.

The 155/39 Bofors FH77/B02 gun/howitzer equipped at least twenty artillery regiments in 1999 and these guns were the single heaviest artillery piece deployed by India during the conflict. The Bofors gun was the subject of much controversy at the time of purchase and plans to license produce over a thousand guns in India were scrapped, thus totally disrupting the Indian Army's artillery modernization plans for decades. The gun, however, delivered excellent performance in the mountainous terrain of Kargil and the range and shell-weight of the weapon was greatly appreciated by the Indian Army. Indeed, post-Kargil, the weapon was unequivocally praised.

Rocket regiments, of which the Indian Army operated five in 1999, were equipped with BM-21 multiple rocket launchers firing locally manufactured ammunition. Light regiments were each equipped with a dozen local versions of the Brandt AM-50 mortar and these were assigned initially on the basis of one per division, with some additional units earmarked for the mountains. A single heavy mortar regiment equipped with 160mm Tampella mortars was also on strength, the last unit operating the type.

In 1999, the new Indian military doctrine emphasized attrition warfare over the previous manoeuvre policy. This meant that the artillery, which used to be a combat support arm, was now classed as a combat arm with priorities shifting between direct support and counter-bombardment. The new army tactical doctrine had moved from deep thrusts with mechanized forces to maximum attrition of enemy forces, limited manoeuvre and attacks on strategic and operational targets. Artillery, therefore had a central role to play in any attrition-based doctrine.

The real modernisation of Indian artillery was in the development of surveillance and target acquisition (SATA) batteries. These were supplied with indigenously manufactured battlefield surveillance radar as well as artillery locating radars. This dramatically enhanced the effectiveness of the Indian artillery. Last but not least, as of 1999, the Indian Army operated a number of Israeli made remotely piloted vehicles (RPVs or 'unmanned aerial vehicles', UAVs), custom-tailored for obtaining and providing the targeting data for the Prithvi surface-to-surface missiles (SSMs).

The changes being made in Indian artillery give some indication of Indian Army's tactical thinking. They also give some clues about India's new military doctrine. The problem is that, to the outside observer, there seem to be many contradictions in what has publicly been revealed about this military doctrine, especially regarding the artillery.

### Infantry

The Indian infantry has, since the 1980s, felt itself a neglected service. The major re-equipment programs that affected the armoured regiments and, to a lesser extent, the artillery, did not come to the infantry. This is not to say that the Indian infantry remained unchanged. The infantry's anti-tank, night fighting and target acquisition capabilities had been substantially enhanced in the 1990s, and some expansion of mechanized infantry units was undertaken.

Indian infantry units in 1999 were still armed with the Ishapore 1A1 – a version of the 7.62mm FN-FAL – as its primary infantry weapon. Each section of 11 men was also issued with one or two 7.62mm 1B – local versions of the L4A4 light machineguns – and one 84mm Carl Gustav recoilless rocket launcher.[9] Platoon level firepower was augmented by a 51mm mortar and each battalion had eight 7.62mm FN-MAG (known as the Ishapore 2A1) machineguns assigned to it along with six 81mm mortars. All weapons were made in India. In many ways, at section, platoon, company and battalion level, the Indian army was almost completely supplied with local products. While there were issues with delivery schedules and often the quality of weapons supplied, the Indian infantry was relatively well-equipped with infantry equipment and was moving slowly towards an upgrade of their basic weapon. Of interest is that the Sterling submachine carbine – known locally as the 9mm 1A1 – was in widespread service as a personal defence weapon for section leaders.

In 1999, India was in the throes of replacing some its infantry weapons. The most extensive project was to replace both the standard battle rifle and light machinegun throughout the army. The 5.56mm INSAS family of rifles and light machineguns had begun to enter service in quantity. Quality control was a major factor affecting acceptance of weapons into the army but by 1999, over 90,000 rifles had been successfully inducted into service along with a limited number of light machineguns. However, although production had been significantly enhanced and over 20,000 rifles were produced per month in a surge of production, the Indian Army still had the 1A1 as its standard battle rifle.

An infantryman of the Indian Army as seen on the street of a town in the Indian-controlled Kashmir in 1999. Notable is his camouflage uniform and a ballistic helmet based on the US-designed M1, combined with a Kevlar-vest and the usual assault rifle of Kalashnikov design. (Albert Grandolini Collection)

The performance of the INSAS has been shrouded in controversy but interviews with personnel who served during the Kargil conflict all indicate general satisfaction with the weapon and appreciation of its light weight compared to the 1A1 SLR. Some believed the latter to be more robust, but most viewed the INSAS as a reliable and effective replacement.

In addition to trying to replace the 1A1 with the INSAS, the Indian Army had inducted well over 100,000 Kalashnikov variants in 7.62mm x 39mm caliber. These weapons were preferred by Special Forces units and had increasingly made their way into elite infantry formations and became the standard weapon for the counterinsurgency force known as the Rashtriya Rifles. These Kalashnikov variants, used and new, were procured in the aftermath of the Indian Army's experience in Sri Lanka and in internal security operations within India. They proved to be extremely popular in army service and were a much sought-after infantry weapon.

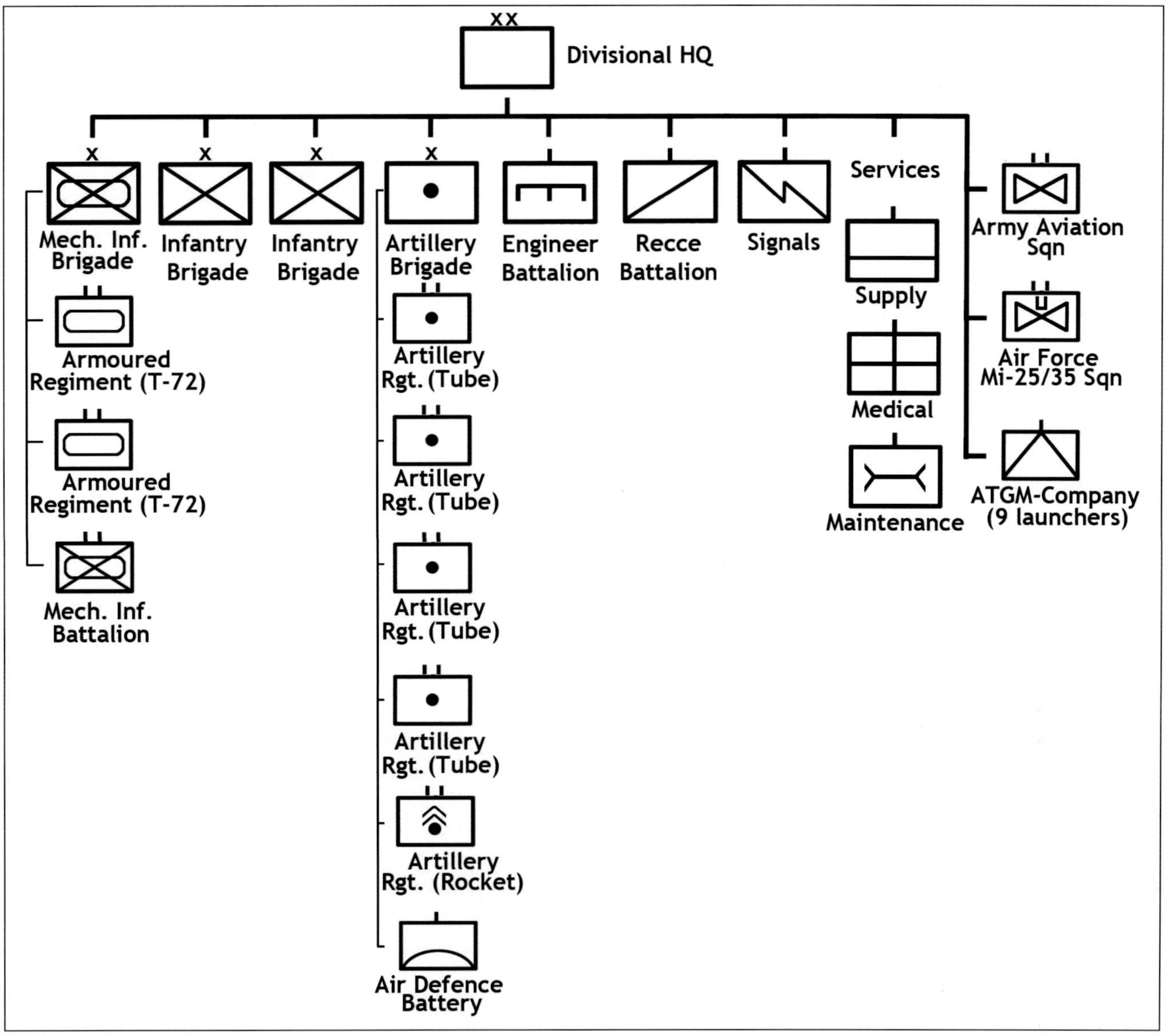


**Table 7: RAPID Structure of the Indian Army**

Battalion support weapons were in the main unchanged, with the FN MAG machinegun and 81mm mortars dominating. However, battalion and support company firepower were being augmented with the induction of 30mm AGS-17 automatic grenade launchers, of Russian origin, which were to prove invaluable for fire support during the Kargil conflict. In addition, the anti-tank weapons of the infantry battalion were being changed. The 106mm M40A1 recoilless rifles and 57mm M18 recoilless rifles (the latter being assigned to mountain formations) were being completely phased out and replaced at battalion level by eight MILAN ATGM launchers, although Russian Fagot systems were also used. The MILAN, with its MIRA thermal sight, would be used effectively in the direct fire role. In addition, there is some evidence that the Indian Army was making use of the larger Konkurs ATGM in the ground role for long-range engagements. The Konkurs was intended for use on the BMP-2 IFVs but was adapted to use a unified launcher alongside the MILAN system. Both missiles were manufactured in India by Bharat Dynamics Limited and production had long been stabilised and ATGMs were made available in adequate quantities for use by the infantry during the Kargil conflict.

By far the most significant development as far as India's infantry was concerned was the creation of the Reorganised Army Plains Infantry Division (RAPID). This was a uniquely Indian creation for the purpose of deployment on the South Asian battlefield. The basic RAPID had one mechanised infantry brigade and two standard infantry brigades, as described in Table 7.[10]

As of 1999, there were four RAPIDs in the Indian Army, all attached to the Holding Corps in Punjab and Rajasthan. The RAPID provided these essentially defensive formations with an extremely flexible unit that dramatically enhanced their ability to withstand offensive operations by Pakistani armour. Moreover, the RAPID possessed sufficient armoured and mechanised infantry assets to conduct reasonably significant offensive operations. The advent of the RAPID was accompanied by a dramatic upgrade of Indian Army C3I assets and communications. Under the Project Army Radio Engineering Network (AREN), a secure, real-time network was established, significantly enhancing the Army's ability to conduct and manage major offensive and defensive operations.

Indian officers viewed the infantry as being particularly significant for wars of the future and substantial investments were – finally – made in terms of equipment upgrades and enhanced training. The Indian Army made the acquisition of better anti-tank and personal weapons, communications gear and night-fighting capabilities for its infantry a top priority.

Another interesting aspect of India's infantry modernization was the lesser importance of mechanization. Mechanized infantry units, mounted in Soviet-made BMP-2 infantry combat vehicles were critical components of the Strike Corps and the RAPIDS; however, they had not made their way into the rest of the Army in any major way.

### Special Forces

As of 1999, the Parachute Regiment had included one special forces, five airborne battalions, two territorial army battalions and one COIN battalion (the latter being the Rashtriya Rifles). Additional battalions could be raised, but as of that time the ratio between airborne and special forces battalions was in flux, with some units on the cusp of transition from regular para units to para/special forces (Para SF). Indeed, at the time no fewer than ten battalions were designated Para or Para (SF) and of these, nine were committed to action during the Kargil War – with great effect.

Plans emerged in the mid-1980s to take the three para commando battalions from the Parachute Regiment and bring them together under a single specialised organisation, the Special Forces Regiment. However, these plans were abandoned, and they continued to be trained and recruited by the Parachute Regiment and thus perforce remained part of the Parachute Regiment's order of battle.

The total strength of the regiment stood at about some 4,500 personnel in the Paratroopers (Airborne), while the Para (SF) included about 1,200 operatives.

Obviously, the 50th Parachute Brigade was something of a hybrid. While Western parachute regiments – most notably the British 'Paras' – are airborne light infantry, the Soviets and then the Russians evolved their airborne units as airborne mechanized infantry. The Indian paratroopers were initially organized as light infantry but with the attachment of BMP-2 ICVs, standard 105mm LFG guns and their associated equipment, one may legitimately ask whether some genuflection towards the greater firepower and staying power of mechanized units was being bestowed upon India's Parachute Brigade.

### Para Special Forces Battalions

The Indian Army established its first Para Commando units in 1966. During the Indo-Pakistani War of 1965, a small ad hoc force comprising volunteers from most infantry units operated along and behind enemy lines. The performance of this force proved to the higher authorities that such forces had much utility and as such there was greater emphasis placed on the raising of unconventional forces.

On 1 July 1967, 10 Para Commando was raised by splitting 9 Para Commando at Gwalior. The Para Commandos were first deployed in the Indo-Pakistani War of 1971, with 9 Para Commando capturing a 122mm howitzer battery at Mandhol in Poonch, Jammu and Kashmir. 9 and 10 Para Commando took part in the 1984 Operation Blue Star and were deployed in Sri Lanka in the 1980s during India's involvement in the civil war, as part of Operation Pawan. They also saw action in Operation Cactus in 1988 in Maldives and in the 1999 Kargil War. It is of interest that much focus has been placed on the Para Commandos (now Para SF) units as these are much more flexible in counterinsurgency and counter-terrorist operations. The Para (SF) battalions of the Indian Army as of 1999 are listed in Table 9.

| Components |
|---|
| 1 Para (SF) |
| 2 Para (SF) |
| 3 Para (SF) |
| 4 Para (SF) |
| 9 Para (SF) |
| 10 Para (SF) |
| 11 Para (SF) |
| 21 Para (SF) |

**Table 9 Para SF Battalions of the Indian Army, 1999**

| Components | Notes |
|---|---|
| 1 airborne infantry battalion | |
| 1 airborne infantry battalion | |
| 1 parachute field regiment (artillery) | 9 and 17 Parachute Field Regiments in rotation |
| 60 Parachute Field Hospital | |
| 411 (Independent) Parachute Field Company | Bombay Sappers |
| 622 Parachute Composite Company | |
| 50th (Independent) Parachute Brigade | ordnance section |
| 50th (Independent) Parachute Brigade Signals Company | |
| 2nd (Independent) Parachute Field Workshop Company | electrical and mechanical engineering section |
| 252nd (Parachute) Air Defence Battery | |
| 50th (Independent) Parachute Brigade Provost Section | military police |
| President's Bodyguard | pathfinder company |

**Table 8: 50th Parachute Brigade, 1999[11]**

### The Ghatak Platoons

The Ghatak Platoon, or Ghatak Commandos, was a special operations-capable infantry platoon attached on the scale of one such platoon to every infantry battalion in the Indian Army. They could be described as an elite group of infantry and acted as shock troops and spearheaded assaults ahead of the rest of the battalion. The role of the Ghatak Platoon was similar to that of the scout sniper platoon or STA platoon of the United States Marine Corps, or the patrols platoon of the British Army. The Ghatak Platoon could be tasked by the battalion or brigade commander to carry out tasks which may include special reconnaissance, raids on enemy artillery positions, airfields, supply dumps and tactical headquarters. They are also capable of directing artillery and air attacks on targets deep within enemy lines and have been equipped with laser-designator units for the guidance of laser-guided bombs.

A Ghatak Platoon was usually 20-men strong and consisted of a commanding captain, two non-commissioned officers and some specialists, such as snipers and spotters, light machinegunners, a medic and a radio operator. The remaining soldiers acted as assault troopers for the platoon. As might be expected, only the most physically fit and motivated soldiers in an infantry battalion were selected to be part of the Ghatak Platoon, and it was mandatory for all of their officers to pass the commando training course.

During the Kargil War, not only were nine out of the ten Para (SF) battalions committed to action, but so also were the Ghatak platoons of each infantry battalion. These commando units were used to spearhead assaults, often either forming the bulk of the assaulting units or a disproportionate number of the

The backbone of the CADA's air defence formations were SA-6 self-propelled SAMs: a brigade controlling 3-4 SA-6 SAM-sites was assigned to each Strike Corps of the Indian Army as of 1999. (Albert Grandolini Collection)

volunteers selected for the final assaults. The Ghatak concept was an unqualifiedly successful experiment at battalion level.

## Air Defence

While the Indian Army already possessed one of the largest arsenals of air defence weapons, as of 1999, its CADA units (nowadays the Army Air Defence troops, AAD) were one of the newest formations. At the time, the CADA had, as its pride of place, two huge missile groups equipped with 2K12 Kub (ASCC/NATO-codename 'SA-6 Gainful') surface-to-air missiles. These were assigned to the Strike Corps' and represented a powerful deterrent to any attack aircraft. In addition, there were 30 regiments with Bofors L40/70 towed anti-aircraft guns, four with ZSU-23/4 self-propelled AA guns and a number with towed ZU-23 guns. These were complemented by a number of mobile point-defence missile regiments with SA-8b and SA-13 missile units.

## Chemical, Biological, Radiological and Nuclear Warfare

India's 60 armoured regiments and 26 mechanized infantry battalions had significant levels of protection from chemical, biological, radiological, and nuclear (CBRN) attacks. The Arjun and T-72 tanks had all received CBRN protection systems, as did the BMP-1 and BMP-2 infantry fighting vehicles (IFVs).[12] India also fielded a number of indigenously developed CBRN reconnaissance and decontamination vehicles: however, its army relied on towed artillery, which is far more difficult to operate in CBRN conditions, and placing an excessive physiological strain on artillery crews operating in what were – usually – high ambient temperatures. That said, respiratory protection was feasible as even the primitive and claustrophobic respirators used in the First World War were employed by artillery crews during chemical bombardment during hot summers, which although not comfortable, were not debilitating.

With respect to infantry formations, in the 1980s, the Army began some tentative preparations for CBRN warfare. A quantity of CBRN equipment was imported from the USSR but proved to be useless in Indian environmental conditions. In 1987, the Defence Research and Development Organization (DRDO) produced prototypes of CBRN suits, decontamination suits, facelets, overboots and CBRN tents. This equipment entered production and was in service with the armed forces by 1999. Meanwhile, from 1987 onwards, the Army – through its College of Military Engineering – began running familiarization courses in CBRN warfare, while DRDO scientists conducted theoretical courses at the brigade level. Over time, this became practical training.

The Ministry of Defence allocated priority to the indigenous production of CBRN gear. This also involved the participation of the private sector in the manufacture of CBRN suits. India seems to have purchased 50,000 S6 and S10 respirators and No.1 Mk3 suits from the UK in the 1980s (the types being identified through photographic evidence), 150,000 Draeger Kareta Nova respirators in the early 1990s, and subsequently a larger order of 334,000 full sets of Individual Protective Equipment (IPE) sets with CBRN suits and locally produced variants of the Kareta Nova respirator.

Despite all of the above, the exact status of CBRN preparedness and training in the Indian Army remains unclear and, for instance, it is unclear as to whether training and equipment had gone down to the battalion level. It was certainly the case that outside of CBRN exercises, Indian troops did not carry CBRN haversacks. Since the late 1990s, some exercises were conducted with troops in full CBRN gear and with decontamination vehicles in operation. However, in the 1990s these exercises had not been widely publicised and their extent was not clear.

## Unmanned Air Vehicles and the Army Aviation Corps

One area where India was peculiarly lacking was in the deployment of UAVs for surveillance tasks. The Indian Army had long seen the need for such systems and the DRDO was developing a small surveillance drone known as the Nishant. However, this was intended for use in the plains and units in the mountains were not intended to operate the type. Instead, India was forced to rely on the ageing Cheetah helicopters of its Army Aviation Corps because of their excellent high-altitude performance. As a result, at one point during the conflict, FLIR turrets from Nishants were fitted to the Cheetahs to enhance their capabilities during night and poor weather conditions.

## The Pakistani Order of Battle

In 1999 the Pakistani Army was organized into nine corps and the Force Command Northern Area. These contained a total of 22 divisions, 15 independent brigades (6 armoured and 9 infantry), 9 corps artillery brigades, 7 engineering brigades, and 15 army aviation squadrons (including two equipped with attack helicopters), as listed in Tables 10 and 11. Furthermore, the Pakistani Army had eight air defence brigades. It must be pointed out, however, that Pakistani brigades and divisions were somewhat smaller than their Indian counterparts.[13]

The two principal fighting formations were the Army Reserve North (ARN) and Army Reserve South (ARS): each was an approximate equivalent to the Indian Strike Corps in terms of size and composition. These had, as in the case of their Indian counterparts, a nucleus of a

| Corps | HQ Location | Major Corps Formations |
|---|---|---|
| **I Corps** | Mangla, Punjab | 6th Armoured Division (Gujranwala) |
| | | 17th Infantry Division (Kharian) |
| | | 37th Infantry Division (Kharian) |
| **II Corps** | Multan, Punjab | 1st Armoured Division (Pakistan) (Multan) |
| | | 14th Infantry Division (Okara) |
| | | 40th Infantry Division (Okara) |
| **IV Corps** | Lahore, Punjab | 2nd Artillery Division (Gujranwala) |
| | | 10th Infantry Division (Lahore) |
| | | 11th Infantry Division (Lahore) |
| **V Corps** | Karachi, Sindh | 16th Infantry Division (Pano Aqil) |
| | | 18th Infantry Division (Hyderabad) |
| | | 25th Mechanised Division (Malir) |
| **X Corps** | Rawalpindi, Punjab | Force Command Northern Areas (Gilgit) |
| | | 12th Infantry Division (Murree) |
| | | 19th Infantry Division (Mangla) |
| | | 23rd Infantry Division (Jhelum) |
| | | Special Security Division (Chilas) |
| **XI Corps** | Peshawar, Khyber Pakhtunkhwa | 7th Infantry Division (Peshawar) |
| | | 9th Infantry Division (Kohat) |
| **XII Corps** | Quetta, | 33rd Infantry Division (Quetta) |
| | | 41st Infantry Division (Quetta) |
| **XXX Corps** | Gujranwala, Punjab | 8th Infantry Division (Pakistan) |
| | | 15th Infantry Division (Sialkot) |
| **XXXI Corps** | Bahawalpur, Punjab | 26th Mechanized Division (Bahawalpur) |
| | | 35th Infantry Division (Bahawalpur) |
| **Army Air Defence Command** | Rawalpindi, Punjab | 3rd Air Defence Division (Sargodha), 4th Air Defence Division (Malir) |
| | | 4th Air Defence Division (Malir) |
| **Army Strategic Forces Command** | Rawalpindi, Punjab | 21st Artillery Division (Pano Aqil) |
| | | 22nd Artillery Division (Sargodha) |

**Table 10: Pakistan Army ORBAT, 1999**

single armoured division and up to two infantry divisions with numerous brigades.[14]

## Status of Pakistani Combined Arms

As in the case of the Indian Army, the Pakistani Army of 1999 possessed three armoured divisions and a number of armoured brigades. These operated almost 2,500 Main Battle Tanks of bewildering variety and from various generations. The most recent acquisitions were 320 T-80UD MBTs from Ukraine.[15]

## Armour

The T-80UD was a major improvement over the existing Pakistani tank fleet. The most modern units, until the arrival of the T-80UDs, were license-made Chinese T-85II tanks. An indigenous MBT – the Al-Khalid – failed to materialise. The rest of the fleet consisted of over a thousand Type-59/69 tanks of Chinese origin, which had been upgraded with 105mm guns, and a mixture of vintage US-made M47 and M48 tanks. While the later were serviceable, they were no match for even the older armour in the Indian arsenal. Moreover, the bulk of the Pakistani tank fleet lacked modern fire control equipment and advanced night-fighting capabilities, even if the

Over 1,000 Type-59 and Type-69 tanks of Chinese origin formed the backbone of the Armoured Corps of the Pakistan Army as of 1999. All of these were upgraded through the addition of British-designed 105mm L7 guns. (Albert Grandolini Collection)

As of 1999, the Artillery Corps of the Pakistan Army was better equipped with self-propelled artillery pieces than that of the Indian Army. This photograph shows a double column of 203mm M110 howitzers of US origin. (Albert Grandolini Collection)

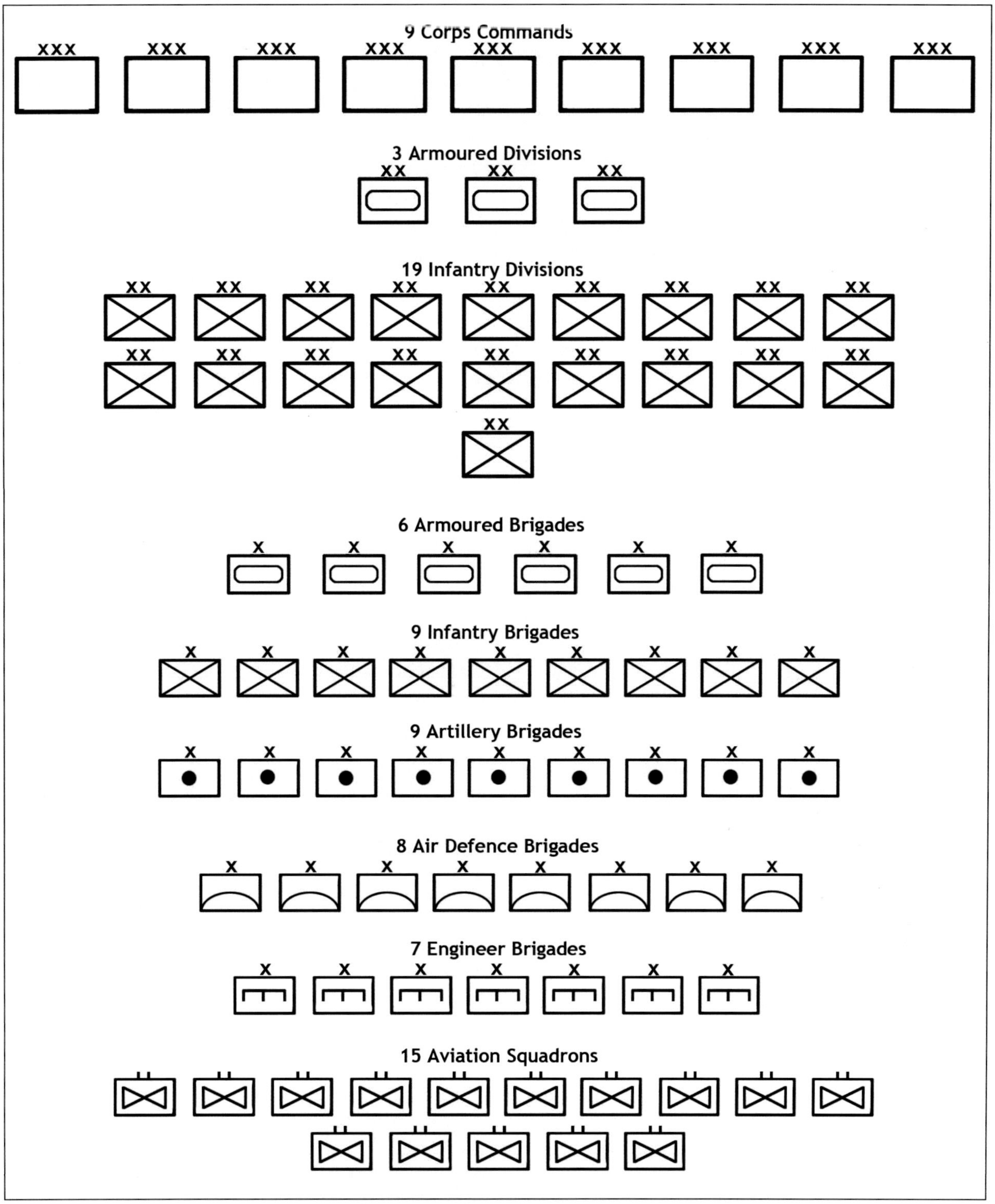


**Table 11: Composition of the 9 Corps HQ & Force Command Northern Area, Pakistan Army**

Pakistani Armoured Corps was making serious efforts to rectify these shortcomings.[16]

## Artillery

As in the case of its Indian counterpart, Pakistan's regiment of artillery had undergone a tremendous re-organization and modernisation programme by 1999. While substantial quantities of new equipment had been inducted, large numbers of completely obsolete artillery pieces – long since relegated to reserve/storage status in the Indian Army – remained in service. While Pakistan had far fewer artillery tubes than the massive Indian artillery park, it is interesting to note that it was responsible for a major organisational innovation: the Pakistani Army created the subcontinent's first artillery division using a core component of two artillery brigades and an air defence unit.[17]

The most noteworthy feature of Pakistan's artillery was the number of 155mm and 203mm self-propelled guns: over 200 of these were in service, providing it with an integral artillery capability that was then lacking in Indian armoured units. Moreover, these guns were more easily operated in a CBRN environment than towed guns. Pakistan's artillery also comprised an assortment of older pieces, including many of vintage 25-Pounders. However, the Artillery Corps made considerable progress through the introduction of fire control computers and other surveillance and target-acquisition equipment, like US-made AN/TPQ-36 and AN/TPQ-37 mortar and artillery

Pakistani infantry on exercise advance with the support of three US-made M48 main battle tanks. (Albert Grandolini Collection)

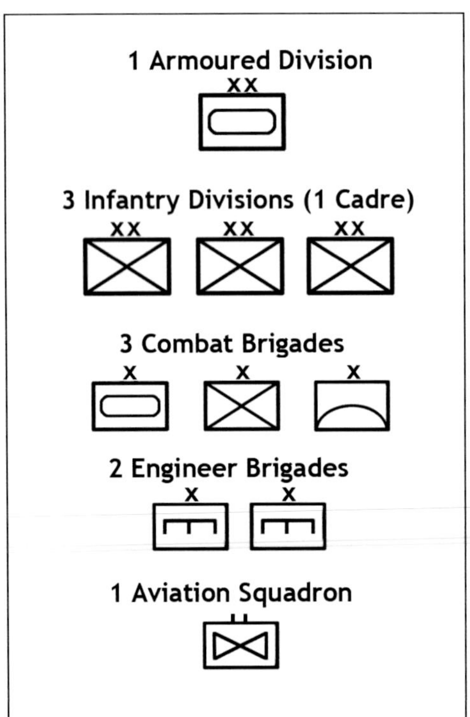


**Table 12: Nominal Composition of the Army Reserve North & South, Pakistan Army**

locating radars, for which the Indian Army had no equivalent at the time. This, of course, dramatically enhanced the efficacy of the artillery – no matter how old the guns were.

### Infantry

There was little difference between Pakistani and Indian army infantry formations. Pakistan did not develop an organization equivalent to the Indian RAPIDs and had not attempted the massive modernisation programme – in terms of modern night vision, target finding and anti-tank weaponry – that the Indian Army was undertaking in 1999.

Pakistan's infantry was equipped with locally manufactured G-3 and Type 56 assault rifles with the MG3 being its standard machinegun. Large numbers of magazine-fed Chinese Type 56 light machineguns were also in widespread service and battalion support weapons were comparable to their Indian counterparts. Pakistani infantry also made extensive use of heavy machineguns for use in the surface role. These were a combination of .5"cal/12.7mm Browning M2HB machineguns and Chinese made copies of the 12.7mm DShK design of Soviet origin. Pakistani forces also made extensive use of jeep-mounted 106mm recoilless rifles and US-made BGM-71 TOW ATGMs. The only really noteworthy aspect of the Pakistani infantry was the fact that it was the first to introduce mechanized units to the subcontinent, provided with over 800 M113 armoured personnel carriers. While not as capable as India's BMP-2s, they provided Pakistan's infantry with a reasonable degree of battlefield mobility.

Acquired soon after the MiG-23BN, the MiG-27M became the most numerous strike platform in the IAF's service during the 1980s and 1990s. (Albert Grandolini Collection)

As of 1999, the MiG-21 – available in variants including the MiG-21FL, MiG-21M and MiG-21bis (visible here) – was still the most numerous and thus the most important point-defence-interceptor and fighter-bomber of the IAF. (Albert Grandolini Collection)

### Air Defence

Unlike the Indian Army, Pakistan lacked any medium self-propelled surface-to-air missiles and modem self-propelled air-defence guns. The Pakistani Army air defence units remained constrained in their ability to obtain advanced self-propelled air-defence assets since Russia, the principal producer of these items, would not sell these items to Islamabad. Therefore, Pakistan's six air defence brigades were equipped with a wide variety of MANPADs and thousands of towed air defence guns, supported by both Western and Chinese-made fire-control radars.[18] Nevertheless, MANPADs were to prove their worth during the Kargil War.

Not the most numerous, but definitely the most advanced fighter-bomber in service with the IAF of the 1990s was the Jaguar IS, locally designated the 'Shamsher'. About 110 were available to a total of five squadrons as of 1999. This example (registration JS110) was operated by No. 5 Squadron ('Tuskers'). (Albert Grandolini Collection)

The third primary fighter-bomber type in service with the IAF of the 1990s was the MiG-23BN, about 70 of which were available. Lacking compatibility with advanced armament, the type was on the way to being replaced by MiG-27Ms. (Albert Grandolini Collection)

# 2
# RIVAL AIR FORCES

The Indian and Pakistani air forces that confronted each other in 1999 were both affected by sanctions following their nuclear tests. These had a significantly more serious impact upon the Pakistan Air Force F-16s, but India also experienced some difficulties sourcing certain Western subsystems. Yet, the most interesting aspect of the state of the air forces was their relatively modest technology levels. The bulk of the two air forces were comprised of relatively low technology platforms such as the MiG-21, F-6 and F-7 which while undoubtedly useful, were very much assets of diminishing utility and capability on the modern battlefield.

Nonetheless, one striking feature of both air forces was their strong professional ethos. Both air forces were thorough professionals and had extremely well developed and established training establishments which produced very well-trained operators, maintenance crews and other support personnel. Both air forces were, of course, rooted in British traditions, having their origins in the Indian Air Force of the pre-Partition India. While there was a divergence in arms supply, with India favouring Soviet/Russian equipment, the training regimens of both forces remained essentially Western with a commensurate ability to make extremely effective use of their equipment despite the limitations thereof.

One striking difference between the Indian and Pakistani air forces was the large force of transport aircraft and medium-lift transport helicopters available to the IAF. The transport force of AN-32, Il-76 and Dornier aircraft was to prove invaluable in supporting Indian troops in Kargil. Moreover, the availability of a large force of helicopters of the Mi-8 and Mi-17 families, enabled Indian units to move significant forces and payloads over short distances, thus endowing them with great flexibility. While possessing assets of its own, the PAF was never able to match the IAF in its ability to support its army counterparts.

| Type | Quantity | Nav/Attack System | Payload | Combat Radius |
|---|---|---|---|---|
| **Jaguar** | 5 squadrons = 110 aircraft | DARIN (all weather attack and ranging) | 2 x R.550 Magic overwing, 4,500kg external stores | 852km on hi-lo-hi profile and internal fuel or 537km on lo-lo-lo profile on internal fuel |
| **MiG-27ML** | 8 squadrons = 200 aircraft | PrNK-23 (weapons aiming), RSBN-6S (nav/attack system), DARIN in the process of being added | 4,000kg external stores | 540km on lo-lo-lo profile with 1 drop tank; 225km on lo-lo-lo profile on internal fuel |
| **MiG-23BN** | 3 squadrons = 70 aircraft | PrNK-23 (navigation and attack) | 3,000kg external stores | 400km on lo-lo-lo mission with 1 drop tank |
| **Total** | **380** | | | |

**Table 13: Primary Fighter-Bombers of the IAF, 1999**

## Indian Strike Assets

In 1999, India operated a large number of strike aircraft. The IAF, then as now, the fourth largest in the world, operated no fewer than sixteen squadrons of nuclear capable strike aircraft. These comprised five Jaguar squadrons, eight MiG-27M squadrons and three MiG-23BN squadrons – numbering well over three hundred aircraft.[1]

The MiG-23BN squadrons were earmarked for the Offensive Air Support (OAS) role and could thus probably be discounted for the nuclear strike role. Some of the MiG-27 squadrons were also earmarked for the OAS task, however, the Indian MiG- 27Ms were fitted with a RSBN-6S navigation system which is associated with the nuclear strike role and Mikoyan has openly acknowledged that the MiG-27 is nuclear capable.[2] The Jaguars were also known to be capable of carrying nuclear weapons, and the 'toss bombing' technique used to deliver nuclear weapons was practised by IAF aircraft during exercise Hammerblow in 1988.[3]

After the nuclear tests of 1998, it is likely that a squadron would have been earmarked for an emergency nuclear role rather than a permanent nuclear alert system with its requirements for a sophisticated command structure. Given the Indian Army's need for air support, plus interdiction and attacks against special targets, the MiG-23/-27 squadrons were likely to be fully occupied. It is, therefore, probable that the main deep strike aircraft would have been the Jaguar, with support from whatever MiG-27Ms could have been spared.

It should be noted that even the vast fleet of Indian MiG-21 combat aircraft could theoretically be used for the strike role. These aircraft would have a very limited range and payload, and as such could not be seriously considered as candidates for anything more than a tactical OAS support role. The then ongoing, and very comprehensive, upgrade program for the MiG-2lbis aircraft of the Indian Air Force which culminated in the MiG-21 Bison added little to their ability to deliver air-to-surface weapons. The fleet of Dassault Mirage 2000 fighter-bombers of the IAF could also be diverted for the deep strike role, but these had air-superiority as a major role and would be at a premium

The 1996 purchase of Sukhoi Su-30MK (I) aircraft and the technology transfer agreement to enable their manufacture in India was highly significant. However, since the Su-30 was originally designed as a long-range interceptor, in 1999 it was unclear as to how the Indian Air Force intended to use them. The Su-30 could, however, carry a very heavy weapons load – including nuclear weapons – over a very long range. In 1999, only a single squadron of Su-30Ks was operational.

## Strengths and Weaknesses of the IAF's Strike Forces

Despite the large number of aircraft at its disposal, the IAF was peculiarly underequipped for modern strike operations. While the MiG-27s were purchased with ordnance that included Kh-25MP, Kh-25, Kh-23 and Kh-29L missiles, the number of these missiles procured

The PAF acquired a total of 40 F-16A/Bs in the mid-1980s, and these entered service with three squadrons. While primarily deployed as interceptors, they still possessed a significant ground-strike capability, as nicely demonstrated by this pre-delivery photograph showing one releasing a total of 12 US-made Mk.82 250kg bombs. (Pakistan Air Force, via Albert Grandolini)

Originally acquired as interceptors armed with air-to-air missiles in the late 1960s, the PAF's Mirage IIIEPs were largely relegated to fighter-bomber roles by the 1990s. (Albert Grandolini Collection)

with unguided munitions and no upgrades to either the MiG-23BN or MiG-27 fleets had been undertaken at the time, with the sole exception that some of the aircraft were finally fitted with chaff/flare dispensers.

The Jaguar fleet comprised the core of India's deep penetration strike assets and with its DARIN Nav/attack system, the Jaguar excelled at delivering unguided munitions with great accuracy. Unfortunately, in the Kargil sector, the fully-loaded Jaguar was extremely sluggish and its utility was perforce limited for mountain strikes. Like the MiG-23BN fleet, and like most of the MiG-27 fleet, India's Jaguars lacked stand-off munitions and integration with laser-guided bombs, although India had been moving towards integrating such weapons at the time of the Kargil conflict.

The bulk of the Indian air effort was always viewed as being borne by the MiG-21 fleet, but this force – while being quite useful as point defence interceptors with their R-60 and R.550 air-to-air missiles – was not particularly capable. Lacking an effective all-weather nav/attack system, the MiG-21 fleet was limited to using unguided 57mm and 240mm rockets and 250kg bombs. The MiG-21MF fleet did have the ability to launch Kh-23 missiles (ASCC/NATO-codename 'AS-7 Kerry'), but it is unclear if any were still operational in 1999.

Pending the induction of the Su-30MKI with its arsenal of guided weapons, the most potent strike asset for precision work in the IAF was the Mirage 2000. Already armed with French-made BLG-66 Belouga submunitions, this fleet proved compatible with the US and British-made Paveway laser-guided bombs, guided with help of the French-made ATLIS II laser designators. However, the quantity of laser-guided bombs, guidance kits and designator pods was relatively small. Moreover, while the ATLIS designator pod and Matra 1,000kg laser-guided bombs delivered with the aircraft were deemed to be extremely effective, they were also seen as exceedingly expensive and thus used only sparingly. The characteristics of the three major types of Indian strike aircraft available as of 1999 are outlined in Table 13 on page 19.[4]

In addition to the remaining Mirage IIIEPs, Mirage 5s of several sub-variants formed the backbone of the PAF's fighter-bomber fleet as of 1999. As indicated by the insignia low on the fin of the jet in the rear, these two examples were assigned to the Combat Command School (the fighter-weapons school of the PA). (Photo by Peter Steineman, via Albert Grandolini)

| Type | Quantity | Payload | Combat Radius |
|---|---|---|---|
| **F-16A/B** | 34 | 7,575kg | 547km on hi-lo-hi profile with 3,000kg of bombs |
| **Mirage III/V** | 140 | 4,000kg | 685km on lo-lo-lo profile with 800kg bombs and 3 drop tanks |
| **A-5C** | ~60 | 1,000kg | 400km on lo-lo-lo profile with 1,000kg bombs and 2 drop tanks |
| **Total** | **~250** | | |

**Table 14: Primary Fighter-Bombers of the PAF, 1999**

was relatively small in number. The aircraft had no capability, at the time, to deliver laser-guided bombs and were largely deployed with unguided munitions such as 57mm, 68mm and 240mm unguided rockets, 250kg and 500kg unguided bombs, and French-made BAP.100 runway denial bombs. Of interest is the fact that both the MiG-27 and MiG-23BN fleets operated much the same unguided ordnance. The MiG-23BN, despite being in service in substantial numbers, did not have any stand-off munitions capability and was employed solely

### Pakistan's Strike Assets

As in the case of its much larger counterpart, the Indian Air Force, Pakistan's Air Force operated a large number of very capable strike aircraft. In 1999, Pakistan's aircraft, like India's were a mix of some extremely sophisticated types and a larger number of older types, the cutting edge being composed of American supplied F-16s.[5] Forty of these extremely potent aircraft had been delivered to Pakistan and about thirty-four remained in service in 1999.[6]

The second most-numerous fighter-bomber in service with the PAF as of 1999 was the Chinese-manufactured Shenyang A-5C. This pair are shown releasing four 250kg bombs each. (Albert Grandolini Collection)

As impressive as these aircraft were, the Pakistani Air Force faced a major dilemma when considering them for the dedicated strike role. The F-16A/B was not only Pakistan's most potent strike aircraft, but also the PAF's only truly effective all-weather interceptor. In fact, of the three squadrons equipped with the type, all had air superiority as their primary role.[7] This meant that the nuclear strike role had to be relegated to some of the older types in the Pakistani Air Force. In 1999 Pakistan operated over 70 Dassault Mirage III and 70 Dassault Mirage V aircraft. These were augmented by ex-Spanish aircraft used as sources of spares. Certainly enough, all the Mirages were of vintage design, but they were still viable combat aircraft and many were equipped with advanced nav/attack systems.

The bulk of Pakistan's tactical attack force was made up of three squadrons of Nanchang A-5 attack aircraft.[8] Grouped within 36 Tactical Attack Wing, they were dedicated to the ground support of the Pakistani Army. These aircraft could theoretically be used for the delivery of strike weapons, but they lacked any advanced avionics and possessed only an extremely basic countermeasures suite. As such, they were thus of very limited use over a battlefield likely to become saturated by advanced air defence systems.

The bulk of the Pakistan Air Force consisted of a large number of Chinese F-6s and F-7s – clones of the MiG-19 & MiG-21, respectively.[9] The F-7s were being upgraded with a new radar, but these two types possessed a very short range and were not equipped with modem countermeasures: indeed, they were extremely unlikely to be committed to any but the most basic strike role.

The primary characteristics of the PAF's strike aircraft as of 1999 are summarised in Table 14.[10]

### Weaknesses of Pakistan's Strike Force

The Pakistani F-16 and Mirage III/V fleets were very capable strike platforms and were able to employ laser-guided bombs and some stand-off munitions such as the Maverick missile. Moreover, the F-16 and Mirage fleets had undergone periodic upgrades to their countermeasures suites and were fitted with chaff/flare dispensers. Both the Mirage and F-16 fleets were also capable of accurate delivery of unguided munitions and were quite capable of excellent results even with standard 250kg or 500kg bombs.

The same cannot be said for the Nanchang Q-5 fleet which was suffering from severe spares problems and was at best a mediocre tactical attack platform. Based on the Shenyang F-6 clone of the MiG-19, the Nanchang Q-5 was a significant improvement in respect of range and ordnance capacity over its stablemate. On the other hand, it lacked modern countermeasures and had no capability to deliver precision guided munitions or stand-off munitions. Equipped solely with unguided rockets and bombs, it offered no improvement in quality of munitions over the F-6 which still had a secondary attack role, or even over the F-7 which was a rather modest improvement over the MiG-21 in every practical military aspect.

### Strategic Air Defence Assets

In 1999 both nations faced financial constraints, although this did not prevent them from acquiring sophisticated air defence equipment. In addition, both India and Pakistan had to contend with the increasing sophistication of the attacking force available to the opposing side. In the 1990s, India embarked on a two-fold approach. Its strike forces were dramatically upgraded with the Prithvi SSMs and upgrades to the Jaguar and MiG-27 fleets. In addition, Indian air defences were being expanded and re-equipped with weapons and sensors that would render an attack by either Pakistani missiles or aircraft an extremely risky proposition. Pakistan, on the other hand, had been unable to procure modern surface-to-air missiles in any meaningful numbers.

### Strategic Air Defences in India[11]

India, with its vast airspace, maintained an advanced, integrated Air Defence Ground Environment System (ADGES). This system, along with the civilian Air Traffic Control. (ATC), was responsible for the detection, identification and, if necessary, the interception of aircraft in Indian airspace. As of 1999, the ADGES was in the process of being upgraded to cater for ballistic missile threats. Before examining the system in detail, a quick overview is in order.

Essentially, India's air defence network was divided into two parts:

- ADGES, and
- Base Air Defence Zones (BADZ).

These two components were closely linked, and shared information related to air defence tasks. The Air Defence Ground Environment System consisted of an array of radars along the western and northern borders as well as a network of mobile systems in the north east and

In reaction to the US sale of F-16s to Pakistan, the IAF rushed to acquire MiG-23MF interceptors from the USSR. The type proved to be something of a disappointment and although retained in service for nearly two decades, was never pressed into action. (Albert Grandolini Collection)

south of the country. The ADGES network was responsible for overall airspace management and detection of intruders: it also controlled and coordinated the air defences deployed for protection of major urban areas. The Base Air Defence Zones, as the name implies, were tasked with the defence of high value targets – air bases, nuclear installations and key military installations. Essentially, each of the BADZ was a scaled down ADGES network, limited to an arc of 100km. The BADZ were providing a much more concentrated air defence environment than the ADGES and provided the only gap-free air defence cover.

## Indian Air Defences: Sensor Network

The ADGES of 1999 employed a three-tier detection network. The first layer consisted of Mobile Observation Posts (MOPs).[12] Each of the MOPs consisted of a two-man team equipped with a HF/VHF radio set and field glasses.[13] The personnel in the MOP were very well versed in the visual identification of aircraft as well as their general direction of flight, and they were deployed along the borders at random intervals, ranging between 25 and 45 kilometres. The MOPs gave the first warning of airborne intrusion, the general direction of the attack and, more often than not, the number of aircraft and their type. The MOP-teams were assisted in this task by personnel from the Indian police forces and Railway Protection Force, who were given some training in aircraft identification. These agencies reported via a communications system based on both HF/VHF radio sets as well as telephone lines. A more advanced communications system based on fibre optic cables and satellite communications was also available to assist the MOPs in reporting to the radar picket line.

The radar picket line, which lay about 150km behind the MOPs, consisted of a number of radar clusters. These comprised three radar stations separated by a distance of the sum of their radii, such that their coverage overlapped. The equipment issued to these clusters generally comprised one license-made Soviet-designed ST-68/U and two P-18 or P-19 radars.[14] These were then flanked by two P-12 or P-15 radars. The ST-68/U acted as the control and reporting centres (CRC). This may have changed somewhat as the ST-68U, which was plagued with some nagging development problems, largely replaced older Soviet-made equipment. Moreover, India had been license producing the French designed TRS-2215D 3-D surveillance radar for a number of years and derived an indigenously built radar – the PSM-33 Mk.2 – from it. These had probably supplanted most of the older Soviet-bloc equipment by 1999.[15] Such 'radar pickets' were responsible for giving accurate information on any intruding force to the Air Defence Control Centres (ADCC) located behind the radar picket line. The picket line and the ADCC were separated by a first layer of air defence weapons, which were planned to be the first to engage any potential intruders.

However, the backbone of the ADGES were the THD-1955 3D long-range surveillance radars.[16] Originally of French design, these were licence manufactured in India for a number of years. Although somewhat aged, the THD-1955 was still providing sterling performance and proved capable of maximum detection ranges of up to 1,000 Kilometres – even if during the peacetime the IAF usually limited its power-output to about 400 kilometres range.

The BADZs also consisted of three layers, including the MOPs, a mixed layer of air defence weapons and their associated radars, and a picket line of radars capable of detecting low-flying aircraft, in turn supported by air defence weapons (the centrepiece of each BADZ was one ST-68U radar). As such, they provided comprehensive and gap-free coverage over their assigned areas of responsibility, and some observers compared their overall capability with that of a carrier battle group of the US Navy: any attacking aircraft not only had to get past the ADGES, but then also to penetrate the far more formidable BADZ.[17]

## Manned Interceptors

India's air defences in 1999 relied on a mix of MiG-21/-23/-29 and Mirage 2000 interceptors and thirty-eight squadrons of surface-to-air missiles (SAMs). The SAM units comprised 30 squadrons of S-125 Pechora (ASCC/NATO-codename 'SA-3 Goa'), and 8 squadrons of 9K33M3 (ASCC/NATO-codename 'SA-8b Gecko') systems and were deployed to protect key air bases as well as some major military/industrial centres. Though the SAMs were old, they had been updated periodically and, when operating as part of the BADZ, were deployed in such a manner as to minimize their shortcomings. In addition, a large number of L40/70 radar directed 40mm anti-aircraft guns and Igla-1M MANPADs ware deployed to provide a 'last-ditch' tier of 'hard-kill' defences. It should be pointed out, however, that this system was geared up for the defence of point targets and not for overall area defence.

Two self-propelled launchers, each for four R.440 Crotale SAMs of the Pakistan Air Force. (Albert Grandolini Collection)

The first signs that India was modernizing its air defences came when a massive order was placed for Sukhoi Su-30 combat aircraft. These aircraft, the first batch of which was in the process of being delivered in 1999, were primarily long-range interceptors, capable of intercepting targets at ranges exceeding 120km. When this was added to the fact that India's ongoing MiG-21bis upgrade program was primarily aimed at enhancing the aircraft's air defence capabilities and India's program for an airborne early warning aircraft had been resurrected after many years in the doldrums, it can be seen that India's fighter defences were about to be dramatically enhanced.

The IAF's interceptors were equipped with a mix of French and Russian air-to-air missiles. All aircraft were cleared to launch R-60 (ASCC/NATO-codename 'AA-8 Aphid') and Matra R.550 Magic short-range missiles while the MiG-29, Su-30 and Mirage 2000 were cleared to launch R-73 (ASCC/NATO-codename 'AA-11 Archer'), R-27 (ASCC/NATO-codename 'AA-10 Alamo') and Matra Super 530D

| Unit | Aircraft Type | Base | Notes |
|---|---|---|---|
| **Central Air Command** | | HQ Allahabad | |
| No.1 Sqn Tigers | Mirage 2000H/TH | Gwalior | |
| No.7 Sqn Battle Axes | Mirage 2000H/TH | Gwalior | |
| No.16 Sqn Cobras | Jaguar IS | Gorakhpur | |
| No. 27 Sqn Flaming Arrows | Jaguar IS | Gorakhpur | |
| No. 35 Sqn | MiG-21M, Canberra PR.Mk.57 | Bareilly | |
| No.102 Sqn Trisonics | MiG-25RB/U | Bareilly | |
| No. 11 Sqn Rhinos | HS.748 | Gwalior | |
| No. 12 Sqn Bisons | An-32 | Agra | |
| No. 44 Sqn Mountain Geese | Il-76MD | Agra | |
| No. 106. Sqn Lynxes | HS.748 | Agra | |
| No. 105 HU Golden Eagles | Mi-8 | Gorakhput | |
| **Eastern Air Command** | | HQ Shillong | |
| No.20 Sqn Thunderbolts | MiG-27M | Kalaikunda | |
| No.22 Sqn Swallows | MiG-27M | Hashimara | |
| No.222 Sqn Tiger Sharks | MiG-27M | Hashimara | |
| No.8 Sqn Eight Pursoot | MiG-21FL | Baghdoghra | |
| No.29 Sqn Scorpions | MiG-21FL | Jorhat | |
| No.30 Sqn Charging Rhinos | MiG-21FL | Tezpur | |

**Table 15: IAF Order of Battle, 1998-1999**[25]

| Unit | Aircraft Type | Base | Notes |
|---|---|---|---|
| No.33 Sqn Caribous | An-32 | Gauhati | |
| No.43 Sqn Ibexes | An-32 | Jorhat | |
| No.49 Sqn Para Spears | An-32 | Jorhat | |
| No.50 Sqn Hornbills | Do.228 | Gauhati | |
| No.122. HU | Mi-8 | Andaman | |
| **South-Western Air Command** | | HQ Jodhpur | |
| No.24 Sqn Hunting Hawks | Su-30K | Poona, Ambala | |
| No.28 Sqn First Supersonics | MiG-29A/UB | Poona | |
| No.47 Sqn Archers | MiG-29A/UB | Poona | |
| No.10 Sqn Winged Daggers | MiG-27M | Jodhpur | |
| No.32 Sqn Killers | MiG-27M | Jaisalmer | |
| No.51 Sqn Sword Arms | MiG-21M | Jamnagar | |
| No.226 Sqn | MiG-23MF | Jodhpur | |
| No.4 Sqn Orioles | MiG-21bis | Jaisalmer | |
| No.6 Sqn Dragons | Jaguar IM, Canberra B(I).Mk.8 | Poona | |
| No.107 HU Desert Hawks | Mi-8 | Jodhpur | |
| No.115 HU | Cheetah | Jodhpur | |
| No.116 HU Tankbusters | Cheetah/Mi-35? | Jodhpur | |
| **Western Air Command** | | HQ Palam (Delhi) | |
| No.223 Sqn Tridents | MiG-29A/UB | Adempur | |
| No.2 Sqn Winged Arrows | MiG-27M | Hindan | |
| No.9 Sqn Wolfpack | MiG-27M | Hindan | |
| No.18 Sqn Flying Bullets | MiG-27M | Hindan | |
| No.31 Sqn Ocelots | MiG-23BN | Halwara | |
| No.220 Sqn Desert Lions/Tigers | MiG-23BN | Adempur | |
| No.221 Sqn Valiants | MiG-23BN | Halwara | |
| No.224 Sqn Warlords | MiG-23MF | Adempur | |
| No.5 Sqn Tuskers | Jaguar IS | Ambala | |
| No.14 Sqn Bulls | Jaguar IS | Ambala | |
| No.3 Sqn Rattlers | MiG-21bis | Pathankot | |
| No.15 Sqn Flying Lancers | MiG-21bis | Chandigarh | |
| No.21 Sqn Ankush | MiG-21bis | Chandigarh | |
| No.23 Sqn Cheetahs | MiG-21bis | Ambala | |
| No.17 Sqn Golden Arrows | MiG-21M | Bathinda | |
| No.101 Sqn Falcons | MiG-21M | Adempur | |
| No.108 Sqn Hawkeyes | MiG-21M | Palam | |
| No.25 Sqn Himalayan Eagles | Il-76MD | Chandigarh | |
| No.41 Sqn Otters | Do.228 | Palam | |
| No.48 Sqn Camels | An-32 | Chandigarh | |
| No.104 HU Pioneer Rotorians | Mi-25/35 | Pathankot | |
| No.114 HU Siachen Pioneers | Cheetah | Siachen | |
| No.125 HU | Mi-25/35 | Pathankot | |
| No.126 HU Featherweights | Mi-26 | Pathankot | |

**Table 15: IAF Order of Battle, 1998-1999** (continued)[25]

| Unit | Aircraft Type | Base | Notes |
|---|---|---|---|
| **Southern Air Command** | | ? | |
| No.19 Sqn ? | An-32 | Tambaram | |
| No.109 HU Knights | Mi-8 | Palam | |
| **Balance of the IAF** | | bases unclear | |
| No.26 Sqn Warriors | MiG-21bis | ? | |
| No.36 Sqn | MiG-21bis | ? | |
| No.37 Sqn Black Panthers | MiG-21bis | ? | |
| No.45 Sqn Colts | MiG-21bis | ? | |
| No.52 Sqn Sharks | MiG-21bis | ? | |
| No.110 HU Vanguards | Mi-8/17 | ? | |
| No.111 HU | Mi-8/17 | ? | |
| No.112 HU | HAL Cheetah or Chetak | ? | |
| No.117 HU | Mi-17 | ? | |
| No.118 HU | Mi-17 | ? | |
| No.119 HU | Mi-17 | ? | |
| No.120 HU | Mi-8 | ? | |
| No.121 HU | Mi-8 | ? | |
| No.125 HU | Mi-25 | ? | |
| No.128 HU | Mi-8 | ? | |
| No.129 HU Nubra Warriors | Mi-8 | ? | |
| No.130 HU | Mi-8 | ? | |
| No.151 HU | Mi-8/17 | ? | |
| No.152 HU Mighty Armour | Mi-8/17 | ? | |
| No.153 HU Daring Dragons | Mi-17 | ? | |

**Table 15: IAF Order of Battle, 1998-1999** (continued) [25]

| Unit | Aircraft Type | Base | Notes |
|---|---|---|---|
| **Northern Air Command** | | Peshawar | |
| HQ. Flt. | PAC/MFI-17 | Peshawar | |
| **33. Fighter Wing** | | | |
| No. 14 Sqn Shaheens/Tailchoppers | F-16A/B | Kamra | |
| No. 15 Sqn Cobras | F-6/F-7P | Kamra | |
| **36. Fighter Wing** | | | |
| No. 16 Sqn Panthers | A-5III | Peshawar | |
| No. 26 Sqn Black Spiders | A-5III | Peshawar | |
| No. 81. Sqn | Alouette III | Peshawar | |
| **37. Wing** | | | |
| No. 1 FCU | FT-5 | Mianwali | |
| No. 19 Sqn Warhawks/Sherdils | F-6/F-7P | Mianwali | |
| No. 25 Sqn Black Eagles | F-7P | Mianwali | |
| No. 86 Sqn | Alouette III | Mianwali | |
| **Central Air Command** | | Sargodha | |
| 34. Fighter Wing | | | |
| No.5 Sqn | Mirage IIIEP/RP/DP | Rafiqui | |
| No.18 Sqn | F-7P | Rafiqui | |

**Table 16: PAF Order of Battle, 1998**[26]

| Unit | Aircraft Type | Base | Notes |
|---|---|---|---|
| No.20 Sqn Cheetahs | F-7P | Rafiqui | |
| No.33 Sqn Skybolts ? | Mirage 5PA2 | Rafiqui | |
| No.83 Sqn | Alouette III | Rafiqui | |
| No.456 Sqn | Crotale SAM | Rafiqui | |
| **38. Fighter Wing** | | | |
| No.9 Sqn Griffins | F-16A/B | Sargodha | |
| No.11 Sqn Arrows | F-16A/B | Sargodha | |
| No.24 Sqn Blinders | Falcon 20 | Sargodha | |
| No.82 Sqn | Alouette III | Sargodha | |
| No.451. Sqn | Crotale SAM | Sargodha | |
| **Combat Command School** | F-6, Mirage 5PA | Sargodha | |
| **Southern Air Command** | | Faisal | |
| **No.31 Fighter Wing** | | | |
| No.17 Sqn Tigers | F-6/F-7MG? | Samugli | |
| No.23 Sqn | F-6/F-7MG? | Samugli | |
| No.85 Sqn | Alouette III | Samugli | |
| No.454 Sqn | Crotale SAM | Samugli | |
| **32. Composite Wing** | | | |
| No.2 Composite Sqn Flt. A | F-7P | Masroor | |
| Flt. B | T-33A/RT-33A | Masroor | |
| No.7 Sqn Bandits | A-5III | Masroor | |
| No.8 Sqn | Mirage 5PA3 | Masroor | |
| No.22 OCU | Mirage IIIDP/5PA/ 5PA2/5DP/ 5DPA2/O | Masroor | |
| No.84 Sqn Dolphins | Alouette III | Masroor | |
| No.453 Sqn | Crotale SAM | Masroor | |
| No.4?? Sqn | HQ-2B (SA-2) | Masroor | |
| **35. Composite Wing** | | | |
| No.6 Sqn Antelopes | C-130B/E, L-100-20 Hercules | Chaklala | |
| No.12 Sqn | Fokker F.27, Falcon 20 | Chaklala | |
| No.29 Sqn | Atlantic 1, P-3C | | |
| No.41 Sqn | Boeing 707-340C, Beach King Air 200, Cessna 172N, Piper Seneca, Beech Baron | Chaklala | |
| No.4 Sqn | Mi-8/17 | Dhamial, Rahwali | |
| No.84 Sqn | Alouette III, SA.315B, HH-43B | Chaklala | |
| No.455. Sqn | Crotale | Chaklala | |
| No.4?? Sqn | HQ-2B | Chaklala | |
| Balance of PAF | | bases unclear | |
| No.17 Sqn | A-5III ? | ? | |
| No.23 Sqn | F-6/FT-6/F-7P? | ? | |

**Table 16: PAF Order of Battle, 1998** (continued) [26]

guided air-to-air missiles. India had also already ordered Russian-made R-77 (ASCC/NATO-codename 'AA-12 Adder') missiles for its upgraded MiG-21bis and Su-30 aircraft, and the first batch of these arrived either in late 1998 or early 1999. To these dedicated interceptors – which routinely carried air-to-air missiles – must be added India's tactical strike aircraft: the Jaguars, MiG-27s and MiG-23BNs could all be armed with R-60s and R.550s. Owing to their large numbers, their secondary air defence role could not be ignored. Overall, by 1999, the IAF's air defence network was relatively advanced, even if not gap-free outside the BADZs.

### Strategic Air Defences in Pakistan[18]

Pakistan's Air Defence Command was formed in 1975 – over a decade before that of India. It was based at Chaklala near Rawalpindi and exercised control, surveillance and coordination over all of Pakistani airspace. The ADC HQ was based in bunkers constructed between five and ten metres under the ground, and its centrepiece had four rows of consoles with 20-25 men operating the main terminals.[19] Indeed, as of 1999, the ADC HQ's set-up was regarded as being one of the most modern in existence.

Subordinate to the ADC HQ were four Sector Operations Centres (Quetta, Sargodha, Karachi and Peshawar), which in turn controlled seven control & reporting centres (CRCs).[20] As in the case of India, Pakistan had a comprehensive radar network which could also accept data from the civilian air traffic control radar. The radar network was established from 1976 onwards as part of Project Crystal which aimed to give Pakistan a modern air defence network. Pakistan operated a bewildering variety of radars from varying sources. In 1999, the most modern units were six Westinghouse AN/TPS-43G 3-D long range radars. These were supplemented by some older American, Chinese and British long-range radars.[21]

In regards of low-altitude radars, in 1979-1980, as the first stage of Project Crystal, Pakistan purchased 45 mobile pulse doppler radars from Siemens of Germany. These systems were of the MPDR 45/E type – an extremely capable radar – and were controlled by six CRCs. They greatly enhanced Pakistan's ability to detect aircraft operating at low altitudes[22] However, because most of Pakistan's major military and civilian facilities were located close to the border to India, the ADC always had very little time to react: this was a problem for which Pakistan simply could not find a solution. Moreover, despite major investment into advanced radar systems, the ADC had a major gap in its coverage along the border from Sialkot to Suleimanike, where several major facilities were located.[23] In attempt to bridge this gap, the PAF hoped to purchase Grumman E-2C Hawkeye airborne early warning (AEW) aircraft from the USA, but this order failed to materialise.

Pakistan's air defences were centred around three squadrons of F-16A/B aircraft, backed up by large numbers of Chinese F-7s and French Mirage III/Vs. These aircraft, while reasonably effective, were all handicapped by the lack of medium- and long-range air-to-air missiles and, in the case of the F-7 and Mirage fleets, the lack of truly modern radars. Pakistan had hoped to obtain up to 40 Mirage 2000-5 aircraft from France, but the deal never materialised. Thus, the PAF was forced to launch an upgrade of its Mirages and F-7s with the hope of making them more viable in the all-weather interceptor role.

As of 1999, Pakistan's SAM defences were also peculiarly thin – comprising only between six and eight squadrons of the French-made R.440 Crotale mobile SAMs and one squadron of HQ-2Js (Chinese versions of the Soviet-made S-75 system, codenamed 'SA-2 Guideline' by the ASCC/NATO).[24] This lack of SAMs was quite surprising, and probably caused not only by the lack of sources for such weaponry, but also their high operating costs.

The Pakistani SAMs were backed up by a very large number (up to 43) air defence regiments equipped with tube artillery, and a number of reserve formations, largely operating Chinese-made anti-aircraft guns ranging in calibre from 12.7mm to 37mm. While these provided some defence against aircraft, they were of no use against missiles.

# 3
# NUCLEAR FACTOR

By 1999, both India and Pakistan had deployed large nuclear arsenals. However, assessments of their nuclear capabilities were still largely confined to views that only fission weapons in the form of free-fall bombs in the 15-20 kiloton range were available for deployment. With the benefit of hindsight, it is now quite well established that both countries had deployed nuclear weapons in either the late 1980s or at the latest, the mid-1990s. What changed, however, was that in May 1998, both countries tested nuclear weapons, thus refining and experimenting with their designs as well as confirming their nuclear status.

### India[1]

On 11 May 1998, India announced that it had tested a fission device, a low-yield device and thermonuclear device. Two days later, these tests were followed by two sub-kiloton tests. Known as 'Operation Shakti-98', the five tests had a recorded seismic magnitude of 5.0+/-0.4 on the Richter scale.[2] By May 14, Indian seismologists at the Bhabha Atomic Research Centre (BARC) stated that an analysis of the data received at the Gauribidnaur Seismic Array indicated that the yield of the 11 May blasts was around 55 kilotons.[3] They also indicated that the seismic waveform was very complex because the explosions were carried out simultaneously. The first group of tests – Shakti I,II & III – consisted of a two-stage thermonuclear device with a yield of 43-45 kilotons (kt), a lightweight fission device with a yield of 12-15kt and a low-yield device of 0.2kt. These were placed in two shafts, one kilometre apart, and simultaneously detonated from a control located 3.5km away.[4] Shakti IV & V had yields of 0.5 and 0.3 kilotons respectively and were conducted to provide additional data for improved computer simulation of designs.

Almost immediately a somewhat unseemly row erupted between Indian scientists and certain American seismologists regarding the yields of the devices. Preliminary estimates put the combined yields at anywhere between 10 and 25 kilotons and some questioned whether India had actually tested a thermonuclear device based on these yield estimates. This row continues with an American scientist – Dr Terry Wallace – giving a yield of 10-15kt and practically accusing the Indians scientists of lying.[5]

| Reactor | Capacity | Plutonium Output | Weapons Potential |
|---|---|---|---|
| **Cirus** | 40MW | 9-10kg/year | 1-2/yr |
| **Dhruva** | 100MW | 20-25kg/year | 4-5/yr |
| **MAPP – Madras** | 2 x 235MWe | 2 x 60kg/year | 2 x 12 = 24/yr |
| **NAPP – Narora** | 2 x 235MWe | 2 x 60kg/year | 2 x 12 = 24/yr |
| KAPP – Kakrapar | 2 x 235MWe | 2 x 60kg/year | 2 x 12 = 24/yr |
| Total | | 389-395kg/yr | 77-79kg/yr |

**Table 17: Indian Nuclear Capability in 1999**

| Source | Stockpile in 1991 | Stockpile in 1995 |
|---|---|---|
| **Cirus Reactor** | 245kg | 280kg |
| **Dhurva Reactor** | 100kg | 190kg |
| **CANDU (First Discharges)** | 15kg | 30kg |
| **Total** | 360kg | 500kg |

**Table 18: India, Available Weapons-Grade Plutonium**

| Source | By 1991 | By 1995 |
|---|---|---|
| **1974 test** | 10kg | 10kg |
| **Processing losses (3%)** | 10kg | 15kg |
| **Fast reactor** | 50kg | 50kg |
| **Total consumption** | 70kg | 75kg |
| **Total Stockpile** | 290kg | 425kg |

**Table 19: India, Consumption of Weapons Grade Plutonium**

According to David Albright, a scientist at the Institute of Science and International Security in Washington D.C., the lower estimates were largely due to the fact that a few Western scientists were of the view that India's first atomic test in 1974 fizzled and produced a yield of only 2kt.[6] However, P.K. lyengar, former chairman of India's Atomic Energy Commission, has stated that the yield was between 8-10kt based on radiochemical analysis of samples of bomb debris taken from the shaft.[7]

Soon after Wallace's article, three Indian scientists writing in *Current Science*, gave a detailed account of why Wallace was wrong. These scientists pointed out that there was a very large variation in the estimates of the body-wave magnitude made by different seismic stations. The variations at stations at similar distances from the explosion site varied by a staggering factor of 30 – or three times as much as expected.[8] The scientists pointed out that seismic stations located to the east and west of Pokhran recorded lower magnitudes than those located to the north and south of Pokhran. Since two large explosions – the thermonuclear device and the fission device – were detonated in separate shafts one kilometre apart in an east-west direction, delays between the two signals could result in seismic stations recording lower strengths than the actual values.[9]

The article went on to say that seismic stations to the north and south of Pokhran would have the least time delay and so would record the highest signal strength, while those to the east and west would have the maximum delay. Averaging out all seismic stations would therefore lower the value. Moreover, the true body-wave magnitude would have to be obtained by superposing the signals from the two powerful explosions.[10] The scientists, Dr S. K. Sikka, Dr Falguni Roy and Dr G. K. Nair of the BARC High Pressure Physics Division, believed that a true estimate of the body-wave magnitude could only be obtained by taking the data from seismic stations to the north and south of Pokhran. The data from the ten stations to the north and two to the south indicated a body wave magnitude of 5.36. If the reading of one station was excluded because the signal to noise ratio was too low, the average value rose to 5.39 which tallied with BARC's own measurements at Gauribidanaur. This data agreed with the yield claims made by Indian weapons scientists.[11] To complicate matters further, Dr Roger Clark, a seismologist at Leeds University, stated that after data from 12 seismic stations was considered, the yield estimate was close to 60kt. 'The US Geological survey indicated that the body-wave magnitude was 5.2 which suggested a yield of 30-60 kiloton'.[12]

Of great concern was the fact that the 13 May explosions were undetected. This has led to scientists like Wallace alleging that these tests never took place. However, Clark points out that if the Indians tested in a sand dune, as claimed by Dr Chidambaram, or if the devices were exploded in a large cavity, then the tests could have been completely concealed. The other possibility was that the tests were hydro nuclear or sub-critical tests as was claimed by Dr Raja Ramanna.[13]

There was another major controversy over India's nuclear tests. There was considerable doubt that India had detonated a thermonuclear device. Once the yield estimates were more or less verified, doubts focused on the fact that the device seemed to have a low yield. The yield of 43 kilotons was said by some to be too small for a thermonuclear device and questioned whether India's device had worked as planned. This is factually incorrect .The United States, for example, tested two thermonuclear devices in 1953 with yields of 23kt

| Source Type | Location | Capacity | Notes |
|---|---|---|---|
| **Ultracentrifuges at Uranium Enrichment Plants** | Kahuta | 50kg of weapons grade uranium per year | Second plant reported as under construction |
| **Plutonium Reprocessing Plant** | Chasma | 100-200kg of plutonium per year | Incomplete; work continuing with Chinese support |
| **Power Reactor** | Karachi | 125MWe | Safeguarded |
| **Research Reactor** | Kushab | 50MWe | Under construction with Chinese assistance; start-up date unclear |
| **Power Reactor** | Chasma | 300MWe | In planning |

**Table 20: Pakistani Nuclear Capability in 1999**

The major Pakistani nuclear plant in Kahuta. (Albert Grandolini Collection)

and 43kt. Doctor Frank Barnaby, writing in Jane's Defence Weekly also disagreed, stating that thermonuclear devices did not need to be tested at full yield and could be limited to firing the nuclear-fission trigger and producing a small amount of fusion energy.[14] Moreover, from chapter two of the same thesis, it has been shown that India had all the components in place for a thermonuclear design. As such, scepticism in this regard seemed unwarranted. Bamaby suggested that an operational Indian thermonuclear weapon was likely to contain a boosted-fission nuclear trigger giving an explosion of 50kt which would produce 500kt in the fusion stage.[15] He further suggested that a variable yield nuclear weapon could be produced in this way, allowing a yield of 5kt, 50kt or 500kt to be chosen.[16] An Indian nuclear scientist claimed that the device tested was a 'third- generation' fusion device. Moreover, it has also been suggested that if India's stocks of weapons grade plutonium are used to make triggers for thermonuclear weapons instead, reactor-grade plutonium could be used to dramatically increase India's available fissile material stockpile. Overall, as of 1998-1999, India's nuclear capability rested on the potential use of reactors listed in Table 17.[17]

It should be noted that the power plants at Madras, Narora and Kakrapar may or may not have been used for the manufacture of weapons grade plutonium. However, they were definitely capable of such production and unsafeguarded reactors of this type remain a potential factor in calculations of India's nuclear weapons potential. Whether India used any of these power reactors for weapons production is debatable but it is suspected that reactor grade plutonium was used in at least a couple of the Shakti-1 tests to determine whether it could be usefully used to bolster fissile material stocks for weapons production.

Available weapons grade plutonium was estimated in 1995 as listed in Table 18. At the time, this was estimated as sufficient for about 85 nuclear weapons.[18]

### Pakistan[19]

Much of what has been said regarding yield analysis of India's nuclear tests can also be applied in the case of Pakistan. Pakistan claimed to have conducted a total of six tests between 28 May and 30 May 1998. Dr A. Q. Khan claimed that the largest test had a yield of 30-35 kilotons and was a boosted fission device, while four others were tactical weapons with a low-yield. Allegedly, there was also another 12 kiloton fission device.[20] Once again, the seismic data showed major variations, with an indication that the total explosive yield was between 7 and 8 kilotons.[21] The alleged boosted-fission test apparently gave a seismic reading of only 2-3kt.[22] Given that Pakistan had been in possession of a viable nuclear weapon design from China, with a yield of 20-25kt, it is rather surprising that the seismic readings were so low. However, just as there were many factors that rendered the seismic analysis of India's tests somewhat suspect, the same would probably hold true for Pakistan as well, though Pakistan's scientists did not come out as vociferously in defence of their claims as India's. Bamaby pointed out that the yield discrepancies may have been due to the fact that Pakistan conducted its test in a horizontal tunnel rather than a vertical shaft and that this would reduce the detectable yield.[23]

Moreover, there is no reason to doubt that Pakistani nuclear-weapons designers could produce a boosted-fission weapon. As discussed in chapter two, Pakistan had been trying – apparently: successfully – to obtain tritium, a key component in boosted fission weapons. Bamaby estimated that a Pakistani operational boosted fission weapon would have a yield of about 150kt.[24] Certainly enough, as of 1999, Pakistan was unlikely to deploy any weapons with such a yield.

Another important point to pay attention to was that as of 1998-1999, Pakistan's domestic nuclear weapon designs used highly-enriched uranium. Shortly thereafter and with substantial Chinese assistance, Pakistan switched its main fissile material to plutonium and invested heavily in plutonium production and reprocessing facilities. Therefore, the conclusion is that as of 1999 Pakistan had not quite moved down the path of tactical nuclear weapons for battlefield use. However, conceptually, the idea seems to have been considered and while neither side moved towards the development of low-yield battlefield weapons, the potential use of smaller fission weapons against enemy military formations was being considered.

In 1998-1999, Pakistan's nuclear capability rested on the potential of the assets listed in Table 20.[25]

Contemporaneous assessments of the nuclear weapons potential of Pakistan give a theoretical maximum of over 30 weapons. However, the RAND corporation estimated Pakistan's weapons potential at the end of 1995 at about 13 weapons, but Pakistan was rapidly increasing its weapons potential and capabilities.[26]

### New Missiles Add to the Delivery Options

In 1999, India had, in addition to its manned aircraft, deployed Prithvi Short-Range Ballistic Missiles (SRBMs) and the Agni-1 and Agni-2 ballistic missiles. The latter had only been tested earlier in 1999.

The 'Prithvi' was a mobile heavy battlefield support system with a range of 150-350km and a payload of 500kg to 1000kg.[27] The system is mounted on an 8x8 wheeled transporter-erector-launcher

(TEL), based on a Czechoslovak TATRA truck chassis. The utility of such tactical SSMs depends on the nature of the payload carried and on the accuracy. The 'Prithvi' had a payload sufficient for a nuclear, biological or chemical warhead. India's first operational Prithvi variants, such as the SS-150, SS-250 and SS-350, were relatively widely produced, with perhaps 180 of the SS-150 variant and 60 of the SS-250 and SS-350 variants being produced. However, it is less clear on whether any of these variants had anything more than a secondary nuclear role. Anecdotal evidence suggests that four SS-150s were armed with 15kt fission warheads during the 1999 Kargil war.

| Designation | Range | Payload | Status |
|---|---|---|---|
| **Prithvi I** | 150km | 1,000kg | Operational |
| **Prithvi II** | 250km | 750-1,000kg | 2 successful tests |
| **Prithvi III** | 350km | 750kg | Under development |
| **Agni** | 1,5000-2,500km | 1,000kg | 3 flight tests (2 successful) out to 1,450Km |

**Table 21: India's Ballistic Missiles, 1999**

| Designation | Range | Payload | Status |
|---|---|---|---|
| **Hatf-1** | 80km | 500kg | operational |
| **Hatf-2** | 300km | 500kg | status unclear |
| **M-11** | 290km | 500kg | 30-60 delivered |
| **Hatf-3** | 600km | 500kg | under development |

**Table 22: Pakistan's Ballistic Missiles, 1999**

Development of the missile began in 1983. The missile was 8.56 m long, 1.1 m in diameter and weighed 4,000kg. Unlike the later Indian missiles, the Prithvi family used a single-stage, liquid propellant engine, which was essentially two liquid propellant motors side-by-side that provide aerodynamic control as well as thrust vectoring. This engine control allowed the missile to stop climbing when it reached an altitude of 30km, travel horizontally at this altitude and dive on its target at an 80° angle. The missile had a minimum range of 40km and in its later variants, a maximum of 350km.

The missile had a reported accuracy of 50m circular error probable (CEP) against targets at 150km. As of 1999, it used an inertial guidance system and was launched from a TEL, which took approximately two hours to prepare. The usual firing unit consisted of two TELs, supported by about 18 other vehicles – including warhead carriers, power suppliers, fuel carriers, cranes, and others.

The Agni-TD was a much larger system with a range of 2,500km and a payload of 1,000kg. However, it was not at all certain if the Agni was a military missile or a 'technology demonstrator', as claimed by Indian officials. The Agni-TD was an amalgam of the Prithvi and the SLV-3: it was perfectly possible that it was actually a cheap test vehicle for re-entry and guidance technology for future use on a more advanced platform.[28] Then, on 19 February 1994, India ran a test of the Agni-TD, in the course of which the missile covered a range of 1,450km, and included a manoeuvrable re-entry vehicle with terminal guidance for increased accuracy: this was definitely a major technological breakthrough. This terminal guidance system with a reported CEP of 300m, is reported to have been based on a scanning correlation optical system using a scanning focal plane homing head in the infrared and millimetric wavelengths of the electromagnetic spectrum.[29]

However, it was soon realised that the Agni-TD was not a practical weapon owing in large part to its hybrid propulsion and the inherent problems of keeping such a system in a state of readiness, or at least in a state of near-readiness. Moreover, it would appear that India, learning the lessons of the 1980s, decided against deploying its land-based deterrent in static-hardened silos and opted for mobile systems. It should be noted that while unlikely, the Agni-TD could have been weaponised. Admittedly, it was far from an ideal system, but it appeared that its designers were always cognisant of the possibility of the need to weaponize it.

The Agni-2 on the other hand was a 2,500km range IRBM that was completely solid fuelled. This missile came to form the backbone of the Indian IRBM force even to the present day. Deployed on a rail-mobile launcher, the Agni-II was first tested on 11 April 1999 at 09:47 IST (Indian Standard Time).[30] In service it was deployed on a converted rail carriage with a sliding roof to allow the missile to be raised by two large hydraulic pistons into the vertical position. Splash down occurred 2,000-2,100 km away in the Bay of Bengal, on a trajectory designed to simulate a range of 2,800-3,000 km.[31] The Agni-II was India's first viable production IRBM.

At the time of the Kargil conflict, however, production and deployment of the Agni-2 would have been at best limited, if at all. Yet, as will be discussed, both Prithvi and Agni missiles were prepared for a potential nuclear role in the event of an escalation of the conflict. While the number of missiles so prepared was very limited, the fact that it was done at all is indicative of the potential for escalation that always lurked.

A word is also in order about India's manned aircraft. While the Jaguar, MiG-27, and MiG-23BN fleets of the IAF could theoretically be adopted for the nuclear delivery role, and the Jaguar having been the original choice for that task, the IAF now centred its efforts on the Mirage 2000 for that role and, in 1994, demonstrated the ability to deliver nuclear weapons from the said aircraft.[32]

A Prithvi I as seen during a test-launch. (DRDO)

The Hatf-1 missile was a short-range weapon of relatively simple design and was fired from a towed trailer. (Mark Lepko Collection)

While India had developed a stockpile of some 15 to 20 nuclear gravity bombs in the period 1974-1985 – all of which were in the 15-20 kiloton range – it became an effective nuclear weapons state in May 1994. It might have been thought that this milestone would have been achieved earlier, and indeed it was certainly possible for this to be done. However, mating the nuclear weapons with the delivery aircraft proved to be challenging. India's first deployed air-delivered nuclear weapons were earmarked for use from the Jaguar strike aircraft. One would have assumed that in the 1980s and into the early 1990s, the Jaguar with an excellent navigation-attack system and a very good payload capacity would have been an ideal choice. However, the type's less than stellar flight performance, combined with practical problems of ground clearance – the Armament and Research Development Establishment (ARDE) concluded that not only was the 'bomb' too heavy, but the ground clearance of a mere two inches was unsafe – lead to the Mirage 2000 being chosen to perform this task, with active trials of the system being undertaken in 1994. Therefore, the IAF picked its Mirage 2000H and Mirage 2000THs for the nuclear delivery role.[33]

It was with this aircraft that India finally completed its development of a fully combat ready system and deployable system for delivering nuclear weapons with the IAF conducting acceptance trials. The ARDE developed the bomb case, while the implosion system developed by the Terminal Ballistic Research Laboratory (TBRL) was successfully mated with a modified Mirage, and test dropped at Balasore using a toss-bombing technique. The bomb, minus its plutonium core, was fused for an airburst and released over the ocean. With this test, India had a reasonably reliable delivery system and by 1994, the IAF had an arsenal of at least several dozen operational nuclear bombs.[34]

Development of India's air launched deterrent was somewhat chaotic. At the urging of General Krishnaswamy Sundarji, the then Chief-of-Staff, Army, Prime Minister Rajiv Gandhi had instructed DRDO to start development of a rugged, miniaturized, safer nuclear weapon and to develop more reliable components and subsystems for what was termed as to 'keep the country's nuclear capability at least at a minimum state of readiness'.[35] While some argue that it stopped short of ordering the building of a weapon or integrating it into a delivery platform, this could be debated ad nauseum as that period of Indian nuclear history is still somewhat unclear. However, eventually, in 1989 weaponization was approved after Rajiv Gandhi's disarmament plan for the globe met with abject failure in March 1988, because, 'Pakistan was in possession of at least three nuclear devices of 15-20 kiloton yield.'[36]

No missiles were yet in the offing and the instructions from India's Prime Minister were to concentrate on the development and certification of air-deliverable weapons and the creation of an aircraft delivery package that was safe and reliable.[37] Whether true or not, it is widely believed that up to 1998, the air force was the only military service with any knowledge of India's nuclear weapons program and that was only because of its role in delivering the weapons.[38] While there was much unofficial knowledge of the fact that weapons were available for use, Gaurav Kampani noted that:

> A senior Indian defense official privy to this effort disclosed that, until 1999, the air force had no idea (1) what types of weapons were available; (2) in how many numbers; and (3) what it was expected to do with the weapons. All the air force had was delivery capability in the form of a few modified Mirage 2000s.[39]

In fact, Kargil was to be an eye-opening experience where the Indian nuclear deterrent took nearly a week to achieve any degree of capability – transitioning from a recessed deterrent to an employment mode – as opposed to an earlier calculation of seventy-two hours. Indeed, Kampani notes that the air force was not ready until the end of June 1999 to commence nuclear operations against Pakistan if ordered.[40]

However, the IAF was not the only agency involved as DRDO had readied one Agni and four Prithvi missiles for the nuclear strike role against Pakistan, with a trajectory for the Agni being worked out so that its discarded stages did not fall in Indian territory. Activation of this Readiness State 3, while taking longer than anticipated, marked the deployment of an operational air and missile-based deterrent for India.[41]

## Pakistan's Nuclear Delivery Capability

When dealing with the Pakistani missile program, one is faced with the same problems as with the Pakistani nuclear program: there is a considerable confusion over the state of deployment in 1999. It remains uncertain if either of the two Pakistani missiles, 'Hatf-1' and 'Hatf-2' had actually entered production by 1999.[42] Moreover, in the late 1990s there was a flurry of rumours concerning the transfer of Chinese M-11 missiles to Pakistan, and reports that China was helping to construct a missile manufacturing plant. Pakistan's space program

A test-firing of the Hatf-2 missile: originally, this was envisaged as a two-stage version of the Hatf-1 but its development stagnated as of 1999. (Mark Lepko Collection)

played virtually no role in its missile program: unlike that of its rival, the Pakistani space program possessed very limited capabilities and was incapable of assisting in any meaningful way. After a slew of strenuous and somewhat implausible denials, it was later confirmed that between 30 and 60 – though some suggest a higher figure of 84 – M-11s were delivered to Pakistan, and that by 1999 the country thus deployed the missiles listed in Table 22.[43]

The Pakistani missile program first came into prominence in 1989, roughly a year after the first launch of the Indian Prithvi, when it was announced that the country had flight-tested two surface-to-surface missiles. On 11 February of that year, Pakistan claimed that two SSMs, one with an 80km range and the other with a 300km range, each carrying a 500kg payload, had been successfully tested. One thing, however, was abundantly clear, the Hatf-1 appeared to have a limited capability and, with a range of 80km, very limited flexibility. The Hatf-2 seems to have been supplanted by imported Chinese M-11 missiles. Indian analysts were uncertain whether or not the Hatf-2 was discontinued entirely, due to the lack of testing over the following years – although, with a range of 300km and a payload of 500kg, it was comparable to the Prithvi in size and capability. Eventually, the flight-testing of the Hatf-2 and Hatf-3 was barely completed by 1999, and it remains highly unlikely that either was anywhere near ready for action. Remarkably, the Chinese M-11 bore resemblance in performance to the elusive Hatf-2: it is possible, if not probable, that at that time the import of M-11 missiles forestalled development of the Haft-2 and allowed Pakistan to match India's Prithvi while allowing it to focus on other, longer range missiles.

On 6 April 1998, however, the Ghauri-1 missile, clearly based on the North Korean Nodong-1 design was flight-tested.[44] This missile, with an approximate range of 1,500km, completely transformed Pakistan's nuclear delivery potential and while it was not fully operational as of a year later, its potential was very much evident. It was only later on that additional reports suggested that the Ghauri-1's first test in 1998 was not successful because the heat generated during the re-entry flight phase melted the nose cone of the weapon.[45]

As for aircraft, in 1999, Pakistan's air-deliverable weapons were largely to be deployed from its 34 surviving F-16A/B aircraft, perhaps augmented by its force of upgraded Mirage-III/Vs. These aircraft represented the cutting edge of the PAF and had numerous other commitments that potentially reduced the number of aircraft available for nuclear tasking. Indeed, and as in the case of most of the other nuclear powers, Pakistan's first nuclear weapons were all air-delivered free-fall bombs. The original aircraft earmarked for this task appear to have been the F-16A/Bs. Their potential for use as nuclear weapons delivery platforms was a cause of significant concern, as expressed by the Bulletin of Atomic Scientists:

> Pakistan probably assigns a nuclear strike mission to select F-16A/B and Mirage III/V fighter squadrons. The F-16 was probably the first aircraft in the nuclear role, but the Mirage quickly joined the mission. The F-16A/Bs were supplied by the United States between 1983 and 1987.

Certainly enough, Washington was of different opinion. In 1989, the US State Department reported to Congress 'None of the F-16s Pakistan already owns or is about to purchase is configured for nuclear delivery', and Pakistan, 'will be obligated by contract not to modify', additional F-16s, 'without the approval of the United States…'[46]

However, such claims were quickly disproved by multiple credible reports – including those by the (West) German intelligence officials, who told that nation's biggest weekly, *Der Spiegel*, that Pakistan had already developed sophisticated computer and electronic technology to outfit its F-16s with nuclear weapons. Whether the PAF then did the same with its – substantial – Mirage III/V fleet remains unclear, but it is likely that at least some testing was undertaken to check the feasibility of these as a secondary platform.

### Available Warheads

What can thus be concluded about the warhead types available to India and Pakistan as of 1999? Both countries fielded multiple weapons with a yield in the range of 15-20 kilotons. Most of these were available for delivery by aircraft, while the Indians might have also adapted some on their Prithvi missiles. Moreover, despite the persistent efforts to either belittle or question the yields of the Indian and Pakistani nuclear tests, it is probable that by 1999 some work had been done to develop larger fission warheads as well as boosted-fission and/or fusion warheads.

More specifically, there are strong indications that the first Indian nuclear weapons had a mass of about 1,000kg, with a yield of 12-15kt. However, subsequently – probably by 1982 – the weapon was scaled down to a more manageable mass of between 170kg and 200kg.[47] Moreover, by 1999, it appears that a 100kt fission weapon had been produced for aerial delivery, weighting 200-300kg.[48] Furthermore, shortly after the 1998 Pokhran tests, Indian scientists claimed an entirely plausible capability to build weapons up to a yield of 200 kilotons which they reasserted on occasion.[49]

Pakistan's capabilities were marginally more modest at the time and its ability to fit warheads to missiles may have been somewhat suspect until sometime later.

### Nuclear Weapons during the Kargil War

Neither side has publicly discussed its nuclear weapons deployment during the Kargil War. However, and as observed above, India did ready four Prithvi SRBMs and one Agni-2 IRBM for possible use in a retaliatory role – in the event of the use of a Pakistani weapon – and it prepared some of its Mirage 2000s for delivery of free-fall bombs.

That these preparations were, in fact warranted, can be gleaned from a 2018 statement by Bruce Riedel, a former CIA analyst and a White House aide during the Kargil War, who indicated that the CIA's daily brief for 4 July 1999 indicated that Pakistan was preparing its nuclear weapons for deployment and possible use.[50] In the event, neither India nor Pakistan overtly threatened the use of their nuclear weapons during this conflict and it is possible that the plausible deniability sought by Pakistan, plus India's response in not crossing the Line of Control, were important factors in moderating nuclear rhetoric.

# 4
# WAR PLANS

In two of their major wars - 1965 and 1971 - India and Pakistan conducted large scale operations along and across their international border. Since 1971, however, there have been no cross-border clashes between the rival armies. This has not been applicable to the Line of Control which has seen extensive use as a launch pad for Pakistani based proxies or terrorist groups launching attacks into the Indian state of Jammu and Kashmir and frequent artillery duels and clashes between constabulary and infantry units.

Why has the Line of Control become such an important focus for military action? The genesis for this could lie in the desire to create the space for military operations short of full-scale war and without crossing an international border. In the post-nuclear age, this assumed added importance. The aim would have been geared towards conducting military operations deleterious to the opponent while not crossing any nuclear threshold.

## Possible Theatres of Operations

An India–Pakistan conflict could take place in four major theatres, each varying in geography and, to a lesser extent, in climatic conditions. The potential theatres of operations were:

- Along the LoC and the Northern Kashmir region;
- Southern Jammu and Kashmir and Punjab sectors;
- North and Central Rajasthan, and
- South Rajasthan and Gujarat.[1]

Each of these areas offered a mix of opportunities and challenges, and the Indian military would need to make an appropriate judgement as to the area most suitable for offensive operations. Over the years, India has shown a degree of adaptability in modifying its doctrine to suit the changing circumstances. For example, in 1987, the Army conducted a massive military exercise, 'Brasstacks', which outlined what was then a new doctrine. No longer would it concentrate on operations in Punjab, as it had during the 1965 War: under this new doctrine, it would deploy powerfully armoured formations in the Rajasthan sector with the aim of bisecting Pakistan at its weakest point in Sindh Province. This model is now clearly unworkable as any such existential threat would cross Pakistan's spatial threshold. Nevertheless, the risk of thermonuclear weapons is at its highest in this sector.

By 1999, India had – in acceptance of changed realities – abandoned the 'Brasstacks' concept. The Indian Army would not attempt to make major territorial gains. Instead, it would concentrate on occupying small stretches of territory and in the process take care not to cross Pakistan's spatial threshold. The territory occupied would not threaten Pakistan's existence, but would be enough to force Pakistan to commit its forces where they would be met and engaged by superior Indian firepower. Obviously, in certain ways this concept from the early to mid-1990s presaged the development of the Cold Start Doctrine. By altering its offensive doctrine and potentially opening up new areas for possible offensive action — such as along the LoC — India has sought to nullify Pakistan's threat of nuclear weapons use. This presents challenges of its own in that India's mechanised forces cannot be adequately employed along the LoC, and emphasises the need for infantry and artillery formations to be adequately prepared.

More recently, further evidence of change can be found in India's attempt to reduce the time taken to commence military operations. Concerned at the lengthy mobilisation witnessed, post-Kargil War, during Operation Parakram in 2001, India made significant progress in reducing the time taken to prepare and conduct offensive operations. Despite official denials of its existence, the 'Cold Start' proactive military doctrine seems to be the current incarnation of this approach, aiming to commence military operations within 48 hours of the orders being given, and limiting territorial aims while seeking to engage and inflict attrition on the Pakistani armed forces. It is a fully legitimate question to ask whether this risks crossing the Pakistani 'military threshold' for nuclear use. What, for example, would Pakistan deem 'unacceptable damage' to its military forces? It was therefore, believed that Pakistan's threat to use nuclear weapons in the event of its forces being decimated is a bluff which, in the event of hostilities, India must be willing to call. In this regard, both passive and active chemical, biological, radiological and nuclear (CBRN) measures assume importance.

When looking at these theatres of operations, it must be borne in mind that the LoC in the Northern Kashmir region is not an internationally recognised border. It should also be noted that Punjab and Kashmir are politically very sensitive areas for the political establishments in both countries. It is, therefore, hardly likely that any major loss of territory in either of these two areas would be acceptable. To this end, military operations in these regions would be the most intensely contested with both sides keen to avoid a loss of territory much more than make major gains.

In the southern Jammu and Kashmir and Punjab sectors, stretching down into north and central Rajasthan, there are a series of extremely formidable obstacle defences, which are called ditch-cum-bunds by the Indians and canals by the Pakistanis. These defences, combined with the existing natural ground features, make large-scale mechanised operations virtually impossible.[2] These linear defences are extremely formidable since the ditch-cum-bunds are liberally laced with diffused and well-concealed concrete bunkers which have considerable defensive firepower and are difficult to locate, even with thermal imaging.[3] This effectively limits operations to defensive positions with only a local offensive capability. It is possible that major operations could be carried out if either side was willing to suffer the inevitable losses in equipment that would ensue.

The Rajasthan and Gujarat regions present an entirely different scenario. In the northern/central Rajasthan theatre, considerable scope exists for the large-scale use of mechanised formations in the desert and semi-desert conditions. It is in these sectors, the Thar Desert and the Rann of Kutch that the major armoured battles of the next India–Pakistan war are likely to be fought. It is, therefore, not surprising that a complete Indian Strike Corps is earmarked for use primarily in this area. The Thar Desert and the Rann of Kutch also present the best possible place for tactical nuclear warfare. The barren desert areas are ideal as the so-called collateral damage could be reduced. Moreover, any meaningful Indian gains in this area, which are beyond the major river lines, would threaten the very existence of the Pakistani state, thus prompting Pakistan to actively consider using nuclear weapons in the event of a major Indian breakthrough.

On the other hand, since the Indian Strike Corps would be operating in this area, so would the bulk of India's formidable CADA. This meant that any Pakistani attack against a major Indian formation would be met with heavy resistance from the extremely dense and sophisticated air defence assets — not to mention interceptors of the IAF. Therefore, any Pakistani attack stood a good chance of being repelled without reaching its targets. India could also reduce the risk of nuclear retaliation by limiting its advance to the major river lines, or between 60 and 80km in the north/central Rajasthan sectors.[4] This would mean that the existence of Pakistan would no longer be threatened while India could still occupy chunks of territory. Pakistan would probably be less willing to cross the nuclear threshold for such a limited Indian advance.

It is unlikely that either India or Pakistan would initiate nuclear warfare in either the Punjab or Kashmir regions purely for tactical gain. Indeed, for Pakistan, the use of such weapons in Kashmir would almost certainly alienate the Muslim population of the Kashmir Valley. In the case of Punjab, Pakistan's military and political elite are largely drawn from that province and as such, it is extremely unlikely that they would take a risk as large as this for limited tactical gains. From a purely military standpoint, it should also be pointed out that the ditch-cum-bund defences and their network of concrete bunkers would probably survive a nuclear attack. This would render a nuclear attack in this sector virtually pointless.

Therefore, the only area in which nuclear weapons would be tactically useful is in Rajasthan and Gujarat —for reasons which have already been given. Yet, that land, especially in the Thar Desert sector of Rajasthan, is of virtually no strategic importance. Would any militarily sane nation risk revealing the full extent of its covert nuclear program unless its very existence was threatened? The answer is clearly no. Therefore, if India limited its territorial gains in this area, Pakistan would have no reason to resort to nuclear weapons.

There was one wild card in this scenario: the LoC. If India were to launch a major assault along the LoC —would Pakistan use nuclear weapons? An examination of a possible war scenario will perhaps illustrate Indian planning more clearly.

## India's thinking prior to Kargil: Conceptualizing a War Scenario

In 1987, the Indian Army conducted the above-mentioned Exercise Brasstacks, which outlined what was then a new tactical doctrine. No longer would the Indian Army concentrate on operations in Punjab, as it had during the 1965 war, but would deploy massively powerful armoured formations in the Rajasthan sector with the aim of bisecting Pakistan at its weakest point in the Sindh province. Ever since, this has been the model most often used and quoted by scholars in the literature available on possible war scenarios. Moreover, it has been further argued that thanks to Pakistan's nuclear capability, an Indian offensive in Sindh that met with success would be answered by a Pakistani nuclear strike. Since defences in Punjab are strong, it was argued that as India's military superiority was hardly overwhelming, the nuclear factor may have created an environment where war was almost impossible.

This model is, however, obsolete and, far from creating a certain conventional stalemate, it has simply led to the Indian Army rethinking its tactical doctrine. No longer would the Indian Army attempt to make major territorial gains, but it instead decided to concentrate on occupying a small stretch of territory. Not enough to threaten Pakistan's existence but enough to force Pakistan to commit its forces where they would be met by superior Indian firepower which would then inflict maximum attrition. The reason for this, in part, lay in the risk of nuclear warfare; but, the main reason was in the fact that previous wars in 1965 and 1971 had shown that major territorial gains were unlikely in a short war.

In pre-Kargil War planning – and perhaps still relevant to today – it is likely that if a major Indian offensive occurred, it would occur in Kashmir.

Another point that has to be kept in mind when it comes to the Kargil War is that, in the past neither India nor Pakistan believed that anything would be decided in a war lasting less than four weeks.[5] India based its plans on a period of intense fighting lasting six to eight weeks followed by a period of major, but less intense fighting lasting up to four more weeks. War wastage reserves were calculated on this basis and thus, if a war lasted only two weeks or thereabouts, the most that can be hoped for is for heavy attrition of the enemy forces. However, since then, there was an emphasis on shorter duration conflicts with a desire to achieve realistic objectives within a 14-day period.[6]

India therefore moved away from the Brasstacks plan of bisecting Pakistan in Sindh and threatening Islamabad with encirclement to a more modest objective of destroying as much of the Pakistani military as possible. Pakistan's nuclear weapons provided some deterrence against any Indian move to make deep thrusts into its territory and against any possible bisection of Pakistan, they were of limited use in a war aimed solely at inflicting maximum attrition against Pakistani military forces.[7]

The Indian Army had two strike corps, and one corps assigned to the Rajasthan and Punjab sectors respectively. The strike corps are described in an earlier section, but each was composed of one armoured division and several infantry divisions and supporting units. Each also had an artillery division attached. A third strike corps — 21 Corps was deployable as needed. In the Brasstacks model, these were the two formations Pakistan was most concerned about and their continued presence in the Rajasthan and Punjab sectors would ensure that Pakistan could not consider any major troop redeployments in either sector. Under the then current plans, India intended not to advance more than 60–80km in the north/central Rajasthan sector and only up to the major river lines in south Rajasthan/Gujarat, Pakistan's existence would hardly be threatened. However, it must be remembered that India and Pakistan would be fighting a political war as much as a military one and any loss of territory would be considered a major political embarrassment. This meant that Pakistan would invariably have to attempt a counterattack against the Indian forces occupying any of its territories. Its forces would then be drawn into a battle of attrition against Indian forces, a battle that they would lose.

If the build-up of air defence assets, upgrading of armour and antitank munitions and the increase in artillery within the Indian Army in the 1990s is seen in the light of this post-Brasstacks tactical doctrine, it is abundantly clear that India was building up its forces to ward off any Pakistani counterattack and inflict devastating losses on the attackers.[8] In the southern Jammu and Kashmir and Punjab sectors, the huge fixed fortifications described previously would have effectively limited the scope of any Indian operation. India was highly unlikely to have attempted a major offensive in this sector for two reasons. The first is the extent of the fortified defences in this sector, but the second is far more significant and goes to the core of Pakistan's vulnerability versus India. The real vulnerability of Pakistan therefore lay not in a lack of 'strategic depth', but in the fact that so many of its major population centres and politically and militarily sensitive targets lay very close to the border with India: this negated even the use of nuclear weapons for tactical purposes (especially so in the Punjab sector). However, should India have threatened Lahore, for example, Pakistan may have been compelled to attempt a nuclear strike against an Indian urban area. As such, it was hardly likely that India would want to risk a major advance in Punjab: aims in this sector would have been limited to holding Pakistani forces in a defensive deployment pattern while inflicting maximum attrition with 2 Corps and 21 Corps.[9]

Along the LoC, however, the situation was very different. One of the consequences of the Kashmir insurgency was that India had transferred several divisions to the area to reinforce the troops already there and brought the total troop strength in that sector to over 250,000. The Indian divisions and brigades also brought their supporting artillery with them and this combination—which was far in excess of what was needed for defensive operations — enabled Indian planners to contemplate a major offensive along the LoC with every chance of success. The importance of the term LoC cannot be understated. Pakistan clung to the illusion, in official pronouncements at any rate, that its part of Kashmir was not really part of Pakistan. As such, it always refused to recognise the LoC as the international border with India. This is something that India intended to exploit to the fullest. Pakistan, on the other hand, appeared to work on a different strategy. From the time of the 1965 and 1971 wars, up until India's Brasstacks exercise, the emphasis was placed on the static defence of the LoC and the border. However, in light of India's substantially enhanced offensive capabilities, Pakistan realised that this 'stand and fight' doctrine would lead to serious Indian penetration of Pakistani territory with the Pakistani Army being unable to manoeuvre to meet the threat: counterattacking formations would then be destroyed piecemeal.[10]

Pakistan therefore adopted a new strategy: the Riposte. This was remarkably simple in concept, in that Pakistan would accept the loss of territory to Indian penetrations, but would conduct a limited advance along narrow fronts with the aim of occupying territory near the border to a depth of 40–50km. Pakistan believed that this would give it a bargaining chip to be used in the aftermath of a ceasefire brought about by international pressure after 3–4 weeks of fighting. The Pakistanis, to some extent, assumed that India would attempt deep penetrations into the territory. Moreover, it appears that though the Pakistani Army was well prepared for this new doctrine: at least there was an inadequate appreciation of the threat posed by Indian air power to the attacking formations. Some planning had been based on the highly unrealistic assumption of local air superiority and as such, these plans may have gone seriously awry.

There are a number of good books on the 1965 and 1971 wars and some excellent accounts of the tactical thinking behind Exercise Brasstacks are available. Subsequently, however, India's military strategy was revamped and was geared towards an attrition based warfighting model as detailed below.[11]

Holding formations in both India and Pakistan could man their forward defensive positions and fortifications in less than 24 hours. However, corps-level reserves with large stockpiles of amunition would take between 24 and 72 hours for mobilisation after being given their orders. In this regard, both armies would be evenly matched in the first 24 hours since the Pakistani units would have to have travelled a shorter distance to their forward positions. Pakistan's Army Reserve North (ARN) was based in the Kharian/Mangla complex and would need to have travelled only 200km to their forward concentration areas or even their assembly areas, for regrouping before an offensive was launched.[12] This would be done on extremely short notice and was consistent with Pakistan's preconceived offensive plans as outlined in the Riposte Doctrine. Army Reserve South (ARS), which was based in the Multan area, could also have been available for operations in a similar timeframe. While many of India's formations would have taken up to 72 hours to be fully deployed, two out of India's three strike corps, 1 Corps and 2 Corps, were so positioned as to match the mobilisation timings of ARS. As of 1999, it was not known if the three Strike Corps and 21 Corps would be available at such a short notice.

India could, in theory, have disrupted the early deployment of ARN if the Indian Army's Northern Command denied it deployment space with the pre-emptive mobilisation and deployment of Northern Command's theatre reserves. In 1994, analysts were unconvinced that this was possible owing to the employment of so many units of the Indian Army on internal security duties in Jammu and Kashmir. However, after 1994, the number of paramilitary units in Jammu and Kashmir grew and the Indian Army deployed almost 30,000 officers and other ranks from the Rashtriya Rifles' battalions. These would have been able to take at least some pressure off the regular army in counterinsurgency operations. Moreover, the number of regular army troops in the state appeared to have grown. These could have provided the Indian Army with sufficient troops in theatre to deny Pakistan's ARN deployment space, thus neutralising any advantage Pakistan had in this regard.[13]

The problem with assessing whether or not Indian troop strength would have been adequate to the task of neutralising ARN's deployment is that the internal security situation in Jammu and Kashmir was very variable. It was possible that the paramilitary forces and the Rashtriya Rifles would free a large number of troops for conventional operations. Moreover, it was possible that up to three divisions, with over 40,000 men, could have been moved from the Chinese border without seriously degrading India's defences against a Chinese assault. These troops were held by Central and Eastern commands and had actually been earmarked for out-of-theatre operations.[14]

In the case of the ARS, the IAF had the potential to cause havoc with their deployment by beginning an intensive interdiction campaign in the Gujarat (Punjab)–Sialkot–Gujranwala area. However, this would have made India the aggressor in any conflict, which was something the government in New Delhi was not expected to permit. On the other hand, the Indian government might have been hard-pressed not to find an excuse, however flimsy, for the IAF to begin such an interdiction campaign. In order to further reduce the risk of a Pakistani nuclear strike, it was contemplated that India, through the United Nations, might make certain pledges to Pakistan. These might have included a pledge not to deliberately attack a civilian target, to refrain from attacking civilian nuclear installations and a promise not to initiate the use of weapons of mass destruction unless attacked with such weapons. India could also make it clear that it would abide by these terms only if Pakistan agrees to do the same. Should Pakistan not agree, India would probably assume that a nuclear strike would be forthcoming.

In the event that India failed to deny deployment space to the ARN and that the Indian government did not sanction the launching of pre-emptive air strikes both India and Pakistan would have had a relative parity in manpower and combat formations at the beginning of any conflict. India would have been able to bring up some very large combat formations from central and eastern India, but Pakistan would have been almost fully committed. A force of three infantry divisions plus some independent brigades under 11 and 12 Corps would have been transferable from the Peshawar and Quetta areas respectively, but with very little artillery and armour. Moreover, if there was any serious escalation of fighting in Afghanistan, Pakistan may have been less willing to denude its Afghan border of all regular army formations.

Indian objectives in the northern sector, in Jammu and Kashmir, would be somewhat unclear. It was argued that the capture of Skardu to cut off the main glacier zone in Baltistan would have been a major objective. Moreover, a strong offensive aimed at capturing Muzaffarabad from the north and the south of the Jhelum, and the neutralisation of the Haji Pir (Bedori) Bulge would have had to be undertaken. The Indian Army would also have attempted to capture the Mirpur-Mangla Complex with the view of presenting a clear and present threat to the Pakistani national capital region. Finally, to cope with the threat posed by ARN, Indian formations would have had to make a penetration into the Sialkot sector with the sole aim of bottling up and denying deployment space to the Pakistani formations, thus ensuring their eventual destruction.[15]

The scenario described above leads to the question as to whether Pakistan would have launched a nuclear strike in response to a threat posed to its national capital. The reality of the war planning went so far as to leak to the Indian press a detailed war scenario.

Analysts, in this scenario, argued that the Indian Army would have had a choice — attacking into either Ladakh–Baltistan or into Pakistan-occupied Kashmir and that the Army would prefer an ingress into the latter along the LoC. They also argued that the main thrust would have been in the Jammu division between Poonch and Chamb with a secondary thrust into the Tithwal-Keran sectors. Northern Command might also have suggested that a limited offensive be conducted to the west of Zoji La in the Dras–Kargil sectors. The aim here would have been to cut off the lines of communications of the Pakistani brigade based near the Shingo and Indus rivers. These operations would have called for troops specially trained and equipped for operations in mountainous and hilly terrain and to this end, the three divisions previously earmarked for use against China would have been invaluable. Moreover, select formations from these forces had already sent divisional reconnaissance groups into Kashmir for terrain familiarisation. That these divisional reconnaissance groups had been conducting terrain familiarisation for quite some time gave rise to the idea that India had been planning for a major offensive in the Jammu and Kashmir sector for a long time.

Analysts assumed that an attack in Kashmir would be launched first with two mountain divisions concentrated to begin operations in the directions of Jhanghar–Mirpur and Nowshera–Bhimber with the ability to switch between the two. A third division would be allocated to the Mendhar–Kotli–Mirpur axis in two columns. Pakistan would probably have understood that some move was afoot at this stage in the sector defended by 19 Infantry Division. The Pakistanis would then have moved the 7 and 9 infantry divisions based at Peshawar to assist in their defence. However, it was not certain that these two divisions would have been available in their entirety since the Afghan border was volatile at the best of times and the situation in Afghanistan was very fluid. Nonetheless, assuming these formations began an eastward movement, Pakistan's ARS would start mobilising at Multan. At this stage, India's three Strike Corps would have begun a forward movement. The plan as envisaged by Indian planners was for 1 Corps to face ARN and 2 and 21 Corps to face ARS. An Indian offensive would have begun in the Ladakh sector with two brigades attacking from Kargil along with two brigades from the northern Kashmir-holding division tasked with straightening the LoC in the Tithwal–Bugina bulge sector. The three mountain divisions mentioned earlier would then have commenced their offensive which would probably have faced extremely stiff resistance from the Pakistani infantry divisions facing them. Compared to the dashing manoeuvre warfare employed during the Brasstacks exercise, the then current Indian Army high command was fully convinced that their offensive plans would be more akin to the 'meat-grinding' assaults of the Second World War.

As Pakistan's strategic depth would have potentially been eroded around Islamabad and with its Army Headquarters at Rawalpindi fixed on the worsening situation at Mirpur, ARN would have been committed to action. ARN would have attempted an offensive aimed at the Jammu–Pathankot corridor while crossing the river Ravi aimed at threatening Gurdaspur–Pathankot. These operations would have been met by India's 1 Corps which would have engaged ARN in a savage battle of attrition, forcing Pakistan to move 9 Division to the Mirpur sector, where the Indian offensive would have continued, while 7 Division would have moved along with 30 Corps to reinforce ARN. In the meantime, the Indian and Pakistani air forces would have engaged in their own battle of attrition, with the former waging a heavy counter-air offensive while engaging in a massive offensive-air-support operation for the Indian Army. With the Indian offensive overcoming its opponents in the Kashmir region, and ARN and its reinforcements engaged with India's 1 Corps in a battle of attrition, Pakistan's Army High Command would have preferred that ARS be kept out of action as long as possible. However, since the whole object of the Indian plan would have been to inflict heavy attrition on Pakistan's armed forces, it would have been essential for ARS to be neutralised.

Analysts believed that India would use its Desert Corps (12 Corps) to draw ARS into action. 12 Corps would have launched a limited offensive aimed south of Rahim Yar Khan to which ARS would respond with a thrust to its north. The Indian Holding Corps, with their Re-organized Army Plains Infantry Divisions (RAPIDS), would probably have found themselves under heavy pressure from the powerful ARS. At this stage, with ARS fully committed, India would have sprung its trap with 2 and 21 Corps, along with massive air support, launching out together along a very narrow front aimed at punching through 31 Corps and falling on the soft underbelly of ARS which would then be destroyed in detail. In this scenario, the fighting which had lasted between two and four weeks would have left Pakistan's armed forces severely depleted, if not almost destroyed. ARS would have been destroyed along with the Pakistani formations in the Rajasthan/Gujarat sector. Indian forces would have made gains along the LoC, severely eroding Pakistan's strategic depth in the region of Islamabad, and ARN and its reinforcing formations would have been mauled by 1 Corps, Indian Holding Corps and the IAF.

What is significant is that Pakistan would not have suffered any major territorial losses. No Indian offensive would have seized much land and in no case was the existence of Pakistan actually threatened. While nuclear threats and counterthreats would probably have been be traded, Pakistan was expected not to have felt quite so compelled to go nuclear as it would if its very survival was at stake. India's gamble was that with such a mauling of its military capability, and since Pakistan had neither the money nor the resources to re-build a large and powerful military machine again, Pakistan might be far more amenable to a permanent settlement of the Kashmir dispute and other outstanding matters. Since India would have held a major advantage in that Pakistan could no longer rival India militarily, such a settlement would probably have gone in India's favour. At least that was the Indian plan. Whether or not any permanent settlement over Kashmir could be achieved after such a war would remain a matter for speculation.[16]

The most important point to note in this scenario is that in no case would India have been seeking to seize large areas of Pakistani territory. Pakistan's existence would not have been endangered. So, would Pakistan have risked using nuclear weapons on the battlefield? Having said this, it should further be pointed out that there was a lot of room for misinterpretation in this scenario. For example, would

Major-General Parvez Musharaf (right), Chief-of-Staff, Pakistan Army, and the mastermind of the Kargil operation – here with two pilots of the Pakistan Army Aviation Corps. (Albert Grandolini Collection)

Pakistan have been able to distinguish between a limited Indian advance and a full-scale invasion? At what stage would Pakistan have considered its existence to be threatened?

After discussions with a number of retired Indian officers — specifically about this question of misinterpretation — the only answers that could be provided revolved around the fact that a limited Indian penetration would have been along a broad front and have limited depth, while a full invasion would have had areas of narrow but deep penetrations into Pakistani territory. The officers believed that Pakistan would have had no difficulty in differentiating between the two and as such, the question of misinterpretation did not arise. However, once Pakistan had developed TNWs, the above scenario was only partially realistic. In 1999 however, the logic was sound, but it was Pakistan which chose to initiate hostile action rather than India, while the latter limited its response by not crossing the LoC.

### Pakistan's Pre-Kargil Military thinking

When examining the previously described war scenario, one must consider that both sides were extremely aware of the other's capabilities, but maybe did not entirely appreciate the intent of opposing military planning and operational deployments. India believed that the LoC offered the potential for military action in the event of a major Pakistani-supported terrorist attack or other such aggression while keeping the escalation to manageable levels.

While Pakistan prepared the necessary forces to deter Indian operations across the international border and possessed operational level parity in conventional forces, it was of course wary of the imbalance along the LoC. India's intent on making the LoC its principal area for offensive operations might not have been thoroughly appreciated.

Pakistan on the other hand viewed the LoC as offering the potential to needle India while at the same time not allowing for the deployment of the bulk of India's forces. The Kargil operation was conceived against a backdrop of these plans. In retrospect, the most surprising thing about the Kargil operation was the total degree of surprise achieved by Pakistan. Running a close second, however, would be the completely woeful underestimation by Pakistan of India's response to the incursion and a complete lack of appreciation as to the international response.

The nuclear tests of 1998 renewed international interest in the region and Pakistan sought to calibrate its operations to avoid a major conventional clash while placing India in a position where it had to retaliate militarily. India's military retaliation would, in the Pakistani calculations, be along the lines of its 1965 operations and cross the International Border. In such a case, while fighting a defensive holding action, Pakistan hoped that as the war progressed, international pressure, fearing Pakistani use of nuclear weapons would compel an end to Indian military operations. In fact, as Kargil showed, none of these calculations were to prove correct and a brilliant operation at the tactical level turned into a strategic fiasco for Pakistan.

Indeed, writing some year's later, General V.P. Malik noted the following as being Pakistan's miscalculations:

- The Nuclear umbrella allows "offensive action" without risk.
- International community would intervene or stop the war at an early stage.
- The coalition government in India, weak and indecisive, would either over-react or under-react.
- India was militarily weak and unprepared.
- Indian frustration would lead to escalation, putting the onus of escalation on India.

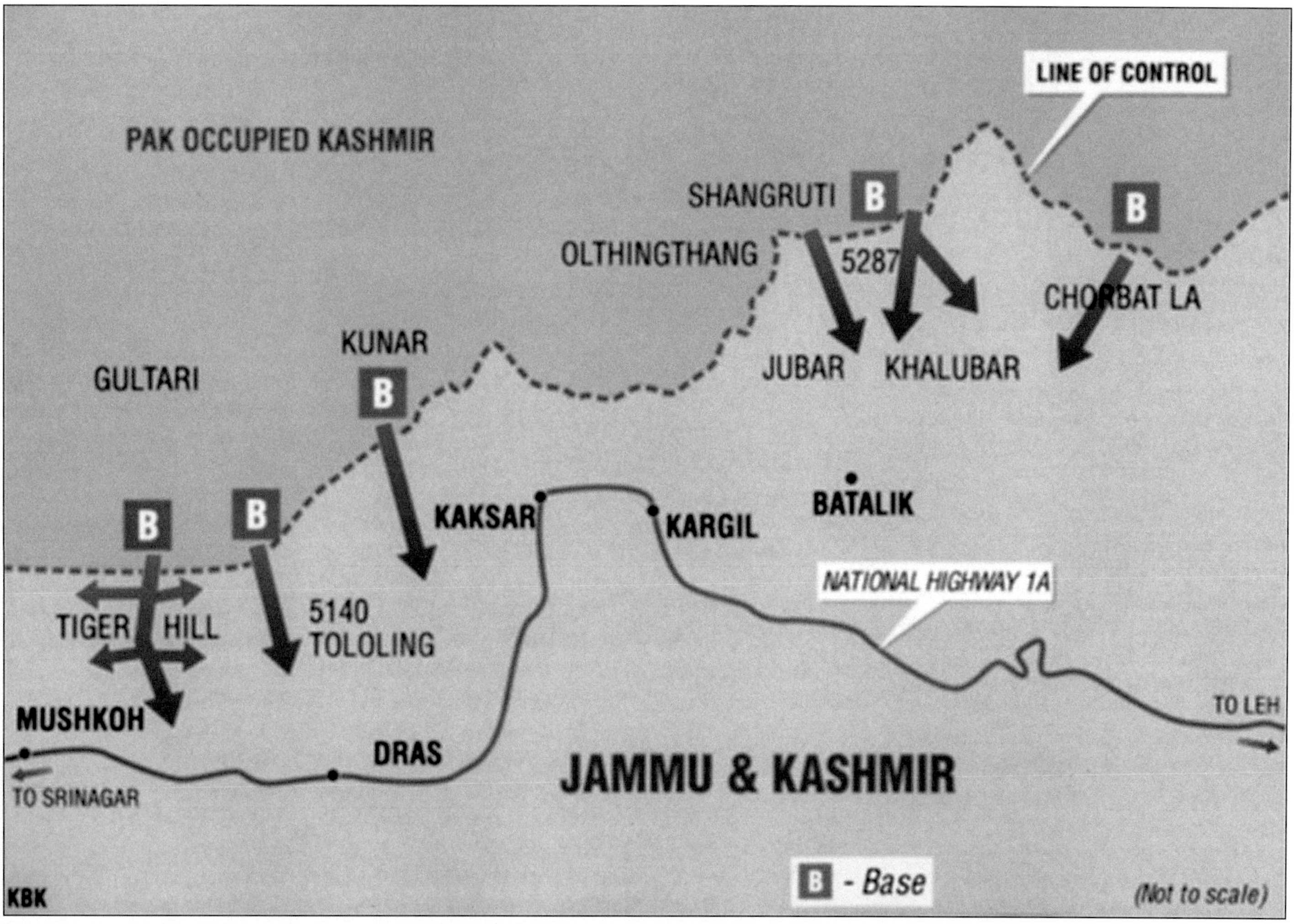

A reconstruction of the Pakistan Army's intrusion plan for the Kargil Sector in 1999. (Courtesy Brigadier Gurneet Kanwal)

- Military operations under the garb of "Mujahidin" would focus attention on Kashmir, and Pakistan would be able to claim this as a victory.[17]

### Pakistan's War Plan: Kargil

It is as yet somewhat unclear as to why Pakistan conceived its war plans for Kargil. This is particularly so given that the summit in February 1999 demonstrated a good deal of hope that the tensions between the two countries could be reduced. What is especially worrisome, even with hindsight is that it remains unclear whether the military-intelligence establishment ever informed the Pakistani Prime Minister Sharif about the Kargil operation. Some Pakistani scholars assert that the plan was only known to Chief-of-Staff, Pakistan Army, Pervez Musharaf, and perhaps a handful of his closest confidantes.[18] In turn, Musharaf claimed that Sharif was briefed on the operation 15 days prior to the Indian Prime Minister Vajpayee's bus trip to Lahore.[19]

Militarily, Pakistan's aim for carrying out the Kargil intrusions was very sound. It was based on exploitation of the gaps that existed in the defences in the sector both on the Indian and Pakistan sides of the LoC. These gaps were made possible by the geography, with the terrain being extremely rugged and very few tracks leading from the main roads towards the LoC making transport and reinforcement difficult. The climate also favoured the timing of the operation as during winter the Kargil area receives very heavy snowfall that makes movement almost impossible. The only mountain pass connecting the Kargil area to the Kashmir Valley, Zoji La, does not usually open until the end of May or beginning of June. This would make the movement of Indian reinforcements by road convoys from Srinagar impossible.

Where the Pakistani Army went wrong was calculating that even if the intrusions were discovered in early May, as they were, the Indian Army's reaction would be slow, piecemeal and limited. This would have allowed the consolidation of the intrusions. In fact, Zoji La was opened in early May, thus allowing a much earlier induction of Indian troops. If the intrusions had been effective, they would have enabled Pakistani troops to secure a number of dominating heights from where the Srinagar-Leh National Highway 1A could be interdicted in multiple places. Moreover, the intrusions would, in Pakistani calculations, tie down large Indian Army reserves as well as drawing in troops from other areas of the state.

If things proceeded according to Pakistani calculations, the status of the LoC would have been irrevocably altered with Islamabad gaining de facto control over strategic tracts of land. This would have enabled Pakistan to negotiate from a position of strength.[20]

General V.P. Malik, then the Indian Chief of Army Staff, summarised the military objectives as follows:

- Occupy approximately 700 sq km area on the Indian side of the LoC in Kargil-Turtuk Sector.
- Interdict Srinagar-Kargil-Leh Road.
- Capture Turtuk and cut off southern and central parts of the Siachin Glacier Sector, and
- Intensify militants' activities in Jammu and Kashmir, which had received a setback after the State Assembly and National Parliament elections in 1997-98.[21]

Although officially 'not involved', several photographs that have surfaced since indicate the extent of the Pakistan Army's involvement in the Kargil operation. This one shows one of its Mi-17 helicopters (serial 58637), refuelling at a forward base along the Line of Control. (Albert Grandolini Collection)

•Give impetus to insurgency in the Kashmir Valley and elsewhere in Jammu and Kashmir.[22]

## Pakistani Planning and Execution

From a tactical and operational standpoint, Pakistan conceived a masterpiece: it kept the plan for the infiltration into Kargil – codenamed Operation Badr – top secret and maintained the element of surprise, totally deceiving multiple Indian intelligence services.[23] Operation Badr envisaged that no additional units of the Pakistani Army would be inducted into the Force Command Northern Area (FCNA): this ensured that India's attention would not be piqued by any movement of troops – not even at battalion level. Artillery units inducted in July to September 1998, during a period of heavy exchanges of artillery fire along the LoC, were not pulled back and as such attracted no fresh attention. Pakistan's army undertook no movement of reserve formations or their support elements and created no new administrative bases. All operations were catered for using existing facilities and made use of existing defensive infrastructure. Logistics were handled along the ridgelines and nullahs, away from Indian units already in position. Moreover, it was only after the Kargil operation had been executed and after the Indian response had started that fresh troops were inducted on the Pakistani side.

Brigadier Gurneet Kanwal, who has written extensively on the Kargil War suggests related but slightly different objectives as follows:

- Phase 1 – Infiltrate militants into the area to subvert locals and initiate insurgency.
- Phase 2 – Launch operations to occupy critical areas around Turtok and the adjacent areas.
- Phase 3 – Launch heliborne/airborne operations in the rear areas of Turtok sector to facilitate operations of ground forces.
- Phase 4 – Declare Turtok and its adjacent areas as part of the Northern Areas.

Kanwal further opined that the Indian Army Headquarters had the view that Pakistan's military aims were:

- Cut off the strategic National Highway 1A (Srinagar-Leh highway).
- Alter the status of the LoC.

Pakistan's Kargil plan was put into action at the end of April 1999. Small sub-groups of platoon size were used to conduct multiple intrusions along the ridgelines and occupy heights dominating Indian positions.[24] The main units were broken into a number of smaller sub-groups of 30 to 40 troops each, for carrying out multiple intrusions along the ridgelines and occupying dominating heights.[25]

The forces earmarked for the intrusion and used therein were a mixture of highly professional soldiers and Islamist combatants. Units involved included the 3rd, 4th, 5th, 6th and 12th battalions of the Pakistan Army's Northern Light Infantry (NLI).[26] The NLI is an old and capable formation with a pedigree going back to the 1950s.[27] Headquarters of 62 Brigade of the Pakistani Army was made responsible administratively for all operations in the Kargil Sector and was responsible for organizing, supporting and where possible assisting the infiltration. Supplementing these were operatives from the elite Special Services Group (SSG) and various Pakistan-based Islamist militants.[28]

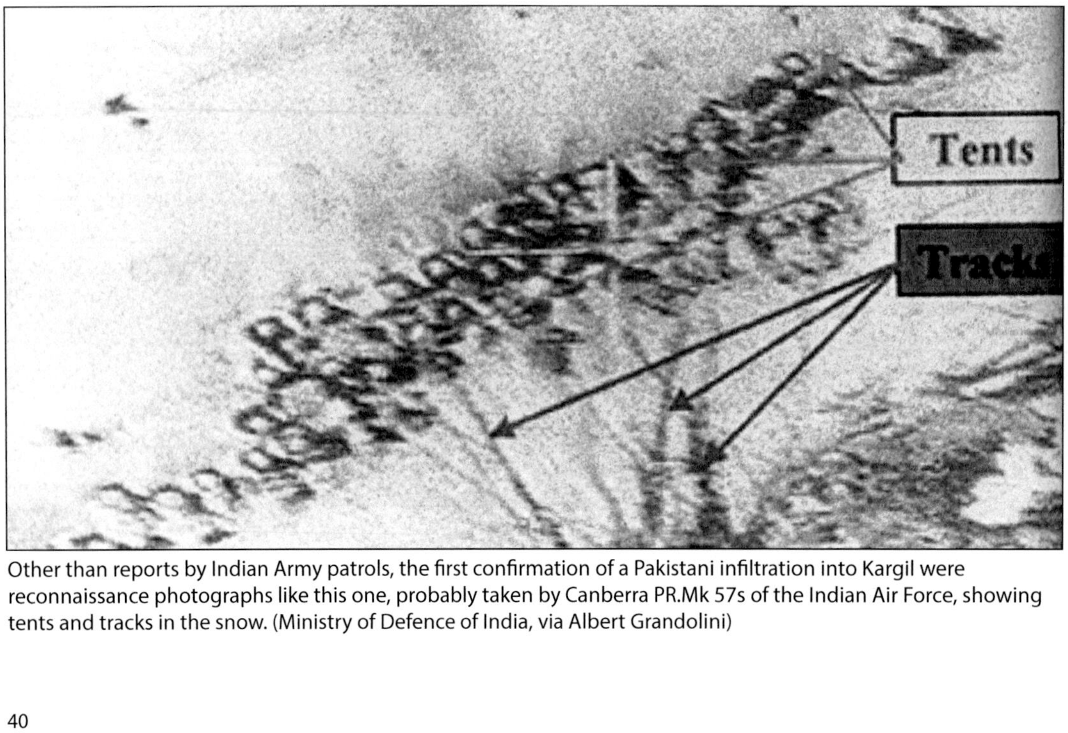


Other than reports by Indian Army patrols, the first confirmation of a Pakistani infiltration into Kargil were reconnaissance photographs like this one, probably taken by Canberra PR.Mk 57s of the Indian Air Force, showing tents and tracks in the snow. (Ministry of Defence of India, via Albert Grandolini)

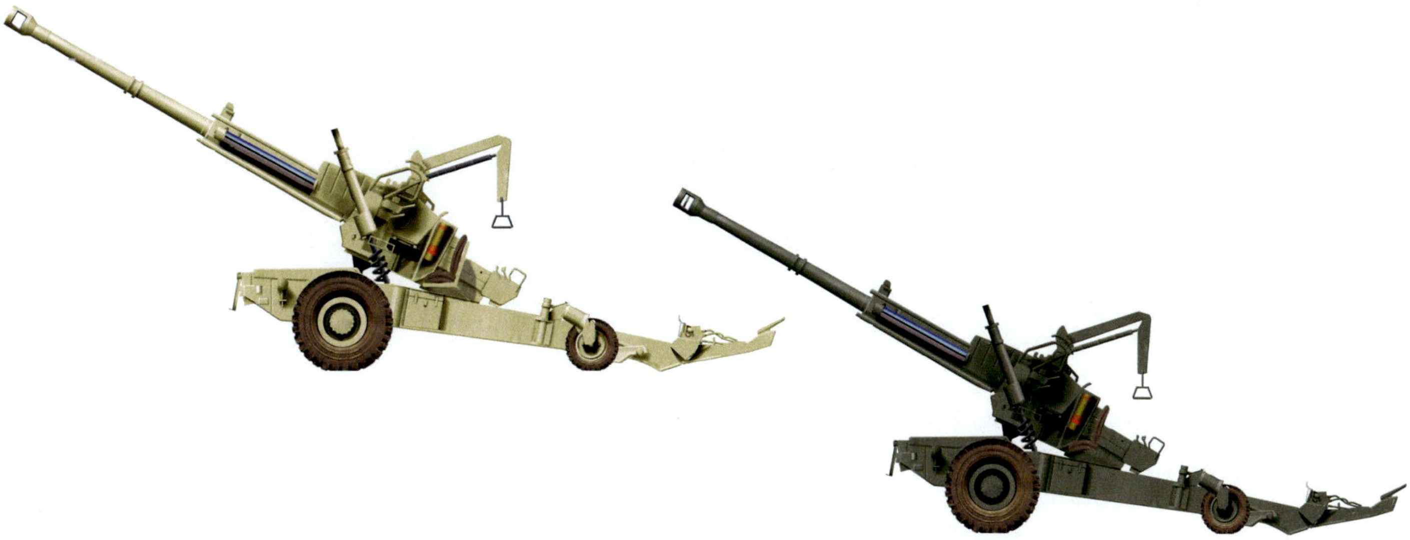

The Indian acquisition of the 155mm Bofors Fälthaubits (Swedish for 'Field Howitzer') FH77/B02 was surrounded by a major weapons-contract scandal that implicated Indian Prime Minister Rajiv Gandi and several other members of the government in receiving kickbacks for placing the order. Therefore, the original plan for acquisition of more than 1,000 examples was scrapped: instead, the Indian Army acquired only 410. In service with about 20 artillery regiments by 1999, it proved highly successful during the Kargil War – in part because of its range of 38 kilometres (when using base bleed-rounds). Generally, most of the examples in Indian service were left painted in dark green overall, as on delivery; however, some were painted in sand overall. (Artwork by David Bocquelet)

While usually towed by the Scania SAB1111 truck for longer distance travel – when it is configured as shown here – the FH77/A also had a Volvo B20A petrol-engine, used as an auxiliary power unit, which enabled it to quickly change position at speeds of up to 7km/h. The weapon was deployed into a firing position by spreading the trail legs, raising the castor wheels and driving it in reverse to anchor the recoil spades. The gun-layer can traverse the barrel 30° left or right from the centreline and elevate it from -5° to +70°. Usually operated by 10-14 troops, the FH77 has a very high rate of fire of up to four rounds in nine seconds, or six rounds in 25 seconds (a more sustained rate of six rounds every two minutes). (Artwork by David Bocquelet)

As of 1999, one of the most numerous pieces in service with mountain artillery regiments of the Indian Army was the 105mm Indian Field Gun. Developed by the ARDE in 1972 on the basis of the British-made L13 105mm howitzer, this had a maximum range of about 15-17km, with a rate of fire of between 6 and 8 rounds per minute. During the Kargil War, its performance surpassed even that of its Soviet/Russian equivalent in the form of the 122mm D-30 howitzer – even if its lighter shell caused less damage to well-protected structures than the 155mm shell of the FH77. Moreover, the IFG – and its lighter variant, the Indian Light Field Gun – proved not only a very rugged design, but also one capable of being transported by helicopters, which greatly increased their flexibility. (Artwork by David Bocquelet)

Still outnumbering the IFG and the LFG in Indian service as of 1999 was the Soviet-made 130mm M-46 field gun, more than 1,000 of which were originally acquired. This weapon proved extraordinarily popular in Indian service, even if not entirely suitable for deployment in the mountains, because its 39-calibre barrel could be elevated up to only 45°. Depending on the type of ammunition, the M-46 had a range of between 22,490 and 38,000 metres (the latter for extended-range full bore, base-bleed rounds). As far as is known, in Indian service, most examples were left in dark olive drab overall, as on delivery. (Artwork by David Bocquelet)

The BM-21 Grad was a 122mm Soviet-made, 40-tube multiple rocket launcher mounted on the Ural-375D six-by-six truck chassis. They formed the primary armament of five rocket regiments of the Indian Army as of 1999: each had a crew of three, capable of deploying the system into a firing position within three minutes of stopping. All 40 rockets could be fired within as little as 20 seconds, or individually, or in small groups in intervals of several-seconds. The Indian Army's rocket units of 1999 used locally-manufactured versions of the M-21 rocket, capable of reaching targets at ranges between 20 and 30 kilometres. As far as is known, all the vehicles were left in dark olive drab overall, as on delivery. (Artwork by David Bocquelet)

Originally based on a design from 1919, and pressed into service in 1940, the US-made M115 203mm howitzer (originally the 8-inch howitzer M1), was still the heaviest artillery piece in the arsenals of the Pakistan Army. More than 30 of them were still in use as of 1999. Weighting about 14.5 tonnes, the weapon was towed by a prime mover, usually a heavy truck, and fired projectiles weighting about 90kg (200lbs) over a range of up to 17km. In Pakistani service, most received a camouflage pattern consisting of dark sand, olive green, and dark green or black. (Artwork by David Bocquelet)

Despite the introduction of camouflage uniforms in the mid-1970s, the Pakistan Army's uniforms had changed little by 1999. This lieutenant of the NLI is shown wearing the kahki set common to all ranks, and black leather boots. His rank is easily recognizable by the straps on his shoulders, and the red circle on the beret was the visual indicator of the Northern Light Infantry. Based on the British models from the Second World War, the webbing shown was widespread among the officers. His canvas holster contains a semi-automatic pistol, probably a local copy of the Berreta 92, while his primary firearm is the Chinese-made Type-56 assault rifle, itself a copy of the ubiquitous AK-47. (Artwork by Anderson Subtil)

This Lance Naik of the Pakistan Army's infantry is shown wearing a heavy woollen pullover typical of the Pakistan Army. His steel helmet is based on the US-made M1 and is covered in khaki fabric and a camouflage net. The canvas belt is typically British, an influence that remains until today. The padded suspenders are of indigenous design and were widely used in the 1990s. The rifle is the local version of the 7.62mm Heckler & Koch G3 manufactured by Pakistan Ordnance Factories. (Artwork by Anderson Subtil)

This Sikh soldier of the 8th Battalion Sikh Regiment is shown as well-equipped for operations in the mountain peaks of the Kargil region, including a double-faced parka and thick wool pants worn over his camouflage uniform. The traditional turban was usually replaced by a woollen cap and a black scarf. His feet are protected by thick socks and special boots for extremely cold climate. On his back is a US-made PRC-25 radio, while his armament includes a 5.56x45mm (NATO) INSAS assault rifle. (Artwork by Anderson Subtil)

India began manufacturing uniforms in the M81 woodland camouflage green of US origin in the 1990s: these replaced the original Disruptive Pattern Material uniforms used earlier. The uniform of this artilleryman of the Indian Army is completed by a standard canvas belt and a Kevlar helmet that emulates the US-made M1 but is covered with standard DPM fabric and camouflage net. He is shown lifting a 155mm ER-HE shell as fired by the highly successful Bofors FH77B howitzer. (Artwork by Anderson Subtil)

The IAF acquired a total of 11 Canberra PR.Mk 57s (a variant with slightly stretched forward fuselage containing reconnaissance equipment) starting in 1957, and they had already provided sterling service during the 1965 and 1971 wars with Pakistan. Always operated by No. 106 Squadron, and rarely shown in public, by 1999 they would have all worn this livery in Tipnis Grey overall (named after Anil Yashwant Tipnis, the Commander of the IAF). Their serials - IP986, IP987, IP988, IP989, IP990, IP991, IP992, IP993, BP745, BP746, and BP744 – were always applied in black atop of the fin flash: roundels were worn in six positions. During the Kargil War, they flewn pre- and post-strike reconnaissance sorties. (Artwork by Tom Cooper)

The HAL Cheetah is an indigenously manufactured variant of the Sud Aviation/Aérospatiale SA.315B Lama (itself based on the SA.315 Alouette II), modified through the inclusion of the Artouste powerplant and rotor system of the SE.316B Alouette III, while retaining a (reinforced) Alouette II airframe. In production since 1972 and operated by both the IAF and the Indian Army Aviation Corps, it proved its worth beyond any doubt during operations high in the Himalayas. As of 1999, most of the AAC Cheetahs were painted in dark olive drab or dark green overall, but some wore very diverse forms of camouflage patterns – usually applied in sand or beige. The national insignia, service title and the registration number were always applied on the cowling below the engine. (Artwork by Luca Canossa)

Locally designated the *Pratap*, the Mi-17 had already proven its worth to the IAF during the Indian peace-keeping operation in Sri Lanka, in 1987-1990. By 1999, they were still usually painted in green overall, and wore service titles in white along the top of the cabin side. Four-digit registrations – always starting with prefix Z – were applied on the boom, in front of the national flag. Most retained their armour plates on the sides of the cockpit, and exhaust diffusers, and had received four banks of chaff & flare dispensers installed under the centre portion of the boom. Their primary armament consisted of either two or four UB-32-57 pods for 57mm S-5M unguided rockets. Inset is shown the insignia of the 129 Helicopter Unit, IAF, nicknamed 'Nubra Warriors'. (Artwork by Tom Cooper)

The 1990s saw the IAF's fleet wearing a wide range of very different camouflage patterns, often strongly influenced by whatever colours were available at the various air bases. One that was applied on a larger number of aircraft overhauled by HAL is illustrated in this reconstruction of the MiG-21bis registration C1539, flown by Flight Lieutenant K Nachiketa Rao from No. 17 Squadron, IAF, when it was shot down by a MANPAD on 27 May 1999. This pattern consisted of beige (BS381C/388), dark brown (BS381C/411) and black green on upper surfaces and sides, and light admiralty grey (BS381C/697) on undersurfaces. The aircraft is shown as armed with UB-16-57 pods for S-5K 57mm unguided rockets – one of the most-frequently deployed weapons of the Kargil War. (Artwork by Tom Cooper)

Like MiG-21s, the IAF's MiG-27Ms wore several different camouflage patterns as of 1999. Illustrated is one of the most frequently used – based on the original pattern applied on MiG-23s exported to the Middle East in the 1970s. This consisted of beige (BS381C/388), dark brown (BS381C/411) and dark green (BS381C/641) on upper surfaces and sides. Sadly, the exact colour applied on the undersurfaces of this example from No. 9 Squadron, IAF, remains unclear: usually MiG-23s and MiG-27s painted before delivery had most of the undersurfaces painted in light admiralty grey (BS381C/697), with the rear lower fuselage in an unknown shade of grey. As usual, the serial number/registration (TS534) was always applied in black above the fin flash, and in black or red on the cover of the forward undercarriage bay, and roundels worn in six positions. Unit insignia was usually applied on the intake, while Individual aircraft received nicknames in white on the lower forward fuselage. (Artwork by Tom Cooper)

No. 223 'Tridents' Squadron was the third (and last) IAF unit equipped with MiG-29. It originally received eight single-seaters and two two-seaters from the second batch acquired in 1989, and then additional aircraft – including the one shown here – from a batch of eight acquired in 1994-1995. While Home-based at Adempur AB, the unit deployed a detachment of MiG-29s to Srinagar during the Kargil War, from where they flew combat air patrols along the Line of Control, usually armed with a pair each of R-27s and R-60s. As usual for nearly all exported MiG-29s, the aircraft was painted in medium grey (FS26373), with a disruptive camouflage pattern in grey-green (FS35352) on top surfaces and sides. Whilst supposed to be standardised, the pattern differed from aircraft to aircraft. Roundels were worn in six positions, with the unit insignia always on the intakes. (Artwork by Tom Cooper)

The Indian Air Force originally acquired 36 single-seat Mirage 2000Hs and 4 two-seat Mirage 2000THs, the first of which arrived in 1985, and were nicknamed the 'Vajra'. These entered service with No. 1 'Tigers' and No. 7 'Battleaxes' squadrons. A follow-up order in 1986 resulted in delivery of nine additional aircraft between 1990 and 1994. Initially at least, all the IAF's Vajras were painted in Celomer 1625 *Gris/Bleu moyen clair* (light medium blue-grey, AFNOR A625) overall, with a standardised camouflage pattern in Celomer 1620 *Gris/Bleu-vert moyen foncé* (dark medium blue-green-grey, AFNOR A620) on upper surfaces and sides (AFNOR is the French colour standard, comparable to the British Standard (BS) or the Federal Standard in the USA). Their radomes were always painted in black. The type flew its first sorties of Operation Safed Sagar on 30 May 1997, initially armed with four 1,000lbs (454kg) bombs, as shown here. Matra R.550 Magic Mk.II air-to-air missiles were carried on outboard underwing pylons in case any PAF aircraft were encountered. (Artwork by Tom Cooper)

Following several losses to Pakistani MANPADs, the IAF rushed its Mirage 2000TH two-seaters into action. Because the French-made 1,000kg BGL Arcole laser guided bombs were developed for release from low altitude, tended to undershoot, and were highly expensive, IAF technicians at Gwalior AB quickly adopted the British-made Paveway II kits to make laser-guided bombs for deployment with help of the ATLIS II. The resulting combination has been described as 'decisive' for the outcome of the Kargil War: Mirage 2000THs usually deployed a single Paveway II (installed on the warhead of the British-designed 1,000lbs bomb) from their centreline pylons; the ATLIS II laser designator was attached to its adaptor on the left 'shoulder' station. This configuration was completed by a pair of 1,300-litre drop tanks (not shown) and a pair of Matra R.550 Magic Mk.IIs on outboard underwing pylons. The IAF also had French-made Thompson-CSF Remora ECM-pod in its arsenal but these were not necessary during the Kargil War. (Artwork by Tom Cooper)

The primary interceptor of the PAF as of 1999 – and also its most important strike platform – was the General Dynamics F-16A/B. Out of 40 acquired in the 1980s, 35-36 were still available. All were painted in grey (FS36270) overall, with a camouflage pattern in dark grey (FS36118) applied on top- and undersurfaces. The radome was painted in ghost grey (FS36320), and all national markings and maintenance stencils were toned down. Their primary air-to-air weapons included AIM-9L (shown on wingtip stations) and AIM-9N/P Sidewinder guided missiles: the 9L had an 'all-aspect' capability. The aircraft also had one 20mm General Electric M61 Vulcan cannon installed internally. Installation of up to three drop tanks was necessary for any extended combat air patrols along the Line of Control. (Artwork by Tom Cooper)

A row of MiG-27Ms waiting for their ground crews to load them with bombs and unguided rockets prior to the next sortie during the Kargil War. (Albert Grandolini Collection)

Troops of 18 Grenadiers with the Indian flag and their CO, Brigadier Kushal Thakur, atop Tiger Hill. The unit was in action almost from the first day of the Kargil War – which is clearly showing in the faces of everybody visible. Notable is the extremely rugged terrain around them: this was almost as dangerous as the enemy. (Brigadier Kushal Thakur Collection)

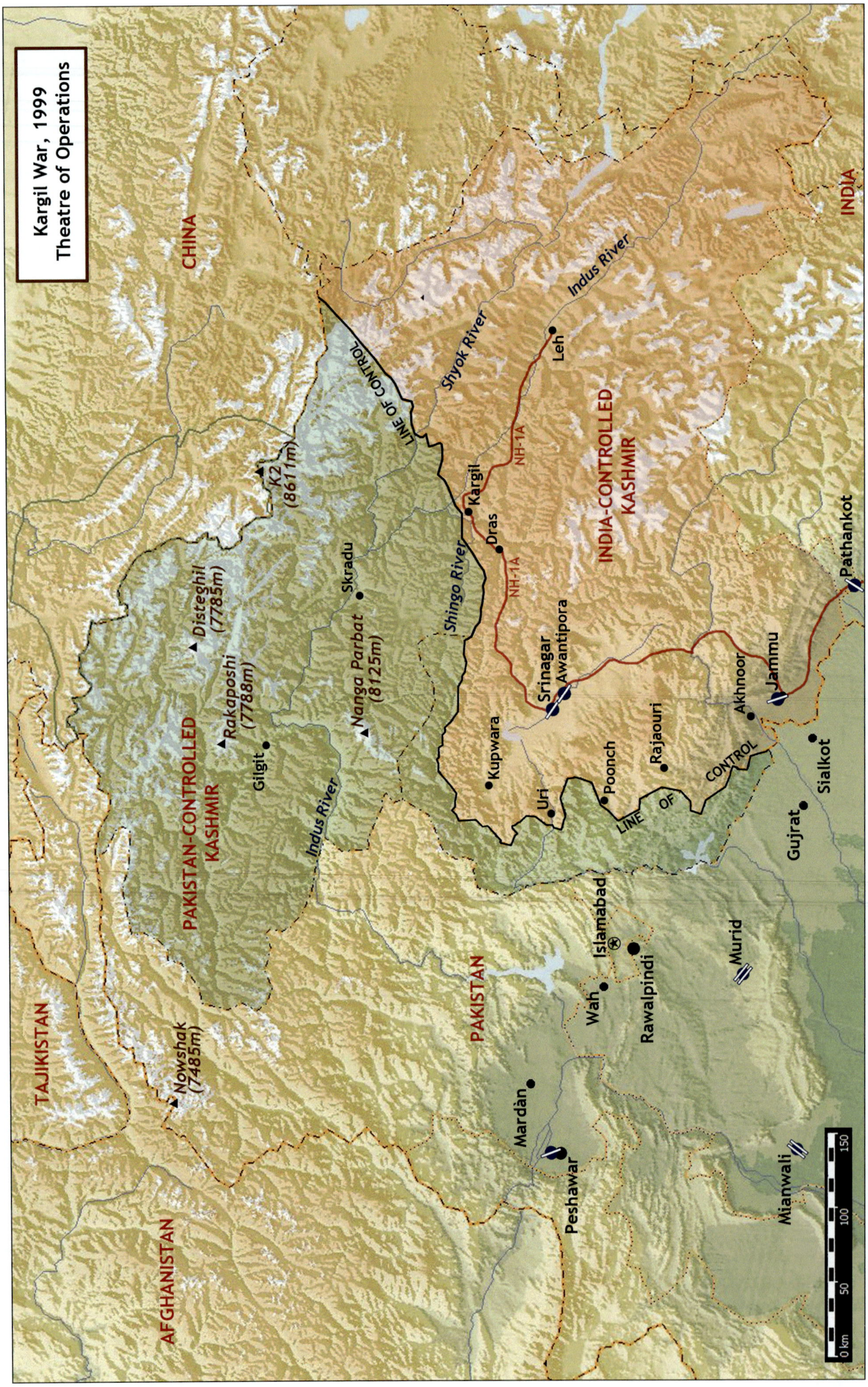

Kargil War, 1999
Theatre of Operations
CHINA
INDIA
TAJIKISTAN
AFGHANISTAN
PAKISTAN
PAKISTAN-CONTROLLED KASHMIR
INDIA-CONTROLLED KASHMIR
LINE OF CONTROL
Shyok River
Indus River
Shingo River
K2 (8611m)
Disteghil (7785m)
Rakaposhi (7788m)
Nanga Parbat (8125m)
Nowshak (7485m)
Skradu
Gilgit
Leh
Kargil
Dras
NH-1A
Srinagar
Awantipora
Kupwara
Uri
Poonch
Rajaouri
Akhnoor
Jammu
Pathankot
Sialkot
Gujrat
Islamabad
Rawalpindi
Wah
Murid
Mardān
Peshawar
Mianwali
0 km 50 100 150

However, some former Pakistani officers have in retrospect criticised the operation as poorly conceived with ridges being occupied by Pakistani troops with no actual ability to sustain operations if cut-off.[29]

Initial Indian estimates put the number of intruders at between 500 and 1,000. This was a woeful underestimate as later estimates suggest that no fewer than 5,000 personnel had occupied the heights with the area of intrusion extending for 160km.[30] Their weapons included Chinese-made Type 56 rifles, Chinese copies of the DShK 12.7mm and 14.5mm KPV heavy machineguns, mortars, light and medium machineguns, as well as substantial anti-aircraft weaponry in the form of US-made FIM-92A Stinger MANPADs and Chinese-made 37mm anti-aircraft guns.[31] Artillery support was provided from across the LoC by existing Pakistan Army units – including about 20 artillery batteries (about 120 guns in total) – while the intruders were well supplied with food and ammunition.[32]

### Defending Pakistani Positions

Following the end of heavy snowfalls, NLI soldiers crossed the LoC in large numbers in the Mushko Valley, Dras, Kaksar and Batalik subsectors and established positions on the top of high mountain ridgelines. To fortify their positions, the intruders set about building bunkers and sangars and brought forward their heavy weapons which, as was noted earlier, included mortars, heavy and light machineguns as well as shoulder-fired Stinger missiles. In addition, storage dumps of ammunition, rations and other stores were established and a large number of anti-personnel mines were laid. As noted, estimates for the intruders' force size varies, but in May 1999 estimates varied between 800 and 1,000. This increased to 2,000 later on and subsequently to estimates of a full brigade of NLI supported by SSG and Mujahidin. The extent of the intrusion varied from an average four to five kilometres to a maximum of seven to eight kilometres.

Estimates at the time suggested that each major ridgeline was held by a reinforced platoon numbering anywhere between 40 to 60 NLI soldiers under the command of an officer. Each post was amply provided with support weapons: in some cases this might have surpassed the normal allocation of battalion support weapons such as heavy, medium and light machineguns, rocket launchers, automatic grenade launchers, mortars, anti-aircraft guns for use against both aircraft and ground targets, and Stinger MANPADs.[33] The intruders further protected their positions by the deployment, somewhat indiscriminately, of a large number of plastic anti-personnel mines, placed along the expected approaches to the ridgelines.

Further evidence of professional military input was the fact that each post could provide mutual support; with fields of fire being so designed as to ensure that any attack on a single post meant that fire support could be provided by at least one other post. Given the fact that the individual posts were manned by professional soldiers, in entrenched positions at high altitude and supported by ample company and battalion level support weapons, India found itself facing an extremely competent, well-entrenched and very well equipped adversary. The failure to detect this intrusion and to appreciate the size, scale, scope and level of preparation of the intruders was to have serious consequences as India mustered a response to the intrusion that would cost many lives.

### The Detection

Initial Indian Army patrols conducting routine surveillance detected intruders atop ridges in Kargil during the period 8-15 May 1999.[34] Quite early on, the infiltration pattern suggested the participation of regular Pakistani troops as well as that of the Islamist militants. The scale of the infiltration was initially underestimated but it soon became clear that India was facing a major military incursion.

Control of the Kargil Sector on the Indian side rested on the shoulders of a solitary infantry brigade. 121 Independent (I) Infantry Brigade, with its headquarters at Kargil, was responsible for all operations in the Kargil sector.[35] This brigade group formed a part of the 3rd Infantry Division, which was headquartered at Leh, and which was responsible for operations in Ladakh. This included the 140km-long stretch of the LoC in Kargil district up to NJ 9842, along the 110km-long Actual Ground Position Line (AGPL) at Siachen Glacier plus along the Line of Actual Control (LAC) against China. This infantry brigade was a relatively small formation, with only three infantry battalions in its order of battle: indeed, when the dispositions of the 121st Infantry Brigade are studied closely, it is obvious that these included several large gaps in what were considered to be 'less threatened areas'.[36]

# 5
# INTELLIGENCE FAILURE

One of the abiding lessons from the Kargil conflict, at least from the Indian side, was the view that both military intelligence and strategic intelligence agencies had failed to detect the Kargil incursions. Many, including Lt. General Puri, GOC 8th Mountain Division during the war, held the view that: 'The Kargil War happened due to the failure of intelligence agencies, including military intelligence.'[1]

All three of India's principal agencies – Research and Analysis Wing (RAW), Intelligence Bureau (IB) and Military Intelligence (MI) – failed to anticipate and to predict Pakistan's actions in Kargil and must therefore share the responsibility for India's initial failures. The RAW, whose domain was external intelligence, had an extensive network of intelligence operatives in Pakistan and POK and also had control of many of India's SIGINT and ELINT assets. RAW collected an enormous amount of information on Pakistan's activities in Kashmir through its Aviation Research Centre (ARC) headquartered in Sarsawa in western Uttar Pradesh, which flew special electronic intelligence and photo-reconnaissance aircraft of a variety of types. Missions which should have been flown on a regular basis, were only flown after the intrusion had been discovered.

The IB, which handled internal intelligence had a stronger presence in the Ladakh region than RAW, with over 400 intelligence-gathering personnel. As early as October 1998 an IB report from Leh spoke of preparations for Pakistani special operations in the Kargil sector. India's MI also must take a great deal of the blame as its failure began from the time the Pakistanis started to construct supply and logistics bases between January and March 1999 to support the intrusion. Army Aviation Corps helicopters, which should have been used to conduct reconnaissance missions along the LoC during winter were not deployed.

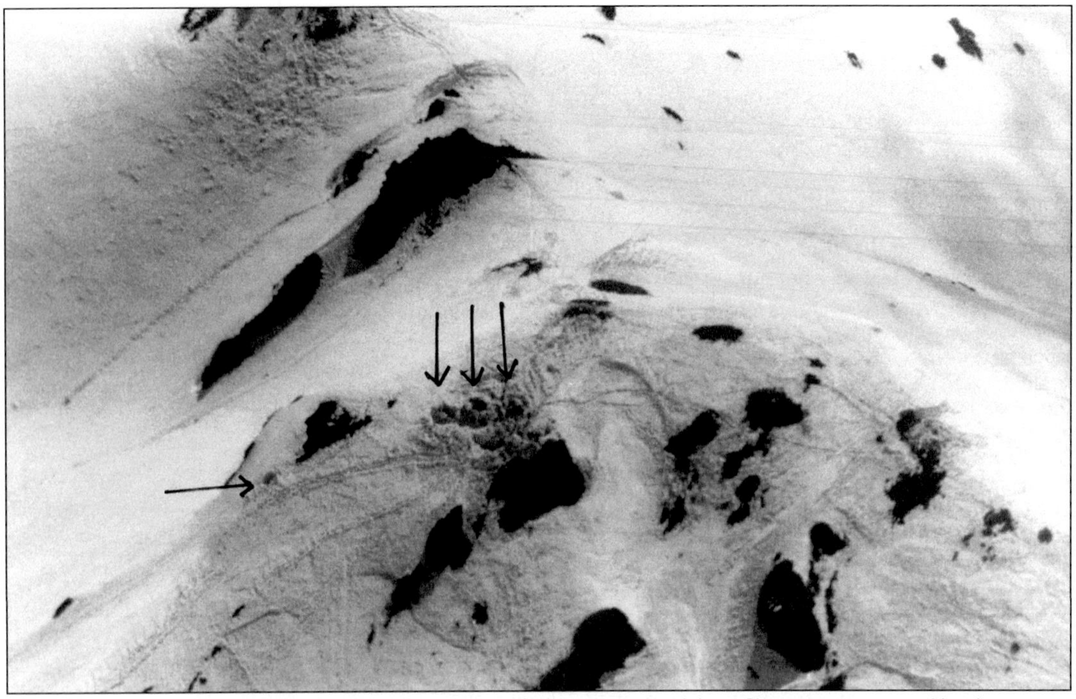

Another reconnaissance photograph made by IAF aircraft, showing one of the infiltration routes used by the Pakistanis. Notable are multiple tracks in the snow, indicating movement of dozens of troops, and as indicated by the three arrows in the centre, what looks like a bivouac area. (Ministry of Defence of India, via Albert Grandolini)

What was clear was that there was a significant breakdown in communications between intelligence agencies and those tasked with conducting operations. Officers of the 121st Brigade, stationed at Kargil, noted that they were prepared for the infiltration of small numbers of militants as opposed to a major incursion by a sizeable regular force. This, despite the fact that IB officers in the sector claimed they shared information on such incursions not only with their headquarters but also with the HQ of the 121st Brigade.

The Kargil Review Committee set up in the aftermath of the conflict was scathing in its assessment of India's intelligence failure and it is worth quoting the section of its executive summary where it notes that:

> The critical failure in intelligence was related to the absence of any information on the induction and de-induction of battalions and the lack of accurate data on the identity of battalions in the area opposite Kargil during 1998. Prisoners of War have disclosed the presence of 5, 6 and 13 NLI battalions and 24 SIND in the FCNA region from October 1998 onwards. The Indian Army has also assessed that elements of 5, 6, and 13 NLI were amongst the units that were initially used by Pakistan to launch the intrusions in April/May 1999. These units did not figure in the Order of Battle (ORBAT) supplied by RAW to the DGMI dated April 1998. Since then, and until Indian troops came into contact with these battalions in May-June 1999, there was no information of their presence in the area. RAW issued another ORBAT on June 1, 1999 which also did not show any changes in the area opposite Kargil between April 1998 and May 1999. An analysis carried out by the Committee on the basis of information now-available shows that there were in fact a number of changes in the ORBAT of Pakistani forces in the FCNA region during 1998/early 1999. These changes included the turnover of some units, induction of two additional battalions over and above the 13 already in the Sector as reported by RAW in April 1998 and the forward deployment of two battalions from Gilgit to Gultari and from Skardu to Hamzigund (near Olthingthang) respectively. In other words, if no de-inductions took place, for which the Committee lacks evidence, there was a net increase of two battalions in the FCNA region over and above RAW's projections as well as a forward deployment of two battalions within the sector during the period April 1998 to February 1999. The responsibility for obtaining information on them was primarily that of RAW and, to a much lesser extent, that of DGMI and the Division or Brigade using their Intelligence and Field Surveillance Unit (IFS) and Brigade Intelligence Team (BIT) capabilities.
>
> It could be argued that given the nature of the terrain, the climatic conditions and the unheld gaps in existence since 1972, there was no way of anticipating the intrusion during the winter provided Pakistan accepted the risk of incurring casualties in avalanches, which it did. However, since Pakistan was focusing upon Kargil, information regarding the induction of two additional battalions in the FCNA region and the forward deployment of two battalions could have proved to be an indicator of the likely nature of Pakistani activity in this sector. In that event, perhaps greater risks in patrolling in snow conditions might have been found acceptable. More focussed intelligence about the activities of Pakistan in the FCNA region would have followed. In the Committee's view, a significant gap in information prior to the detection of the Kargil intrusion was the inability of RAW to accurately monitor and report changes in the Pakistani ORBAT in the FCNA region during 1998 and early 1999 and to a lesser extent that of DGMI, the BITs and IFSUs to notice the additional forward deployment of troops in the vicinity of the LOC.[2]

This suggests that the RAW did not detect the shift in NLI battalions and did not appreciate the increase in Pakistani force levels in the area. This, combined with numerous other defaults by the IB and MI, plus perhaps total complacency in respect of the possibility of such incursions, was to cost the Indian military dearly during the Kargil operations. The late B. Raman, an Indian intelligence operative with great experience and one who was widely respected noted in his own analysis of intelligence failures during Kargil that:

> The recent events have, however, proved this assumption wrong. Consequently, focus on trans-border surveillance in the Ladakh area was concentrated across the Sino-Indian border and little attention was paid to trans-LoC developments in the Northern Areas.
>
> The second observation is that there were major gaps in India's knowledge of the Northern Areas. Indian intelligence was better informed on POK but had difficulty in collecting human intelligence from the Northern Areas because:

> (a) There is very little trans-border traffic across the LoC in this sector in the form of relatives exchanging visits or traders and smugglers clandestinely crossing the LoC with their goods;
>
> (b) Officials posted in the Indian High Commission in Islamabad or visitors from India are not allowed to visit this area;
>
> (c) The Government of India too follows a very restrictive policy by not allowing the people of these areas to visit their relatives and friends in the Kargil tehsil. As such, no one approaches the Indian High Commission to obtain visas;
>
> (d) The Northern Areas has very limited facilities for higher education. As a result, migration from there to earn a living abroad is not common. The Mirpuri diaspora in the United Kingdom and the United States, which is a useful reservoir of intelligence recruits for monitoring developments in POK, has practically no migrants from the Northern Areas.
>
> These difficulties leave little scope for collection of human intelligence and hence, one has to depend on technical intelligence. Unfortunately, till recently, not only successive governments but the intelligence community itself gave low priority to these areas even for strengthening the technical intelligence capability.[3]

Structural issues plagued India's intelligence mechanisms with neither redundancy nor back-up systems being in place to adequately impose quality controls. The Kargil Review Committee stated the following:

> The Indian Intelligence structure is flawed since there is little back up or redundancy to rectify failures and shortcomings in intelligence collection and reporting that goes to build up the external threat perception by the one agency, namely, RAW which has a virtual monopoly in this regard. It is neither healthy nor prudent to endow that one agency alone with multifarious capabilities for human, communication, imagery and electronic intelligence. Had RAW and DGMI spotted the additional battalions in the FCNA region that were missing from the ORBAT, there might have been requests for ARC flights in winter and these might have been undertaken, weather permitting. As it happened, the last flight was in October 1998, long before the intrusion, and the next in May 1999, after the intrusions had commenced. The intruders had by then come out into the open.
>
> The present structure and processes in intelligence gathering and reporting lead to an overload of background and unconfirmed information and inadequately assessed intelligence which requires to be further pursued. There is no institutionalised process whereby RAW, IB, BSF and Army intelligence officials interact periodically at levels below the JIC. This lacuna is perhaps responsible for RAW reporting the presence of one additional unit in Gultari in September 1998 but not following it up with ARC flights on its own initiative. Nor did the Army press RAW specifically for more information on this report. The Army never shared its intelligence with the other agencies or with the JIC. There was no system of Army minorities at different levels from DGMI downwards providing feedback to the Agencies.
>
> There is a general lack of awareness of the critical importance of and the need for assessed intelligence at all levels. JIC reports do not receive the attention they deserve at the political and higher

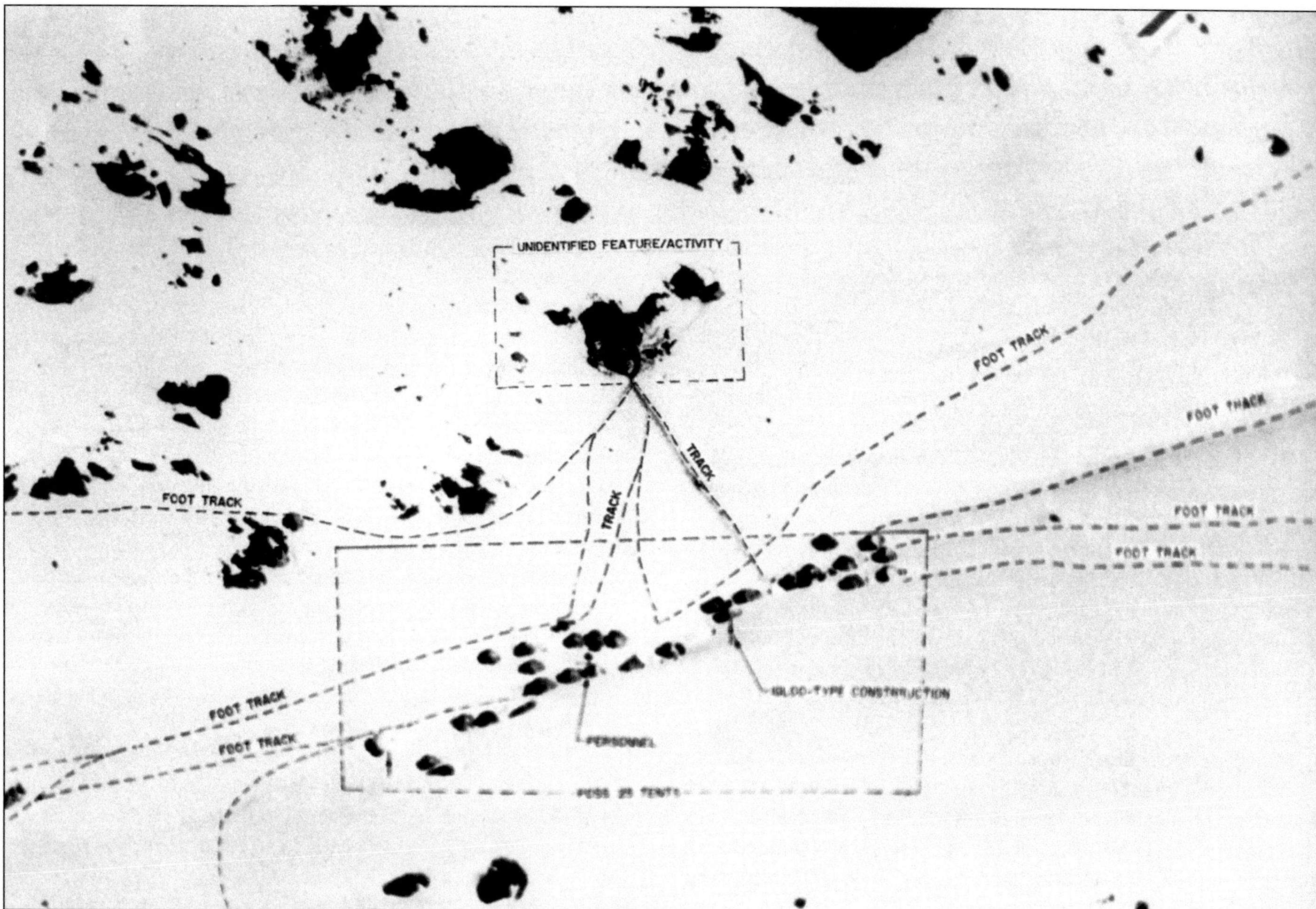

A more detailed reconnaissance photo of one of infiltration routes used by the Pakistani troops, including descriptions of what can be seen: multiple foot-tracks, about two dozen tents, and an 'unidentified feature/activity'. (Ministry of Defence of India, via Albert Grandolini)

bureaucratic levels. The assessment process has been downgraded in importance and consequently various agencies send very junior officials to JIC meetings. The DGMI did not send any regular inputs to the JIC for two years preceding the Kargil crisis. The IC was not accorded the importance it deserved either by the Intelligence agencies or the Government. The Chairmanship of JIC had become the reserve of an IPS officer who was generally a runner-up for the post of Secretary (RAW) or DIB. The post was in fact left unfilled for 18 months until December 1998. During this period, Secretary (RAW) doubled as Chairman, JIC.

There are no checks and balances in the Indian intelligence system to ensure that the consumer gets all the intelligence that is available and is his due. There is no system of regular, periodic and comprehensive intelligence briefings it the political level and to the Committee of Secretaries. In the absence of an overall, operational national security framework and objective, each intelligence agency is diligent in preserving its own turf and departmental prerogatives. There is no evidence that the intelligence agencies have reviewed their role after India became a nuclear weapon state or in the context of the increasing problems posed by insurgencies and ethnic-nationalist turbulences backed with sophisticated hi-tech equipment and external support. Nor has the Government felt the need to initiate any such move.[4]

Nonetheless, despite its initial failings, India's intelligence agencies produced what might be the intelligence coup of the Kargil War when they intercepted conversations between the Pakistani Chief of Army Staff, General Pervez Musharraf (C) and Lt. General Mohammed Aziz, the Chief of the General Staff (P), on 26 May 1999, while Musharraf was in China, with recordings of a similar conversation following on 29 May 1999. In this intercept the two men discussed Pakistan's operations in the Kargil area and the Indian response. Coming at a time when the Pakistanis were trying to indicate to the world that the operation was a Mujahedin incursion, as opposed to one supported and perpetrated by the Pakistani Army, these intercepts came at a most inopportune time and perhaps provided the necessary spike in any Pakistani plans to seek decisive external intervention.[5]

Rather striking was the following excerpt coming from those intercepts of 26 May 1999 which seems to suggest that the Pakistani civilian government was less than fully aware of the Army's plans and that international intervention was at least part of the objective:

C: Was there some other talk of putting pressure on us?

P: No. He only said that they [militants] will be given suitable reception. This term he used. He said they will be flushed out, and every time Tauqir said that please tell us some detail, detail about how many have gone into your area, what is happening there? Then I will ask the concerned people and then we will get back to you. So whenever he asked these details, he would say, we will talk about this when we meet, then I will give details. This means, they are possibly looking forward to the next round of talks, in which the two sides could meet. This could be the next round of talks between the two PMs which they are expecting it....Sir, very good thing, no problem...

C: So, many times we had discussed, taken your [PM's?] ... blessings and yesterday also I told him that the door of discussion, dialogue must be kept open & rest, no change in ground situation.

P: So, no one was in a particularly disturbed frame of mind.

C: Even your seat man?

P: Yes, he was disturbed. Also, Malik Saheb was disturbed, as they had been even earlier. Those two's views were that the status quo & the present position of Gen Hassan [?] no change should be recommended in that. But he was also saying that any escalation after that should be regulated as there may be the danger of war. On this logic, we gave the suggestion that there was no such fear as the scruff [tooti] of their [militants] neck is in our hands, whenever you want, we could regulate it. Ch Zafar Saheb coped very well. He gave a very good presentation of our viewpoint. He said we had briefed the PM earlier & given an assessment. After this, we played the tape of Tauqir. Then he said that what we are seeing, that was our assessment, and those very stages of the military situation were being seen, which it would not be a problem for us to handle. Rest, it was for your guidance how to deal with the political & diplomatic aspects. We told him there is no reason of alarm and panic. Then he said that when I came to know seven days back, when Corps Commanders were told. The entire reason of the success of this operation was this total secrecy. Our experience was that our earlier efforts failed because of lack of secrecy. So the top priority is to accord confidentiality, to ensure our success. We should respect this and the advantage we have from this would give us a handle.
C: Rest [baki], is Mian Saheb okay?

P: Ok. He was confident just like that but for the other two. Shamshad as usual was supporting. Today, for the last two hours the BBC has been continuously reporting on the air strikes by India. Keep using this — let them keep dropping bombs. As far as internationalisation is concerned, this is the fastest this has happened. You may have seen in the press about UN Secretary General Kofi Annan's appeal that both countries should sit & talk.[6]

Further evidence of this desire came in the 28 May 1999 tape, which showed both men conceptualizing a position to be taken in favour of UN intervention:

C: Idea on LoC

P: Yes. Hint is that, given that the LoC has many areas where the interpretation of either side is not what the other side believes. So, comprehensive deliberation is required. So, that can be worked out by DGMOs.

C: If they are assured that we are here from a long period. We have been sitting here for long. Like in the beginning, the matter is the same — no post was attacked and no post was captured. The situation is that we are along our defensive Line of Control. If it is not in his [Sartaj Aziz's] knowledge, then discuss it altogether. Emphasise that for years, we are here only.
C: Yes, this point should be raised. We are sitting on the same LoC since a long period.

P: This is their weakness. They are not agreed on the demarcation under UN's verification, whereas we are agreed. We want to exploit it.

C: This is in Simla Agreement that we cannot go for UN intervention.

P: Our neighbour does not accept their presence or UNMOGIP arrangement for survey for the area. So, we can start from the top, from 9842 (NJ 9842). On this line, we can give them logic but in short, the recommendation for Sartaj Aziz Saheb is that he should make no commitment in the first meeting on military situation. And he should not even accept ceasefire, because if there is ceasefire, then vehicles will be moving (on Dras-Kargil highway). In this regard, they have to use their own argument that whatever is interfering with you. That we don't know but there is no justification about tension on LoC. No justification. We want to give them this type of brief so that he does not get into any specifics.[7]

These transcripts were invaluable to India: they strengthened its position against external intervention and in favour of dealing with the incursion on its own. The release of these transcripts helped to isolate Pakistan on the international level and allowed the government in New Delhi and the military a degree of political and military freedom to deal with the incursion. This was aided by the cautious approach to Indian military operations to ensure that the LoC was not crossed.

# 6
# ORDERS OF BATTLE IN KARGIL

Neither India nor Pakistan deployed more than a small fraction of their military forces in the Kargil theatre of operations. This does not mean that their military forces were not fully mobilized for the operation: the actual participation of units in the battle, however, was rather limited. While both sides remained very wary of escalation and deployed forces along their entire border and frontier – the latter extending north and the former south and west – neither side chose to utilize more than a small core of units for military operations in Kargil. Pakistan in particular, was unable to reinforce its infiltration teams and resupply became increasingly difficult and erratic especially once Indian operations began to isolate infiltrator held positions.

Another aspect of the Kargil operations was the very effective use of troop rotation by the Indian Army. Battalions were kept in theatre but not necessarily all committed to offensive operations simultaneously. This enabled adequate rest and resupply efforts for units while simultaneously ensuring that adequate forces were kept engaging the Pakistani infiltrators. This was to pay big dividends for the Indian Army, which, while having good logistic support, found itself having to engage hostile and well entrenched units uphill and in treacherous terrain. The ability to have well-rested, adequately supplied and equipped troops was to prove decisive in combat.

Pakistan was able to earmark at least four brigades to cover the Kargil operations but only one brigade equivalent actually crossed the Line of Control. It is as yet unclear whether Pakistan intended a larger number of troops to be pushed across the Line of Control but it is evident that a single brigade of NLI, despite excellent artillery support and large stocks of munitions and supplies, would have been inadequate to the task of holding their positions in the face of an Indian counterattack. The inability of either Pakistan's air force or army to resupply the NLI was evident.

## Indian Army Order of Battle

The Kargil Operations fell under the ambit of the Indian Army's Northern Command – in particular XV Corps. In peacetime, the area was the responsibility of 121st (Independent) Infantry Brigade, itself a part of the 3rd Infantry Division, but later attached to the 8th Mountain Division when this assumed a greater share of the burden during the Kargil operations. This Corps had two full infantry divisions attached to it plus an additional artillery brigade at corps level. The 8th Mountain Division had three infantry brigades and an artillery brigade under its command while the two independent brigades – the 121st Infantry and the 50th Parachute – were attached to it temporarily. The second of the Indian divisions – the 3rd Infantry

Two Indian Army troops against the backdrop of the typical landscape of the Kargil area. As always in warfare, the local topography was to play a crucial role in the conflict. (Albert Grandolini Collection)

Division – allocated one full integral brigade and one attached independent brigade to the operations.

During the course of the Kargil operations, numerous infantry battalions rotated through different brigades, and were attached and detached as needed. For example, the Brigade of the Guards provided additional detachments with MILAN ATGMs which were used in the direct fire role. Special forces units as well as India's counter-insurgency force, the Rashtriya Rifles, were also participants in the Kargil operations, with the Border Security Force and Central Reserve Police Force – which are Central Armed Police Forces – supported the Army and helped preserve the integrity of the counter-insurgency grid that is critical to internal security in the state of Jammu and Kashmir.

Infantry battalions deployed in Kargil used the full range of their support weapons. Battalion support companies made very effective use of their mortar platoons while the anti-tank platoons were not only able to use the MILAN missile in the direct fire role, but also to use the MIRA night-sights of the system to augment the limited amount of thermal imaging night vision equipment available to Indian infantry at that time. In addition, firebases using the battalion level medium machineguns – FN-MAGs – as well as the AGS-17 automatic grenade launchers were established to support battalion level assaults on Pakistani held positions.

No fewer than 19 artillery regiments participated in the war and were attached to the artillery brigades of the respective divisions, with XV Corps artillery as well as independent units assigned to fire support. Field regiments were equipped with 105mm Indian Field

Cheetah helicopters of the Indian Army Aviation Corps provided precious support for ground troops during the Kargil campaign and also flew artillery spotting operations. (Colonel Gurmeet Kanwal/Directorate General of Artillery, Indian Army, via author)

Guns or Light Field Guns, medium regiments were equipped with 130mm M-46 guns and 155mm FH77/B-02 Bofors Howitzers. Light regiments operated 120mm mortars, while the sole heavy mortar regiment deployed fielded Tampella 160mm mortars. Some 75/24mm Indian-designed pack howitzers were used in the direct fire role, while a rocket regiment with BM-21 122mm rockets was also deployed.

The deployment of artillery was lavish by Indian standards with some three to four hundred artillery pieces and mortars in action to support Indian operations. This in turn placed a significant strain on India's ability to keep guns supplied with ammunition and spare parts. The use of older weapons was slowly discouraged and whilst the 75/24mm gun might have been deemed suitable for use in mountains, its short range and light shell were less than effective. This also applied, albeit to a lesser extent, to the 105mm field guns which were given less priority than larger calibre weapons.

The artillery units were supported by two Reconnaissance and Observation squadrons (663 and 668) of the Army Aviation Corps, both equipped with HAL Cheetah (license built Aérospatiale SE.315 Alouette II) helicopters. These helicopters, in the absence of UAVs were to prove extremely valuable to the Indian Army. Not only did they provide excellent spotting for the artillery, but they also proved to be a highly effective reconnaissance asset. While the helicopters initially flew with no sensor arrays of any kind, the Indian Army did experiment with fitting the FLIR turret of the Nishant UAV to the Cheetah to dramatically improve its night and bad-weather surveillance capabilities. However even with such equipment, the Cheetah remained a small and relatively vulnerable aircraft and it is almost surprising that none was shot down.

The Indian Army's Corps of Air Defence Artillery also deployed units during the Kargil conflict, with P-18 radars and the 326th Light Air Defence Regiment (Composite) being deployed to give active support in the event of any Pakistani air threat. Being a composite regiment, the 326th operated a combination of 23mm towed ZU-23-2 anti-aircraft guns and Igla-1M missiles and were assigned to defend artillery positions and cover troop and munition-convoys moving into the theatre. Additional support was provided by Bofors L/70 40mm guns of the 323rd Air Defence Regiment which provided cover

A Bofors L70 40mm anti-aircraft gun in position in the Dras sector. (Colonel Gurmeet Kanwal/Directorate General of Artillery, Indian Army, via author)

Indian Army troops assembled at their base in the Kargil area, waiting to move out into action. (Albert Grandolini Collection)

for vital areas and points, and the 146th Light Air Defence Regiment (Self-Propelled) which operated ZU-23-2 guns on 6x6 trucks.

In the absence of a serious air threat, none of India's air defence assets – whether in the Kargil sector or not – were tested and Indian infantry and artillery units operated completely unmolested by Pakistani aircraft. This also meant that India was able to move supplies and reinforcements with relative ease and its lines of supply and communication were safe. It is also possible, but not confirmed, that India used some of its anti-aircraft guns in the ground support role where their high rate of fire and the not inconsiderable destructive power of their ammunition could have been quite effective in supporting infantry assaults. Bofors L70 40mm guns and ZU-23-2 23mm guns have been widely employed against Pakistani formations, bunkers and troops across the Line of Control, with very impressive results when called into action.

| **Table 23: Indian Army ORBAT, Kargil, 1999**[1] |
|---|
| **Unit** |
| **Northern Command** |
| **XV Corps** |
| • **XV Corps Artillery Brigade** |
| |
| **8th Mountain Division** |
| • **121st (I) Infantry Brigade** |
| • 16th Battalion, The Grenadiers |
| • 4th Battalion, Jat Regiment |
| • 3rd Battalion, Punjab Regiment |
| • 10th Battalion, Garhwal Rifles |
| • Unknown Battalion, Border Security Force |
| • ATGM Detachment, 17th Battalion, Brigade of the Guards |
| **56th Mountain Brigade** |
| • 16th Battalion, The Grenadiers |
| • 18th Battalion, The Grenadiers |
| • 8th Battalion, Sikh Regiment |

| **Table 23: Indian Army ORBAT, Kargil, 1999** (continued)[1] |
|---|
| • 1st Battalion, Naga Regiment |
| • 2nd Battalion, Rajputana Rifles |
| • 3rd Battalion, Rajputana Rifles |
| • 18th Battalion, Garhwal Rifles |
| • 13th Battalion, Jammu and Kashmir Rifles |
| • 1st Battalion, 3 Gurkha Rifles |
| • 9th Battalion, Parachute Regiment |
| • ATGM Detachment, 17th Battalion, Brigade of the Guards |
| **50th (I) Parachute Brigade** |
| • 6th Battalion, Parachute Regiment |
| • 7th Battalion, Parachute Regiment |
| • 1st Battalion, Parachute Regiment (SF) |
| • ATGM Detachment, 19th Battalion, Brigade of the Guards |
| **192nd Mountain Brigade** |
| • 18th Battalion, The Grenadiers |
| • 8th Battalion, Sikh Regiment |
| • 9th Battalion, Parachute Regiment |
| • ATGM Detachment, 17th Battalion, Brigade of the Guards |
| **79th Mountain Brigade** |
| • 17th Battalion, Jat Regiment |
| • 28th Battalion, Rashtriya Rifles |
| • 12th Battalion, Mahar Regiment |
| • 13th Battalion, Jammu and Kashmir Rifles |
| • 2nd Battalion, Naga Regiment |
| |
| **3rd Infantry Division** |
| • **3rd Artillery Brigade** |
| • **70th Infantry Brigade** |
| • 1st Battalion, 11th Gurkha Rifles |
| • 12th Battalion, Jammu and Kashmir Light Infantry |
| • 10th Battalion, Parachute Regiment |

Indian Army troops – the two in the foreground are both armed with Ishapore SLRs – marching into the combat zone in Kargil in 1999. (Albert Grandolini Collection)

| Table 23: Indian Army ORBAT, Kargil, 1999 (continued)[1] |
|---|
| • 1st Battalion, Bihar Regiment |
| • Ladakh Scouts |
| • 17th Battalion, Garhwal Rifles |
| • 5th Battalion, Parachute Regiment |
| • 14th Battalion, Sikh Regiment |
| • ATGM Detachment, 19th Battalion, Brigade of the Guards |
| • **102nd (I) Infantry Brigade** |
| • 11th Battalion, Rajputana Rifles |
| • 9th Battalion, Mahar Regiment |
| • 13th Battalion, Kumaon Regiment |
| • 27th Battalion, Rajput Regiment |
| • High Altitude Warfare School (Permanent Cadre Detachment) |
| • ATGM Detachment, 19th Battalion, Brigade of the Guards |
| |
| **Kargil Theatre Artillery Units** |
| • 4th Field Regiment |
| • 15th Field Regiment |
| • 41st Field Regiment |
| • 108th Medium Regiment |
| • 139th Medium Regiment |
| • 141st Field Regiment |
| • 153rd Medium Regiment |
| • 158th Medium Regiment |
| • 197th Field Regiment |
| • 212th Rocket Regiment |
| • 244th Heavy Mortar Regiment |
| • 253rd Medium Regiment |
| • 255th Field Regiment |
| • 286th Medium Regiment |

| Table 23: Indian Army ORBAT, Kargil, 1999 (continued)[1] |
|---|
| • 305th Medium Regiment |
| • 307th Medium Regiment |
| • 315th Field Regiment |
| • 1861st Light Regiment |
| • 1889th Light Regiment |
| |
| **Balance of Battalions** |
| • 5th Battalion, Special Frontier Force |
| • 663rd Reconnaissance & Observation Squadron AAC |
| • 668th Reconnaissance & Observation Squadron AAC |
| • 13th Battalion, Punjab Regiment |
| • 12th Battalion, The Grenadiers |
| • 22nd Battalion, The Grenadiers |
| • 7th Battalion, Jat Regiment |
| • 14th Battalion, Rahstriya Rifles |
| • 17th Battalion, Rashtriya Rifles |
| • 11th Battalion, Sikh Regiment |
| • 3rd Battalion, Jammu and Kahsmir Rifles |
| • 16th Battalion, Dogra Regiment |
| • 5th Battalion, Rajput Regiment |
| • 9th Battalion, Mahar Regiment |

## Indian Air Force Order of Battle

While the Indian Air Force was at its peak strength in terms of numbers of aircraft in 1999, it did not deploy complete squadrons during the operations. Partly due to a lack of infrastructure and largely due to the lack of need, the IAF deployed detachments from several squadrons to the Kargil operation while keeping back the bulk of its forces in the event of escalation. No fewer than 11 combat squadrons sent detachments of between four and six aircraft to participate in the Kargil operations. These included both of the then extant Mirage 2000

| **Table 24: Indian Air Force ORBAT, Kargil, 1999** [3] | | | |
|---|---|---|---|
| **Squadron** | **Aircraft Type** | **Commanding Officer** | **Battle Honours** |
| **Fighter Squadrons** | | | |
| 1 | Mirage 2000H/TH | Wg Cdr S. Neelakantan | Op Safed Sagar 1999 |
| 7 | Mirage 2000H/TH | Wg Cdr Sandeep Chabbra | Op Safed Sagar 1999 |
| 9 | MiG-27M | Wg Cdr Avtar Singh | Op Safed Sagar 1999 |
| 14 | Jaguar IS | Wg Cdr Ashwani Bhakoo | |
| 17 | MiG-21M | Wg Cdr B S Dhanoa | Op Safed Sagar 1999 |
| 27 | Jaguar IS | Wg Cdr H K J S Sokhey | |
| 28 | MiG-29 | Wg Cdr P M Cherian | |
| 51 | MiG-21bis | Wg Cdr Randhawa (until 21 June 1999), then Wg Cdr N K Tandon (from 21 June 1999) | |
| 102 | MiG-25RB/U | Gp Capt S P Ojha | |
| 108 | MiG-21FL | Wg Cdr H S Jallawalia | Op Safed Sagar |
| 221 | MiG-23MF | Wg Cdr Ashit Mehta (from 18 June 1999) | Op Safed Sagar |
| 223 | MiG-29 | Wg Cdr Sandip Sud (until 18 June 1999) | Op Safed Sagar |
| **Transport Squadrons** | | | |
| 25 | An-32, Il-76 | Gp Capt S P Singh | |
| 48 | An-32 | Gp Capt M K Devnath | |
| **Helicopter Squadrons** | | | |
| 114 HU | Cheeta | Wg Cdr A S Butola (until 14 June 1999) | |
| 129 HU | Mi-17 | Wg Cdr A K Sinha | Op Safed Sagar |
| 130 HU | Mi-8 | | Op Safed Sagar |
| 132 FAC Flight | Cheetah | Wg Cdr O S Ahluwalia | |
| 152 HU | Mi-17 | Wg Cdr S Mittal | Op Safed Sagar |
| **Air Bases/Air Stations** | | | |
| Wing | | Commanding Officer | Theatre Honours |
| 1 | Srinagar | Air Cdre Mohinder Khanna | Op Safed Sagar |
| 8 | Adempur | | Op Safed Sagar |
| 9 | Halwara | | |
| 12 | Chandigarh | Air Cdre S K Banerjee | |
| 21 | Leh | | |
| 8 FBSU | Awantipur | Gp Capt K K J Mathews | Op Safed Sagar |
| **Radar- and Signal Units** | | | |
| Squadron | | Commanding Officer | Theatre Honours |
| 228 Sqn | | | |
| 229 Sqn | | | Op Safed Sagar |
| 299 Sqn | | | Op Safed Sagar |
| 256 Sig Unit | | | Op Safed Sagar |
| 305 TRU | | | Op Safed Sagar |
| 311 TRU | | | Op Safed Sagar |
| **Mobile Observation Flights** | | | |
| 411 | | | |

| Table 24: Indian Air Force ORBAT, Kargil, 1999 (continued)[3] | | | |
|---|---|---|---|
| 422 | | | Op Safed Sagar |
| 457 | | | Op Safed Sagar |
| **Air Defence Units** | | | |
| Squadron | | | |
| 2202 Sqn | SA-3 | Wg Cdr R C Pandey | |
| 2214 Sqn | SA-3 | Wg Cdr Ravinathan | |
| 2228 Sqn | SA-3 | | |
| 2255 Sqn | SA-8 | Wg Cdr S Singh | |
| 2307 Flight | SA-16 | Sqn Ldr S C D'Souza | |

squadrons, two of three MiG-29 squadrons, three MiG-21 squadrons, two Jaguar squadrons and one squadron each of MiG-27s and MiG-23BNs. Neither of the two Jaguar squadrons was committed to action, while only one of the two MiG-29 squadrons was involved in actual operations, earning it battle honours largely for its role escorting strike packages and deterring Pakistani operations. Both of India's strategic reconnaissance squadrons – 102 and 106 – were deployed with the latter providing excellent photographic reconnaissance of the area. Transport assets were provided by two squadrons – one a composite unit of An-32 and Il-76 transports and the other an all An-32 unit. The majority of munitions and supplies were moved by road and the military infrastructure in place was able to cope quite easily with the stresses of the Kargil conflict. Helicopter units provided critical transport and combat support and – at between 10 and 12 aircraft each – were smaller than IAF squadrons. Mi-17 helicopters were actively deployed in the combat role armed with unguided rockets, while Cheetah helicopters provided much needed medevac and forward air control. Two Mi-17, one Mi-8 and two Cheetah helicopter units were deployed during the Kargil conflict, with three being awarded battle honours.

The IAF also deployed three Mobile Observation Flights, six radar/signal units, and four squadrons of SAMs (three of SA-3s and one of SA-8s), to cover key assets in the area, plus one flight of Igla-1M MANPADs for close-in base protection.[2]

### Pakistan Army Order of Battle

Pakistan has not quite fully admitted the role of its combat units during the Kargil conflict and thus a detailed order of battle is not available: indeed, much related information remains speculative.

The burden of the Kargil campaign was borne by the Northern Light Infantry which was headquartered at Gilgit in Gilgit-Baltistan. Four NLI battalions – 5, 6, 8 and 12 NLI battalions – were deployed in full strength. Elements of 3, 4, 7 and 11 NLI, together with the Chitral and Bajaur Scouts, were employed for logistic support of the four combatant NLI infantry battalions. These were under the control of 62 Brigade Pakistan Army and were provided with fire support from some 20 Pakistan Army artillery batteries. Each NLI sub-unit involved in the infiltration was provided with lavish quantities of battalion level support weaponry. The units available and employed in the Kargil operation were split into holding units in the POK, and infiltration units crossing the LoC, as listed in Table 25.[4]

PAF F-16s did not become involved in combat operations during the Kargil War. Their constant presence along the LoC was felt by the IAF – if for no other reason than because the F-16s and Indian MiG-29s several times 'exchanged cordialities' by locking their radars on to each other. (Albert Grandolini Collection)

| Table 25: Pakistan Army ORBAT, Kargil, 1999 |
|---|
| **Unit** |
| **80th Brigade** |
| Holding Units |
| • 11th Battalion NLI |
| • 24th Battalion Sindh Regiment |
| • 5th Battalion Baluch Regiment |
| • 18th Battalion Punjab Regiment |
| • 2nd Wing Khyber Rifles |
| Infiltrating Units |
| • 2 companies SSG |
| • 12th Battalion NLI (plus two companies) |
| |
| **28th Brigade** |
| Holding Units |
| • 13th Battalion POK Regiment |
| • 13th Battalion NLI Regiment |
| Infiltrating Units |
| • 1 company SSG |
| • 4th Battalion NLI |
| • 6th Battalion NLI |
| **62nd Brigade** |
| Holding Units |
| • 69th Battalion Baluch Regiment |
| • 32nd Battalion Punjab Regiment |
| • 3rd Battalion NLI Regiment |
| • 7th Battalion NLI Regiment |
| • 8th Battalion NLI Regiment |
| • 10th Battalion NLI Regiment |
| Infiltrating Units |
| • 5th Battalion NLI Regiment |
| • Elements of the 3rd and 8th Battalions NLI Regiment |
| |
| **323rd Brigade** |
| Holding Units |
| • 10th Battalion Baluch Regiment |
| • 12th Battalion Baluch Regiment |
| • 38th Battalion Frontier Force |
| • 2 companies SSG |

| Table 25: Pakistan Army ORBAT, Kargil, 1999 (continued) |
|---|
| |
| **Artillery Units** |
| • 17th Medium Battery of the 8th Medium Regiment (155mm) |
| • 408th (I) Medium Battery and Survey Troop (155mm) |
| • 14th Mountain Regiment (105mm and 25Pdr) |
| • 38th Mountain Regiment (105mm and 25Pdr) |
| • 77th Mountain Regiment (105mm and 25Pdr) |
| • 450th (I) NLI Mountain Battery |
| • 451st (I) NLI Mountain Battery |
| • 452nd (I) NLI Mountain Battery |
| • 161st Mortar Regiment (120mm) |
| • 164th Mortar Regiment (120mm) |
| • 166th Mortar Regiment (120mm) |
| |
| **Air Defence** |
| • 60th Zambaz Air Defence Battery (artillery) |
| • 403rd Light Air Defence Battery (artillery) |
| • 472nd (I) Missile Battery (FIM-92A) |
| • 475th (I) Missile Battery (FIM-92A) |
| • 476th (I) Missile Battery (FIM-92A) |
| • 479th (I) Missile Battery (FIM-92A) |

Pakistan thus deployed an infantry and artillery-dominated, but still considerable, division-sized force during the Kargil War. This might not have committed all of its elements across the LoC, but the fact that infiltrators from the NLI had been assigned to brigade sectors speaks to the level of Pakistani Army support for the operation. In addition, the allocation of artillery was quite substantial for a brigade-level incursion, with the equivalent of perhaps four full regiments of artillery plus three heavy mortar regiments being allocated to the task. Noteworthy is the extent of Pakistan's air defence cover for the infiltration with its guns and MANPADS.

### Pakistan Air Force Order of Battle

Pakistan did not deploy its air force as a combatant unit during Kargil. Nevertheless, the PAF maintained a high degree of alert to respond to any Indian air incursions across the Line of Control. The most active in this effort are known to have been two of its units: No. 9 'Griffins' and No. 11 'Arrows' squadrons, both equipped with F-16A/Bs.

# 7
# OPERATION VIJAY

On the Indian side of the LoC, there is a single 'all weather' road connecting Srinagar in the south to Leh: National Highway 1A. This road is effectively a lifeline, linking the Ladakh region to Srinagar and the rest of the Kashmir Valley. From Srinagar, the route runs 19km north to Ganderbal, east thereafter to Sonamarg for 65km, another 14km to Baltal. The road then climbs to an elevation of 3,529m to the Zojila Pass and runs due east through a valley bordered by steep mountains. From Zojila, the road slopes down through Gumri, Macho, Mianmarg, Mugalpur, Matayin, Pandras, Mamyol, Dras and Kargil, with the distance from Baltal to Kargil being 97km. The total distance from Srinagar to Leh is 427km.[1]

The weather is singularly inhospitable, with Dras being deemed the second coldest place on the planet with winter temperatures falling to 60° below zero centigrade. At Gumri, lying east of Zojila, two nullahs flow into the valley – Bod Gummar Nar from the north and Lokat Gummar Nar from the south. The latter becomes the Gumri Nullah and remains so until the Mushkoh Nullah joins it near Dras and the two become the Dras River. This in turn flows until it meets the Shingo River which then joins the Suru River flowing north from the Zanskar Valley to merge with the River Wakha Rong from Kargil. All flow north to join the Indus. In the west, the Mushkoh Nullah is close to the LoC which then follows the Dras-Kargil road over the

Another reconnaissance photograph taken by IAF Canberras, nicely illustrating the rugged terrain and the problems that the Pakistani incursions caused for the Indian Army. Barely visible at the top of the photograph are four areas with visible infiltration activity; just visible at the bottom is an outpost of the Indian Army. (Albert Grandolini Collection)

Shingo River. This is where National Highway 1A comes closest to the LoC and where it is most vulnerable to interdiction. As the LoC turns north from Kargil, road communications become increasingly poor once the Indus is crossed. It runs on to Shangruthi north-west of the Jubar Ridge Line and thereafter to Chorbat La, where it goes north, crossing the River Shyok eventually to Map Square NJ 9842.[2]

There the LoC is no longer referred to as the LoC but becomes the Actual Ground Position Line (AGPL). The AGPL continues north along the Saltoro Range and is crossed by three passes – Gyong La, Bilafond La and Sia La. It ends at Indira Col on the border of the part of Kashmir gifted to China by Pakistan – the Shaksgam Valley. This makes demarcation of the LoC and following the LoC on maps extremely difficult

The Kargil sector starts at Kaobal Gali, which lies on the ridge line Bot Kulan Ganj Point 5209 to Point 5301, with the latter lying on the LoC. From there the border extends beyond the River Shyok. The peaks along the Indian side of the LoC are an average of 5,000m above sea level. They are devoid of all vegetation and snowbound from November to late April or early May. These areas are inhospitable, cold, and lack any roads or tracks save for seven axes:

- The Minimarg-Gurez sector – opposite Gurez
- The Marpo La sector – opposite Dras
- The Barbat-Dulang sector on the River Shingo – opposite Kaksar
- The Olthingthan sector on the River Sulu – opposite Kargil
- The Marol-Shangruti sector on the River Indus – opposite Batalik
- The Piun-Chorbatla axis – opposite Hondanbrok
- The River Shyok axis, Piun-Siari – opposite Turtok.

It was only along these seven axes that offensive military operations could be conducted by either side with any degree of efficacy. Given the inhospitable terrain, low temperatures, and topographical and climatic difficulties, the Indian view that military operations during winter were unlikely allowed for a degree of dangerous complacency and the inherent vulnerability of NH 1A and the Indian lines of communications made the Kargil region a target.

## Forces in Kargil

While it is known that the Kargil Sector was the responsibility of 121 Independent Infantry Brigade, in 1999 under Brigadier Surinder Singh, the vast area of its responsibility was too much for the limited forces under the control of this Brigade. At the time of the Kargil incursion, like all other Indian brigades, 121 (I) Brigade had under its control four infantry battalions. To this was added one battalion of the Indian Border Security Force – a paramilitary outfit primarily earmarked for border constabulary roles but one which was quite able to fight alongside the regular Indian Army. The four infantry battalions were:

- 16 Grenadiers
- 10 Garhwal
- 4 Jat
- 3 Punjab

These were augmented by 8 BSF. It should be noted that these were fully equipped and trained infantry units with a full complement of personnel and support weapons. However, they would be limited in their mobility due to the constraints of terrain and the temperature,

Forward-deployed observation party of Major Rohit Butalia, from the 17th Parachute Field Regiment, during the action in the Mushkoh Valley. (Directorate General of Artillery, Indian Army, via author)

with foot patrols being the mode of travel. These units were deployed to the following sub-sectors:

- 16 Grenadiers – Dras sub-sector
- 4 Jat – Kakasr sub-sector
- 8 BSF (less one platoon stationed are Chorbatla) – Channigund sub-sector
- 10 Garhwal – Indus sub-sector
- 3 Punjab – Batalik sub-sector

However, these deployments opened substantial gaps between the battalions:

- 42km from Marpola to the boundary with 109 Infantry Brigade west of Kaobal Gali
- 11km from Marpola to Bimbat
- 10km from Bimbat to Bajrang Post (close to Point 5299 in the Kaskar sub-sector)
- 25km from Batalik to Chorbat La in Yaldor

With such gaps, 121 (I) Brigade and its constituent battalions were not only isolated from other Indian units but were covering a large area with significant gaps between the specific battalions' sub-sectors. Given the brigade's winter posture and reduced patrolling, this allowed an opportunity for Pakistani infiltration.

## Understanding the Kargil War

The ground combat in the Kargil war revolved around recapturing peaks. It was not spread over a particularly large geographic area and it was not, despite the intensity of the fighting, a widespread, general conflict between the Indian and Pakistani armies. One may break the ground combat into four phases:

- Discovering the infiltration
- Containing the infiltration
- Building up forces
- Retaking Tololing
- Retaking Tiger Hill
- Retaking peaks at Batalik.

It should be noted that once the infiltration had been discovered some hasty assaults were launched and while ill-conceived and certainly very costly, the Indian Army was able, with its existing forces and without reinforcements, to contain the infiltration without significant compromises to the counter-insurgency and counter-infiltration grids aimed at halting the influx of Pakistani-trained insurgents into Jammu and Kashmir, as well as operations aimed at hunting down those insurgents extant at the time of the conflict.

The truly surprising thing during the Kargil War was how easily contained the Kashmir insurgency was during the duration. While Kargil, being in Ladakh, was hardly a hotbed of insurgency, the lack of insurgent activity was noteworthy. This was partly a result of the higher concentration of troops but also perhaps indicative of a more robust approach to dealing with insurgents. It is interesting that the insurgent groups operating in Kashmir were unable to impede or disrupt, or even distract, Indian military operations in the Kargil sector.

## Discovering the Infiltration

From 10 November 1998 to 4 May 1999, a miserable total of six Winter Air Surveillance Operations (WASO), five operational reconnaissance sorties and thirteen training sorties were conducted by the Indian Army Aviation Corps, totalling some 116 flying hours, many conducted only within a three-hour period – 1100hrs to 1400hrs. Not surprisingly, these discovered little evidence of the incursion and it was only on 3 May that some evidence was seen in Banju.[3]

On this date, the Chief of Staff to the GOC XV Corps, Major General A.S. Sihota, informed the GOC, Lieutenant General Krishan Pal, that there had been a sighting of a possible intrusion in Banju. Sihota was ordered to send out patrols throughout the Kargil Sector with special care taken to confirm reports from the Batalik sub-sector. While this was happening, the 3rd Division had sought to reinforce 121 Brigade with a company of Ladakh Scouts. In the meantime, 3rd Punjab had ordered out a patrol of one Junior Commissioned Officer and 12 men to try to reach Banju through the Garkhun Bar, but they were unsuccessful due to heavy snow. Another patrol was dispatched on 6 May through the Yaldor-Gragario Nullah but this fell out of communication. A third patrol sent out on 7 May under Naib Subedar Sulakhan Singh was able to link up with the missing patrols. They observed radio antennae, defensive positions, and men in black uniforms.[4]

With this information, the CO 3rd Punjab ordered the three patrols to close with the enemy while supporting troops from the protection company of 121 Brigade's HQ as well as a company of 16th Grenadiers were dispatched to encircle the enemy. Four additional columns, comprising a company each of 16th Grenadiers, 10th Garhwal and 1/11th Gurkha Rifles, were ordered to close and deal with the enemy at five locations – Jubar, Point 4517, Point 4924, Kakarthang and Tharu.[5] Major General Bhadwar, GOC 3rd Division, ordered Brigadier Devinder Singh of 70th Brigade to the Batalik sub-sector. Two battalions, 1/11 GR and 12 JAK LI (minus a company), were dispatched to reinforce the same unit, and on 9 May they were followed by 14th Sikh.

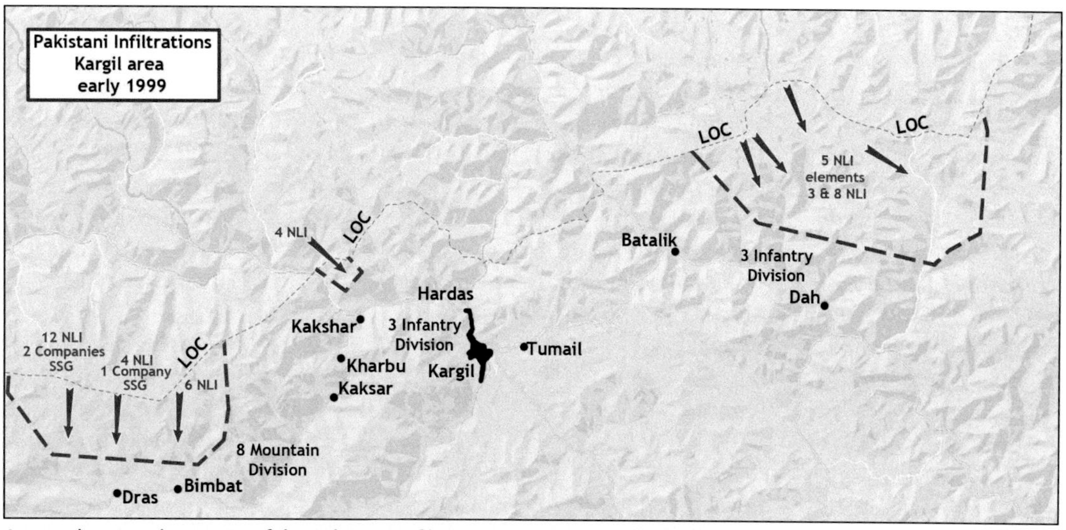


A map showing the extent of the Pakistani infiltrations in the Kargil Sector. (Map by Tom Cooper. Based on sketch by Shivani Badri-Maharaj after Amarinder Singh [see bibliography for details])

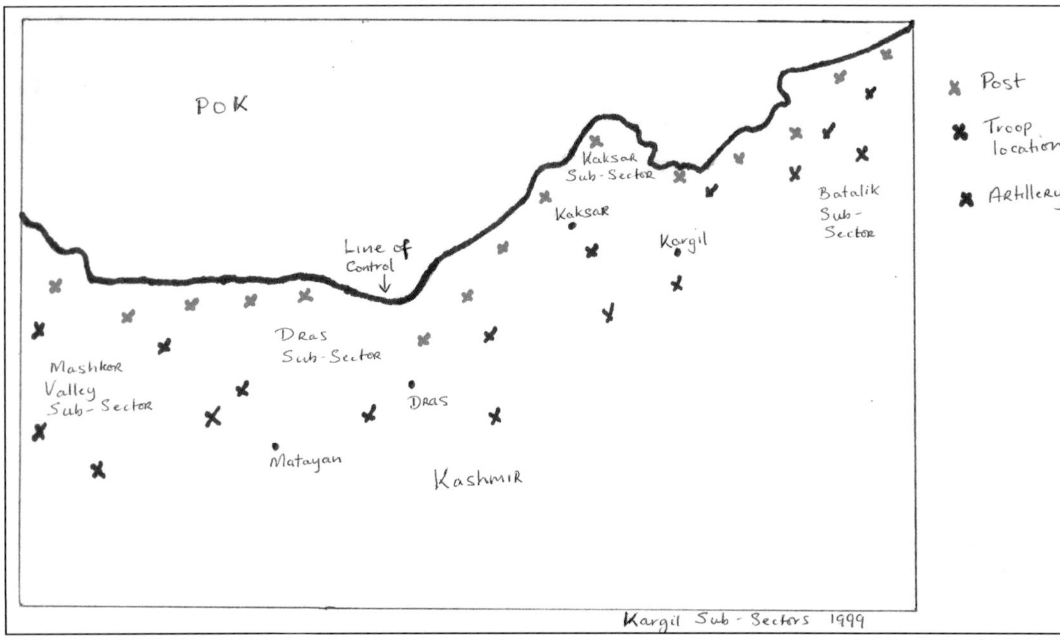

A map of Indian Army outposts, forward bases, and artillery positions in the Kargil Sub-Sector. (Hand drawn sketch map by Shivani after Amarinder Singh [see Bibliography for details])

An Indian Army mortar crew loading a 120mm bomb into their weapon during one of early actions in the Mushkoh Valley sector. (Directorate General of Artillery, Indian Army, via author)

While these troop reorganisations and repositioning were taking place, the Quick Reaction Team (QRT) of the 16th Grenadiers had been ambushed and four of its number killed. These were the first Indian casualties of the war. Major Gaur's company of 10th Garhwal was subjected to severe artillery fire near Jubar and Point 4927, and also suffered four killed along with eight wounded. With these encounters it became increasingly clear that the infiltration was on a larger scale, comprised of larger numbers and was better supported than initial Indian estimates believed. 70th Brigade, correctly, called off its attack and proceeded to conduct a detailed reconnaissance of the Pakistan positions.[6]

## Scale of the Infiltration

It had become increasingly evident that the scale of the infiltration was widespread, with reports coming in from the Dras, Mushkoh, Kaksar and Yaldor sub-sectors of patrols, and helicopters being fired upon and attempts to dislodge intruders being met with heavy resistance supported by Pakistani artillery. GOC XV Corps, Lieutenant General Krishan Pal, viewed this as a major intrusion with the intention of occupying Indian territory. He then ordered that 10 Para (SF), less one team, and a company of 5 Para to reinforce 70 Brigade with 28 RR, minus one company, and 9 Para (SF) arriving between 14 and 17 May. The Dras-Mushkoh sector was then assigned to 56 Mountain Brigade under Brigadier Amar Aul, which moved from its counter-insurgency role, with its two battalions – 18 Grenadiers and 1 Bihar. Battalions were thus being added to flesh out brigades which had been operating with forces more suitable for their role in the counter-insurgency grid. The smaller forces allocated to the Kargil region in peacetime were dramatically enhanced with units from all over India. This did not mean a simultaneous use of all forces, but a careful deployment of combat assets.

## Containing the Infiltration[7]

The 121st Brigade was tasked with immediately pinpointing intrusions within the Dras sub-sector and four columns from 16 Grenadiers, 1 Naga, and the Ladakh Scouts moved up the Tololing Nullah to Point 4080, Sando Nullah and Bimbat on the LoC. The Ladakh Scouts observed 15 intruders on Tololing Ridge at Point 4590. On 12 May the intruders fired a SAM at a helicopter but missed. The pilot was able to report that both ridge lines on either side of the Sando Nullah were occupied by infiltrators. Two more helicopters came under fire on 12 and 13 May from both Point 4590 and Point 5284 while on reconnaissance. The 121st Brigade sought to contain Pakistani positions at Points 4080, 4590 and 5140, as well as to contain Tiger Hill and Points 4195 and 4460. These tasks were assigned to 8 Sikh and 16 Grenadiers. 8 Sikh had arrived from Dras and was not properly acclimatized and lacked proper high-altitude clothing.

By 18 May, 9 Sikh had captured Points 4295 and Point 4460 while 16 Grenadiers secured 4080. They were then tasked with recapturing Tiger Hill. While the Grenadiers secured a strong support base for 8 Sikh, the latter launched a two-pronged attack from the north and east. This was repulsed by heavy Pakistani fire from entrenched positions along the entire ridge. Pakistan Army artillery fire was accurate and heavy, and this ensured that 8 Sikh could make little progress. The CO 8 Sikh, Colonel S.P. Singh, decided to surround Tiger Hill from three sides – north, east and south. The western approach was a very well defended ridge. Several attempts to take the ridge were repulsed with the loss of one officer and twelve men killed and one officer, one JCO, and forty-eight men wounded. 8 Sikh held its position from 21 May to 3 July despite the intense fire from Pakistani troops along the ridges and their artillery support from across the LoC.

In the Indus sub-sector, 3 Punjab was heavily committed to engage the Pakistanis on both Point 4927 and Point 5285. A single company of 8 BSF at Chorbatla was tasked to assist 3 Punjab which was finding itself seriously overstretched for its limited personnel strength. Pakistani efforts to gain the Chorbatla Ridge Line between Sachho and Point 5260 would have enabled them to cut the brigade's lines of communication. In recognition of this threat, two companies of the Ladakh Scouts were dispatched to reinforce Chorbatla. A platoon under Major Ashish Nangia was heli-lifted to occupy Point 5520, on 27 May another platoon occupied Point 5498, while a third occupied the base of Point 5620 on 28 May. By this time, 3 Punjab and 8 BSF had moved to expand their defensive positions on the ridgeline, occupied Point 5512 and Point 5540, and were confronting Pakistani positions on Point 5440 and the Handangbrok Heights.

A more tragic story unfolded in the Kaskar sector on 14 May when a four-man patrol of 4 Jat, let by Lieutenant Saurabh Kalia, moved to an unoccupied Indian post at Bajrang. This patrol was ambushed and the corpses of all four men mutilated. A second patrol of thirty men under Captain Amrit Bhardwaj was dispatched but were also ambushed. Bhardwaj and Havildar Rajbir Singh fought a rearguard action, allowing the rest of the unit to escape. Every man of the unit was wounded and Bhardwaj and Rajbir Singh were killed.[8]

The scale of the Pakistani incursion created severe problems for 121 (I) Brigade which thus found all its battalions committed. Containing the intruders could only be accomplished by thinning out the existing units. A company of 28 Rashtriya Rifles (RR) which was on counter-insurgency duties, was spread along the Chhorokhur and Mumar Shung Nullahs, while a detachment from 14 Sikh was diverted from 70 Brigade and placed at Nirli Shung Nullah in order to prevent the infiltrators from attacking the rear areas of 4 Jat.

To facilitate this, a series of new posts, along with the existing ones at Points 5299, 4885 and 5305, were established with troops from 4 Jat and 14 JAK LI. These battalions came under control of 121 (I) Brigade at this time. It should be noted that the troops of 28 RR and 14 JAK LI were not specialist mountain troops and found the terrain extremely difficult. To this end, eleven teams, each of one officer, one JCO and twenty men drawn from 4 Jat, 14 JAK LI, the Garhwal Scouts and 21 Special Forces (SF) were given specialist mountain training from instructors from India's High Altitude Warfare School (HAWS), with emphasis on rock-climbing. These personnel were readied to spearhead assaults against positions held by infiltrators in hostile terrain.[9]

Major V.S. Shekhawat of 4 Jat, along with a team of twenty volunteers, established a post on Point 5299, overlooking Pakistani posts at SW Spur, Junction and Saddle. With the assistance of 141 Field Regiment, through its attached Gunner Observer Post, Captain PV Vikram, Shekhawat engaged Pakistani posts on Saddle with Konkurs anti-tank missiles and artillery fire. The enemy posts were destroyed by 22 May and this denied all use of the maintenance routes which came under the shadow of Point 5299 to the Pakistanis, thus severely impacting the logistical support available to the infiltrators. Severe Pakistani artillery fire was sustained by the post, with Captain Vikram being killed and Major Shekahwat wounded on 2 June.[10]

In the Chorbatla sub-sector, Pakistani assaults on Point 5620 were beaten off. The ambush of a patrol of the Ladakh Scouts was followed up, with the ambush party and a Pakistani post attacked and eliminated, with the infiltrators suffering three dead. A substantial number of weapons and stores, including a 12.7mm heavy machinegun, were also lost. These small unit operations were very much the hallmark of the Kargil operations; infantry dominated with both attackers and defenders relying on their professionalism, training, skill, and motivation to achieve their objectives with no quarter being given.

By 6 June, the entire watershed of the Ladakh range was in Indian hands and secured. 11 Rajputana Rifles (Raj Rif) from 102 Brigade had reached the Eastern Heights and had linked up 121 (I) Brigade at Point 5620. This enabled the complete clearing of the area from Point 5440 to Turtuk. The hard pressed companies of the Ladakh Scouts, the BSF and 3 Punjab which had borne the brunt of the action in that sub-sector up to that date, were finally relieved on 5 June by 14 Sikh, which on that date came under the command of 70 Brigade.[11]

## The Build Up

The Kargil conflict was the responsibility of XV Corps to which the 3rd Infantry and 8th Mountain divisions were assigned. The 3rd Infantry Division was to take care of the area east of the Dras bowl and had attached to it 121 (I), 70 Infantry and 102 Brigades. The 8th Division was to cater for the Mushkoh and Dras sub-sectors and had 56 and 79 Mountain Brigades attached to it. A third brigade, 192 Mountain, was assigned to the counter-insurgency grid but was moved to Dras and would play an important support role.

As the conflict wore on, the 3rd Infantry and 8th Mountain divisions were reorganized and restricted so as to better deal with their challenges as detailed below.[12]

### 3rd Infantry Division

#### 121 (I) Brigade

The Kaksar Sub-Sector: Covering the Kaksar Defences

- 14 JAK Rifles
- one team 21 SF
- one platoon Garhwal Scouts
- one company 28 RR
- one company 2 RR

The Kargil Sub-Sector: Covering the Kargil Defences down to the Indus River

- 4 Dogra
- 18 Jat
- 2 RR (less one company)
- 10 Garhwal and 4 Jat in the holding role.

#### 70 Infantry Brigade

The Yaldor Sub-sector: From the Indus to the line running from Chorbatla to Hangdangbrok to Hunuthang

- 14 Sikh
- 12 JAK LI
- 1/11 GR
- 5 Para (less two companies)
- 10 Para SF (less one team)
- 1 Bihar
- 22 Grenadiers
- 17 Garhwal
- 4/3 GR
- 5/3 GR
- Ladakh Scouts

#### 102 Brigade

Sub-Sector West (SSW): From Chorbatla, 18km due east to the River Shyok

Brigadier Kushal Thakur and the staff in command of 18 Grenadiers, Indian Army. (Brigadier Kushal Thakur Collection)

Indian Army troops hauling a 120mm mortar and its ammunition into a new position. (Directorate General of Artillery, Indian Army, via author)

- 28 RR (less one company)

Dras: 56 Mountain Brigade
- 16 Grenadiers
- 8 Sikh
- 1 Naga
- one company of the Indus Wing of Ladakh Scouts

Dras and Counter Infiltration Grid: 192 Brigade
- 18 Grenadiers
- 8 Sikh (attached for assault on Tiger Hill)
- 3/3 GR
- one company 9 Para (SF) (attached for the capture of Zulu Spur)

50th (I) Para Brigade (attached from 12 June) with
- 1 Para (SF)
- 6 Para (eventually attached to 192 Brigade)
- 7 Para

From the relatively small forces in theatre at the start of the conflict in May 1999, the Kargil sector had a force level of two divisional headquarters, six brigade headquarters, 52 infantry battalions and the equivalent of sixteen full regiments of artillery (19 regiments participating in total) comprising seven medium regiments less one battery, seven field regiments, two light regiments, one rocket regiment, and one heavy mortar regiment of two batteries. In addition, field engineers, personnel from the Electrical and Mechanical Engineers (EME), the Army Service Corps (ASC), ordnance and medical units were all committed to the Kargil sector.

Sub-Sector Hanif (SSH): From Turtok to a point 10km south-east of the southern glacier
- 11 Raj Rif
- 9 Mahar
- 13 Kumaon
- 27 Rajput
- 5 Vikas
- one company of Ladakh Scouts to which were later added 3 Rajput

**8 Mountain Division**

Mushkoh Sub-Sector:

79th Mountain Brigade
- 17 Jat
- 12 Mahar
- 13 JAK Rifle
- 2 Naga

The artillery build-up was impressive, too, with 121 (I) Brigade initially controlling 141 Field Regiment, 286 Medium Regiment, 1861 Light Regiment and one battery of 307 Medium Regiment: ultimately a total of one hundred and eight 105mm guns in field regiments, one hundred and thirty two 130mm guns and 155mm howitzers in medium regiments, and about 280 other guns, mortars and rocket launchers deployed to support Operation Vijay – in addition to the tube artillery of the CADA, deployed to provide direct fire support.[13]

GOC XV Corps also made a request through Army HQ for air support, duly sent to the IAF on 15 May. However, as this required Cabinet approval, this was not given until 24-25 May. This request for air support was unprecedented in Indian post-independence history, as no such request had hitherto been made, marking a turning point in the conflict. Though there were assets in the area, an initial batch of eight IAF squadrons was allocated for support:

- One squadron each MiG-21M, MiG-23BN and MiG-27 for close air support
- One Helicopter Unit of 10 Mi-17 helicopters operating in the attack role
- One squadron each of Mirage 2000 and Jaguars – for precision strike and reconnaissance
- One squadron of MiG-29s for air defence missions.[14]

### Retaking Tololing – A Turning Point

Tololing, a stark and imposing mountain, rises to a height of 16,000 feet and overlooks the town of Dras. The Tololing ridge was occupied by Pakistani intruders who had built extensive fortifications in the form of concrete bunkers, and reinforced breastworks called sangars. With these fortifications well supplied with weapons and stores, and able to call on very effective artillery support, the infiltrators were in a position to dominate Dras.[15]

From this vantage point, the Pakistani infiltrators were able to direct heavy artillery fire onto NH 1A, which was closest at this point, and bring movement on the highway to a standstill. For India, the recapture of Tololing was an imperative and one which was pursued with single-minded determination. It was a serious and most taxing endeavour, with nearly half of all Indian casualties in the Kargil conflict being suffered in the battle to recapture this location.[16] That India's miscalculations in the initial assaults did not have more dire consequences was a matter of good fortune but above all, the tenacity of Indian infantry, despite setbacks, allowed objectives to be achieved with artillery and air support and effective management of small-unit operations.[17]

### Initial Assaults

Initial Indian attempts to take the ridge were nothing short of disastrous. Shortly after the intruders were detected in the Dras sector on 14 May, 18 Grenadiers were taken off counter-insurgency operations in the valley and ordered to evict the intruders. The Commander of 121 (I) Brigade told the Grenadiers' commanding officer at one of the initial briefings that there were no more than eight to ten infiltrators on the heights. "Just go up," he allegedly ordered, "and bring them down by their neck."[18] This attitude was to lead to most unfortunate consequences with 18 Grenadiers paying a high price.

Three battalions from the Naga, Garhwal and Grenadier regiments tried to make their way up to Tololing in a two-pronged attack. These were met by sustained and highly accurate fire from the infiltrators and their support weapons. It would be unsurprising therefore that these assaults made little headway. 18 Grenadiers began operations on 22 May but were repulsed with losses. It was only after the Grenadiers were repelled that the commanders at 121 (I) Brigade began to appreciate the scale of the threat and the nature of the incursion, demonstrating the consequences of India's intelligence failure.[19]

Attacking troops had virtually no cover and faced the full force of the intruders' fire as they were compelled to advance uphill along narrow tracks or through rocky terrain. The intruders' bunkers, which had been reinforced with iron girders and corrugated iron sheets, offered good protection from some indirect fire and, as they were supported with well-directed artillery fire from across the LoC, the Indian advance was stopped shortly after it began. Two platoons from 16 Grenadiers was stuck for 16 days on a ridge below Tololing, being effectively halted in their advance by gunfire and artillery barrages directed by Pakistani observers among the infiltrators.[20]

The first three Indian assaults were beaten off. Air support in the form of Mi-17 helicopters was made available, but on 28 May, Nubra 3, the third helicopter in a four-ship formation, was shot down by a Stinger while attacking Point 5140 on the Tololing Ridge. This curtailed further helicopter air support. Furthermore, this came only a day after two Indian fighters – a MiG-27 and a MiG-21M – were lost while attacking the infiltrators' main logistics base at Muntho Dhalo. With these losses, air support in the Dras sector was severely restricted to the point of being almost non-existent for practical purposes.

Without air support, relying on Indian artillery and their own battalion support weapons, the three Indian battalions were regrouped and reinforced. However, the initial three assaults were beaten off by the infiltrators.

### Appalling conditions

Indian soldiers had to crawl along narrow ledges along a steep incline with high winds. The temperatures, despite it being May-June, hovered between −5 and −11°C. In this terrain, Indian soldiers had to climb 16,000ft with packs weighing up to 25kgs.

From the base of the Tololing Ridge, it would take at least 11 hours for a fit and fully acclimatised soldier to climb the 16,000ft to the top. For some soldiers who were barely acclimatised, a five-metre trudge would leave them, weighed down by weapons, equipment, supplies, and ammunition making up the aforesaid 25kg or more, panting for breath. Captain Ajit Singh of 16 Grenadiers was to comment: 'Every gram of the weight you carry is extra load, and you have to choose between your ration and ammunition.'[21]

Indian troops were often forced to choose between their 2kg food packs or an additional 100 rounds of ammunition. Captain Singh, like many Indian soldiers, chose the extra ammunition and opted to survive on ice, water, and cigarettes for up to three days in intense climatic and combat conditions. Moving uphill, in treacherous terrain, the Indian troops found themselves very vulnerable not only to gunfire but also to boulders rolled downhill and stones thrown by the infiltrators. Soldiers climbing uphill on ropes were particularly vulnerable as their rifles were slung and as such were unable to shoot back. Several soldiers were apparently crushed in this manner, with the Naga battalion suffering particularly heavily, and while the tenacity of the attacking troops was not in doubt, the tactics employed clearly needed revision. This did not preclude additional acts of almost insane bravery and commitment.

With no headway being made, B Company of 18 Grenadiers, led by 28-year-old Major Rajesh Adhikari, made another assault. Despite two previous assaults ending in total failure and being repulsed, the impetus and intensity of Adhikari's attack succeeded in reaching a point beyond the Hump, bringing him to within 25 meters of Point 4590.[22] However, his unit was now surrounded and outnumbered. A strong Pakistani counterattack led to a vicious close quarter battle in which Adhikari, along with Subedar Randhir Singh, Lance Naik R K Yadav, and Grenadier Parveen Kumar were killed. The rest of the attacking force was pushed back. Captain Sachin Nimbalkar of the battalion's commando platoon was stuck behind a large rock on a ledge on a sheer cliff face for three days before effecting a successful fighting withdrawal.[23]

### Rushed Assaults with Tragic Consequences

Despite the evidence, there was still a level of underestimation of the scale of the situation, the gravity of the circumstances, and the nature and scope of the Pakistani incursion. Moreover, even after the initial setbacks there was still a degree of surreal denial of the difficulty to be faced in evicting the intruding forces. This was to manifest itself in unrealistic and hasty orders which were costly in terms of lives and was particularly preposterous given the fact that air support was

Troops from 18 Grenadiers taking a break in between operations against the Pakistani infiltrators at Point 4590. (Photo by Brigadier Kushal Thakur)

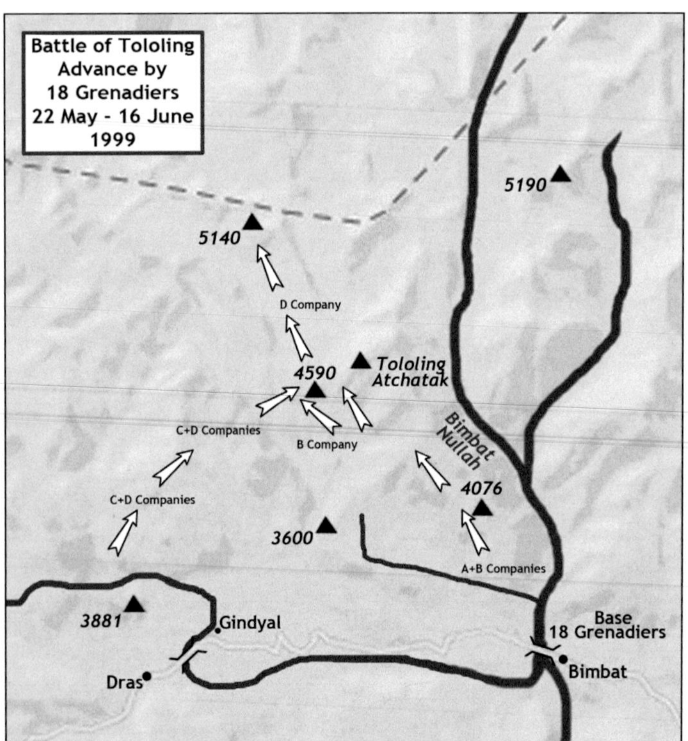


A map of the advance by 18 Grenadiers on the Point 4590. (Map by Tom Cooper. Based on sketch by Shivani Badri-Maharaj after Amarinder Singh [see bibliography for details])

being re-worked and artillery support was still being reinforced with additional regiments.

Indian battalion and company commanders were under no such illusions. However, they were facing intense pressure from brigade commanders – the words of the CO of 121 (I) Brigade to 18 Grenadiers being indicative of the sense of denial among some senior officers. Indeed, Brigadier Surinder Singh of 121 (I) Brigade and Colonel Oberoi of 16 Grenadiers would find themselves relieved of command for their failures to detect and contain the incursions and for their poor handling of efforts thereafter. These senior level failings were most pronounced in the early weeks as 121 (I) Brigade tried to deal with matters alone.[24]

Pressure from New Delhi, which had been relying on information initially supplied by 121 (I) Brigade and the reassurances therefrom, caused another hasty attack to be mounted on 2 June 1999. This time 18 Grenadiers would pay a terrible price. Led by their second-in-command, and despite the objections of their commanding officer and others, 18 Grenadiers reached the top of Tololing Ridge after a six hour climb in difficult, if not impossible conditions. The troops of 18 Grenadiers chose to immediately go into an attack rather than recovering, so as to take advantage of the dark, with tragic consequences.

After a preparatory artillery bombardment, 18 Grenadiers attacked Point 4590. This was spearheaded by Lieutenant Colonel Vishwanathan and a commando section led by Lieutenant Balwan Singh, and was of platoon plus strength – a full platoon under Subedar Randhir Singh providing the bulk of the manpower. Fire support was provided by 81mm mortars and medium machineguns under the command of Subedar Chanda Jat. This level of fire support, augmented by section-level 84mm Carl Gustav recoilless rifles was intended to suppress enemy positions during the actual assault, complementing the limited number of artillery pieces assigned to support the infantry.[25]

The attack was a failure. Despite being pressed home with great tenacity and determination, Lieutenant Colonel Vishwanathan was killed after reaching the forward defences and killing three of the infiltrators. Subedar Randhir Singh neutralized a machinegun position, killing its crew of two before also being killed. Despite breaching the forward defences, the Indian assault faltered in the face of intense resistance from the entrenched defenders and was gradually pushed back with four more Indian soldiers being killed in the fighting. The rest of the attacking force was able to disengage and withdraw successfully. Colonel, later Brigadier, Kushal Thakur, CO of 18 Grenadiers, summarized the situation he faced when his unit was inducted:

> Initially we were told that there were only a few intruders and we should get rid of them quickly. By 22 May we realized that the situation was far more serious. The Pakistanis were well entrenched and their snipers and artillery were extremely effective. We found ourselves engaged in intense and sustained close quarters combat both by day and night.[26]

Lieutenant, later Colonel, Balwan Singh, also of 18 Grenadiers, adds to the situation faced by the unit when it was initially tasked with operations at Tololing:

> The weather was challenging and we had to move in fog. Night vision equipment was inadequate during the initial operations but improved as the campaign went on. Initially, there was no artillery support and we relied on 81mm mortars, medium machineguns and 84mm rocket launchers. We evolved our tactics accordingly to conduct small unit operations moving through ridges and attacking in three to four directions with a view to one attack succeeding and conducting our attacks at night.[27]

### Building up – Artillery inducted

Towards the end of May 1999, Brigadier Lakhinder Singh, Commander of the Dras Artillery Brigade came into the combat zone. One of his immediate observations was that the deployment was wholly inadequate. This was noticeable with the paltry artillery support that had been made available to the disastrous attempts to by the Grenadiers and Nagas to dislodge the enemies.

From the middle of May to the first week of June, artillery strength had been limited to a few batteries of 105mm guns. This was to alter dramatically and by the end of the first week of June, full regiments of medium artillery with 130mm guns and 155mm howitzers were being brought to bear on the target areas. Movement of these guns was difficult as Pakistani observers were carefully watching all traffic on NH 1A from Peak 4875 in the Mushkoh Valley, Tiger Hill and from Tololing Top itself.[28] Deployments were made post-sundown and trucks were moved without headlights, with soldiers with torches moving in front of the Scania trucks to prevent accidents. It should be noted that some of the medium regiments were brought in from the plains and were still in Indian desert camouflage.[29] The switch from field regiment 105mm guns with lighter shells to medium regiments with 130mm guns and 155mm howitzers with heavy shells was indicative of the challenge faced by Indian artillery to effectively neutralise fortified enemy positions.

A battery of 155mm FH77 howitzers preparing. (Albert Grandolini Collection)

Gun positions were carved into the mountain side, not only to enable maximum accuracy but also to avoid Pakistan's counter-battery fire. Ranging shots were fired on 7 June to establish targets and range to targets, aided by artillery observation officers at vantage points. Concerns over Pakistan SSG raids led to intensified security while several batteries of anti-aircraft guns were deployed to ward off any roving UAVs. Indian counter-battery efforts were led by Para SF units tracking and tracing Pakistani gun positions.

The Indian Army went back to standard procedure and did away with hasty attacks. Later units inducted into the Tololing sector were to note:

> There was no pressure on us and we were allowed adequate time to prepare. Units learned from each other and where necessary individual battalions augmented each other's support weapons. Night vision equipment improved and the army began to evolve the 100 gun artillery bombardment concept and multi-directional attacks with emphasis on sub-unit leadership with section leaders being given more responsibility as we evolved the concept of maneuver warfare in the mountains.[30]

### Tololing Ridge

Troops at Tololing were reinforced by a fresh infantry battalion, brought in specifically for the assault – 2 Rajputana Rifles. The Grenadiers consolidated positions at three points some 300 metres below the Pakistani positions which were used to launch the final assault. 2 Rajputana Rifles tested and zeroed their weapons and carried out mock assaults on proximate ridges and also conducted reconnaissance on the positions to be assaulted.[31]

The assault team consisted of 90 volunteers led by Major Vivek Gupta and, surprisingly, eleven members of the Tomar caste, many of whom were unit sportsmen and athletes, were included. A final briefing and pep talk were delivered by the unit CO Colonel Ravindranath and, in an ominous sign, letters home were written in case the soldiers did not return. However, morale was surprisingly high and there was a degree of intense determination to assault the hills. In contrast to the earlier hasty assaults, the final attack on Tololing Ridge was carefully planned, closely supported and well-coordinated. Moreover, learning from earlier failures, the Indian Army prepared its artillery bombardment with a great degree of precision. With H-hour set at 1830hrs IST on

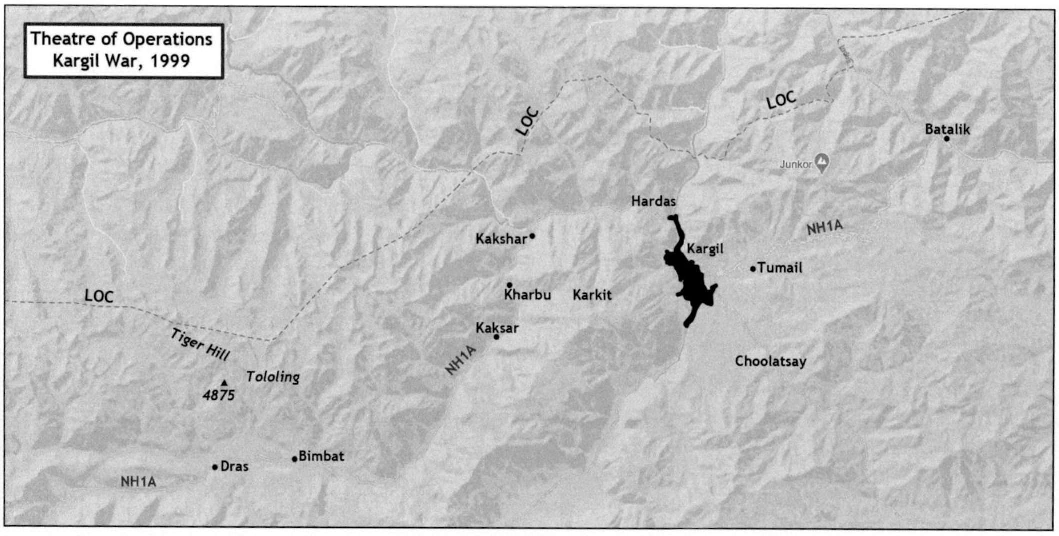

A map showing approximate locations of major points along the LoC in the Tololing Sector. Map by Tom Cooper. Based on sketch by Shivani Badri-Maharaj after Amarinder Singh [see bibliography for details])

12 June, the troops moved into position some 300 metres from the infiltrators and were readied for the final assault.[32]

### The Final Assault

With 120 guns ranged, at 1830hrs the artillery barrage began against Pakistani positions at Tololing Top. With their heavier shells, Bofors 155mm howitzers began the bombardment and, being used in the direct fire mode, they targeted bunkers. These were joined by the 130mm and 105mm guns. When Pakistani counter-battery fire responded, the 155mm howitzers switched to High-Explosive Extended Range (HEER) rounds and began targeting Pakistani gun positions across the LoC which had been located by Para SF units.[33] The Pakistani guns were largely neutralized and, for the rest of the operation, were confined to occasional shots, with mortars trying to augment these efforts.

The bombardment went on for more than five hours. Divided into three teams – code named "Abhimanyu", "Bheem" and "Arjun", Major Gupta led his men into action with one team moving up the heights in a frontal assault, a second cutting of the retreat from a lower ridge and the third attacking from behind.[34] The Grenadier battalion provided covering fire for the assault.

It was not unexpected that, with Pakistani infiltrators in natural caves, the artillery bombardment failed to neutralize all Pakistani troops. These now met the assault with heavy machinegun fire. The Indian troops used craters caused by shell fire for cover as the assault was over exposed terrain and, with entrenched and well protected adversaries, the assault was extremely difficult with bunkers having to be neutralized one at a time with grenades. Communication with unit commanders was impossible as the fighting was at close quarters. Two hours into the assault Havaldar Yashvir Singh Tomar collected grenades from the rest of the men and charged the last Pakistani bunkers. He was killed after tossing in new fewer than 18 grenades.[35] Fierce hand-to-hand fighting ensured but by 0410hrs, Tololing Top had been taken. Of the 90 men in the initial assault, eight had been killed – Major Gupta included. However, even at this stage, and in spite of the joy felt at this victory, there were concerns that a counterattack from the Hump could dislodge Indian troops.

The task of capturing the Hump was given to Major Joy Dasgupta of 'C' company, 18 Grenadiers. This attack began at 2000hrs, while the artillery bombardment of Tololing Top was in progress. Facing heavy machinegun fire, such an assault would be near suicidal but the Bofors 155mm howitzers proved to be highly effective, firing at bunkers and then moving position to prevent hostile counter-battery fire.[36] This allowed the Grenadiers to reach the first bunker and to neutralize it with grenades and close quarters combat. The assault, facing heavy fire from the adversaries, was faltering. However, two NCOs, Havaldar Dashrath Lal Dubey and Havaldar Udham Singh, from two separate companies of 18 Grenadiers, together charged the bunkers and cleared them. Udham Singh was killed in the process but the last enemy bunkers were cleared and with the Hump taken, Tololing Top was secured. Twelve Indian soldiers fell taking this position, but their success allowed the clearing of several other points over the following days.[37]

Tololing was to prove the costliest battle of the Kargil War for the Indian Army. Of the units involved, 2 Rajputana Rifles alone suffered 4 officers, 2 JCOs and 17 OR dead and 70 wounded. The casualties sustained earlier in the rushed attempts to take Tololing Top were unnecessary and could have been averted by better planning and more effective support and coordination.[38]

Of interest is that the battle for Tololing was fought and won largely with small unit actions by platoon and company sized units of infantry with artillery support. It was in such action that company, platoon and section commanders and leaders were able to have a significant impact and where junior leaders were able to shine. The Indian Air Force was not entirely absent in this battle but, after the loss of the Mi-17 in the opening stages of the battle for Tololing, close air support was severely limited and its place taken by fire support from medium artillery pieces.

### Recapturing Point 5203

The success at Tololing was followed up by a series of actions aimed at securing other sectors which were held by hostile forces. In the sector assigned to 70 Brigade, this involved the capture of Point 5203. Two companies – one each from 12 JAK LI and 5 Para were dispatched on the night of 7-8 June along four nullahs to retake the position. This effort failed thanks to heavy fire from the infiltrators and, after the loss of one officer and 13 men from 12 JAK LI, the initial assault was abandoned and the process rethought. Brigadier Devinder Singh, CO of 70 Brigade, took personal command, moving his Tactical Headquarters to the battle area and planned to attack again, this time between 19 and 21 June. Reinforcements were brought in from Ladakh Scouts, with the Demonstration Company under Major Deepak Pandey, 5 Para under Captain Cariappa, and the KK Wing of Ladakh Scouts under Captain Bishnoi, forming three strong columns to approach Point 5203 from the north-west and south-west spurs and south-east respectively. The assault was to commence on the night of 20-21 June. The KK Wing of Ladakh Scouts was also tasked with cutting off any retreat from the northern approach.[39]

After an artillery bombardment lasting an hour, the attack commenced and though the columns came under sustained fire from infiltrator positions on Point 5203, the columns moved forward with covering fire being provided by a company sized column from 12 JAK LI located at Ring Contour some 1,500m south of Point 5203. By 0230hrs, the assaulting columns were beginning to achieve success and by 0700hrs, Point 5203 had been secured after rather intense fighting. Brigadier Devinder Singh was among those wounded and Indian losses were nineteen killed – one officer, one JCO and 17 other ranks – with a like number of infiltrators, later identified as being from 7 NLI, being killed.[40]

The capture of Point 5203 was a significant development and success for India as the pressure on Indian troops from the eastern flank of the Junk Lungpa had been dealt with, thus ensuring that no hostile forces could link up with each other. Moreover, the main intrusion in the Piun-Chorbatla sector could no longer be supported. Thus, the battle for Point 5203 had its own unique importance. The capture of Point 5203 was followed up by 70 Brigade with an operation that commenced on 22 June and involved the capture of Point 4812, the north Khalubar Ridges, Point 5287, Stangba, and Jubar. These assaults were led by 12 JAK LI and 22 Grenadiers with 1/11 GR and the Indus Wing of Ladakh Scouts completing the infantry units assigned.

Initially, the attacks made little progress and were stalled after local counterattacks by the infiltrators. By 7 July, Stangba and Point 5000 had been taken and the assaults on Khalubar, Point 5287, and Point 4812 were readied. After heavy fighting, the objectives were secured by the following day.[41] 1 Bihar was tasked to capture the Jubar Complex and Point 4924 on the night of 7 July. Following the capture of Jubar Top at first light on that day the rest of the complex had been taken by dawn on 8 July.[42]

### Batalik Sector

The Batalik sector was in many ways the saga of 1/11 Gorkha Rifles. This unit, having been recently deployed in Siachen, was fully

A BM-21 Grad in the process of firing: note the rocket that has just emerged from the launcher. (Directorate General of Artillery, Indian Army, via author)

acclimatized and its induction was made relatively swiftly. Its exploits were that of an infantry battalion, supported by others tasked with a wide variety of missions over a relatively small geographic area, but in terrible weather and with virtually no road infrastructure.

The Khalubar Ridge line was cleared and operations to isolate Pakistani forces in the area were mounted between 8-11 July to secure the Jubar-China Nullah axis. 17 Garhwal secured Bumps 1, 2 and 3 by 10 July, 1 Bihar took Point 4927, Kala Pathar and Tharu simultaneously.[43] 1/11 GR secured Kukarthang and captured Chang Chomo (Point 5190) on 10 July. In the meantime, 5 Para captured Point 4100 and took Muntho Dhalo and Ganisbar on 11 July thus clearing all tactically important ground.[44]

The actions of 1/11 GR in Operation Khalubar were nothing short of ambitious, perhaps overly so, reflecting the confidence placed in the unit by the brigade. More interestingly was that Operation Khalubar was not the only task assigned to the unit as it was also required to capture the Garhi Heights – Point 4812 – capture Khalubar North, capture points 5287, 5190 and 5300 as well as capturing the ring contours east of the Kukarthang Ridge and east of Kukarthang and the ring contour south-west of Point 5300.[45]

1/11 GR was led by Colonel Lalit Rai who was on leave at the time of the incursions, returning only on 2 June 1999. In the interim, under the command of Lieutenant Colonel Asthana, they had already deployed a company to secure the Dah-Yaldor axis with another containing the enemy at Kukarthang and a third company being tasked with containing the enemy at Jubar and Point 4297.[46]

Colonel Rai in his recollection of the struggle in these operations noted that there were serious logistics challenges in providing the requisite fire support to 1/11 GR. There was little artillery support, and battalion support weapons had to be moved and positioned manually. Even ammunition for mortars had to be man-packed to their required location and this involved not only the personnel of 1/11 GR but also local civilians who volunteered to assist.[47] Medium machineguns and automatic grenade launchers had to be left at the Forward Assembly Area, with each company leaving one platoon at the battalion FAA east of Khalubar. With the enemy in a dominating position, Colonel Rai's men had to employ their rock-climbing skills to reach objectives, limiting what was carried, with extra ammunition being chosen over rations for the assaults. This, he stated:

> In weather with poor visibility, bitter cold of -32 degrees Celsius and with driving snow and rain, we were hungry for three nights and four days. Special lubricants had to be issued for our weapons. In spite of that, and facing repeated enemy counterattacks, 1/11 GR maintained its elan.[48]

Colonel Rai also recalled being pinned down by an enemy sniper, later identified as a Pakistan Army major, and being targeted by two shots aimed at his heart, which ricocheted off his binoculars. To assist his CO, one young soldier fired to divert the sniper only to be shot and paralyzed. Colonel Rai recalled him calling out, 'Sir, I don't want to die, please save me', and asking for water but there was none to give. The young soldier bled out in the snow.[49]

It is to the credit of 1/11GR that they held off the counterattacks and rallied taking the Bunker Area and Khalubar South (Operation Khalubar) by 6 July. In the battle for the Bunker Area, the name of Lieutenant Manoj Pandey would become virtually a household name in India. He led a platoon action on 3 July, leading attacks on four sangars personally, and with Havildar Bhim Bahadur leading assaults on three more. Pandey was killed clearing the fourth sangar while Bahadur was killed during the assault on his second sangar. The reputation of Manoj Pandey was already high from the unit's Siachen tour where the unit was sent in March 1998 to begin mountain and glacier training. As one person who knew him wrote:

> Manoj volunteered for the most difficult post, called Pehalwan (Wrestler). This post was at an altitude of almost 5,500 meters. It was also closest to the Pakistani deployment right in front, where we could hear the voices from across very clearly at night. Due [to] the highly treacherous terrain and climatic conditions the deployment here was limited to 45 days. It is difficult to describe the dangers on this post, both of the nature and the enemy, suffice to say that, the troops could not make any movement during the daytime without inviting enemy sniper and fierce machinegun fire. Everything had to be done at night. It goes to the credit of him and the team that they managed to open a day route to this post…an achievement widely acknowledged and appreciated by our higher commanders. The citation read "The unit successfully opened a day route to the Pehalwan Post – a unique feat which was not done since Indian Army's first deployment on the glacier in 1984"…. I remember him like the modern day Abhimanyu, fearless, courageous and the unfazed by challenges, his never say die spirit still inspires the men in the unit.[50]

The Khalubar South operation was quickly followed by operations to secure Khalubar North and this was secured by 1000hrs on 7 July. The battalion moved to initiate Operation Garhi to secure Point 4812 immediately thereafter and this was duly accomplished by the Commando Platoon under Lt. Sateesh Kumar and a platoon from B Company commanded by Subedar I.P. Subba.[51]

At last light on 7 July 1999, the Commando Platoon under Lieutenant Kumar and another platoon of B Company, under Naib Subedar Kabindra, began the assault to take Point 5287. Effective fire support from the battalion fire base, and despite having to deal with a gradient of 85 degrees straddling their approach, 1/11GR was able to take the position by 0530 on 8 July, establishing contact with 22 Grenadiers.[52]

Operations to secure Kukarthang were led by A and D companies of 1/11 GR under Majors J.S. Rautela and R.P. Singh respectively, totalling some two officers, eight JCOs and 130 other ranks.[53] These operations commenced on 8 July at 1600hrs and by 0400hrs 9 July, Kukarthang Top had been taken. With this, Operation Kukarthang was completed. The operation to capture Point 5190 began at 0230hrs on 10 July with Commando Platoon of 1/11GR and two platoons from B Company, this time, artillery support being available to suppress enemy troops on the feature. By 1030hrs on 10 July 1999, Point 5190 had been recaptured.[54]

The seventh objective of 1/11GR – taking Point 5300 – was given to D Company to accomplish, with one platoon of A Company in reserve and with support from specialist high-altitude mountaineering troops of 5 Vikas. This operation began on 22 July with a preparatory artillery bombardment. The assault was spotted and subjected to sustained heavy and very accurate enemy artillery fire but to the surprise of 1/11GR, the enemy had fled their positions and by 0830hrs on 23 July the position had been taken unopposed. The final operations undertaken by 1/11GR during the Kargil conflict were those to secure the last avenue of approach open to the enemy through Indian territory via Tekri, this was assigned to A Company, less one platoon, under Major L.C. Katoch and the Commando Platoon with a detachment of medium machineguns. Artillery support was provided by 15 Field Regiment with Major Gurpreet Singh acting as observer. The attack commenced at 0030hrs led by the Commando Platoon and with very effective fire support. The position fell to 1/11GR at 0400hrs on 26 July 1999.[55]

It is of interest that despite being involved in intense platoon and section level action in inhospitable terrain, appalling weather conditions and facing an entrenched, well-motivated, and well-supplied enemy, 1/11GR suffered only 13 fatalities and 58 wounded in its actions lasting over roughly two months.

## Point 4875

There was heavy fighting in the sector assigned to 79 Mountain Brigade as the efforts to capture Point 4875 and its surrounding features "Pimple 1", "Pimple 2", "Flat Top", "Twin Bumps", and Whale Back" got underway. The units assigned were 17 Jat, 13 JAK Rifles, 21 SF and 2 Naga. In addition 12 Mahar, which established fire bases at Point 4540 and Terkri, was augmented by additional AGS-17, 84mm Carl Gustavs, medium machineguns and ATGMs. Rather surprisingly, the attack succeeded quickly and on the night of 4-5 July, and into the day of 5 July, Point 4875, Pimple 1, Whale Back and Flat Top had all been taken. However, an attempt to recapture Pimple 2 was beaten back and the feature was not taken until 7 July. 2 Naga captured Twin Bumps on 6 July and by 9-10 July the features had all been secured by the brigade's formations. Three 105mm howitzers and five mortars – three of 120mm caliber and two of 82mm calibre were captured – at the cost of 79 killed in action.

## Capture of Point 5140

In the sector assigned to 56 Brigade, the objective was to capture Point 5140. Prior to this, a feature known as "Rocky Knob" needed to be secured. This was assigned to 13 JAK Rifles. On the night of 15-16 June 1999, this unit moved towards "Rocky Knob" but was halted by intense fire and the advance stalled, despite forward positions being reached and four hostiles killed. The operation was temporarily halted so that a revised plan could be considered for implementation with additional support and extra artillery. This revised plan began at 1500hrs on 16 June with two Bofors 155mm howitzers firing in the direct fire role against the fortifications held by the infiltrators. These guns fired until the assaulting company of 13 JAK Rifles was within 100m of the target. In the ensuing action, 13 JAK Rifles was able to secure their objectives and surrounding features, as well as "Rocky Knob" itself, falling to Indian troops by 1900hrs on 16 June. This success paved the way for the planning of the assault on Point 5140 itself which was much more onerous and demanding.[56]

For the assault on Point 5140, 56 Brigade was to employ three battalions – 13 JAK Rifles, 1 Naga and 18 Garhwal. These were assigned the following tasks:

- 13 JAK Rifles (minus two companies): to capture Point 5140 from the south and west
- 1 Naga (minus two companies): to capture the features known as "Pyramid" and "Thumbs Up" on the south-west spur of Point 5140
- 18 Garhwal: to launch an attack with two companies along the north and south-east spurs of Point 5140 with a view to capturing the north face of Point 5140 by 0600hrs 20 June.[57]

Artillery support for the operation was provided by fifteen batteries of artillery and heavy mortars which began a one-hour bombardment at 1900hrs on 19 June against all the assault objectives. Simultaneously, diversionary attacks were launched against Point 4700 and Tiger Hill.

The bombardment began as scheduled and two companies of 1 Naga moved into position. Pyramid and Thumbs up were both captured by 0400hrs on 20 June. In the meanwhile, two companies of 18 Garhwal faced intense machinegun fire and accurate artillery fire from across the LoC. This stalled the Garhwali advance but also distracted Pakistani attention from the main assault on Point 5140. While this was going on, the two companies from 13 JAK Rifles crossed their start line at 2130hrs, and after intense fighting the peak of Point 5140 was captured by 0330hrs on 20 June 1999.[58]

## Taking Three Pimples and Point 4700

From Point 5100 to the west of Tololing Nullah there are three main features – Lone Hill, Knoll, and Three Pimples. On 28 June, 2 Raj Rif was assigned to capture Knoll and Lone Hill. 18 Garhwal was to capture Point 4700 and its features Tommy and Saddle. Once this was done, the battalions would go on to capture Three Pimples and Junction Point by 30 June. Supported by sixteen batteries, the attacks were pressed home to schedule and rather surprisingly some of the objectives of phase one were secured by 2200hrs on 28 June. Both battalions had secured their objectives by 0700hrs on June 29. Tommy and Point 4700 were captured by 0400hrs on 29 June. Phase two commenced immediately thereafter with Rocky and Sandra – two other features – being taken by 1900hrs on 30 June. A night attack secured the last feature, Junction Point, by 0300hrs on 2 July.

A ZU-23-2 anti-aircraft gun in its position: while an air defence weapon, the ZU-23 saw lots of action in the direct fire role. (Deepak Das/Directorate General of Artillery, Indian Army, via author)

These successes were a prelude to the major Indian offensive of the war – the recapture of Tiger Hill. This was to become an iconic and important battle for India and marked both in reality and in terms of the perception of the battle, the major turning point of the Kargil War, and the beginning of the end of any hope of a prolonged military stalemate on the part of Pakistan.[59]

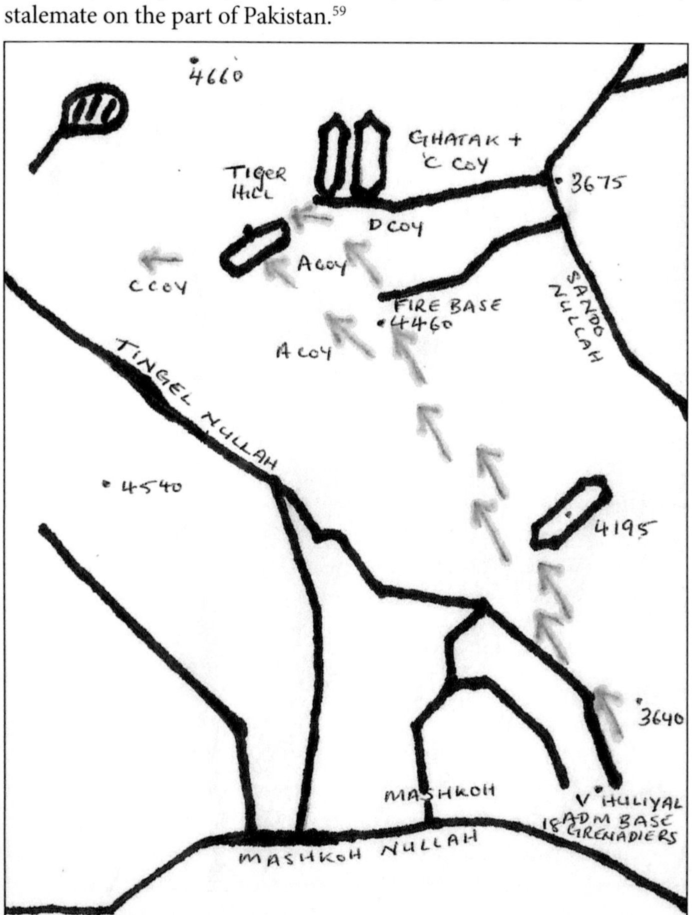


A map of the advance by 18 Grenadiers on the Tiger Hill/Point 4660. (Sketch map by Shivani Badri-Maharaj after Amarinder Singh [see bibliography for details])

## Retaking Tiger Hill: The Beginning of the End

One of the iconic moments of the Kargil War was the recapture of Tiger Hill, also known as Point 4660. This feature is 5,062 metres high with sharp conical features and is located along the mountain tops a few kilometres north of Dras, dominating the landscape. Tiger Hill was to become the best-known geographical feature of the war and its recapture was to be a major victory for India. It became symbolic of the struggle for the peaks of Kargil. While the battle for Tiger Hill was not quite as bloody as that for Tololing, it was a critical strategic point for India. Tiger Hill dominated its surroundings and from that vantage point, troops of 12 Northern Light Infantry, with their supporting weapons at company and battalion level, a detachment of the Special Services Group, plus cross-LoC support from artillery and engineers, were able to get a clear view of NH 1A from the Dras transit camp to Bhimbat, and the road leading to Marpola on the Line of Control (LoC).

With such domination of the terrain, the infiltrating forces were able to interdict vehicular movement on these roads with artillery fire and were able to create sufficient disruption as to make the recapture of the said position a priority. General V.P. Malik, Chief of Army Staff in 1999, was to write:

> It was clear to us from the beginning that unless Tiger Hill and Point 4875, which is located 2 km to its South-West, were secured, movement along NH 1A will never be safe. Although Point 4875 was closer and dominated a larger stretch of NH 1A, Tiger Hill occupied by the enemy was a lot more difficult to attack.
>
> Geographically, Tiger Hill extends about 2200 metres from West to East and about 1000 metres North to South. The main extension is towards West on which there are two prominent protrusions. The first, approximately 500 metres West of Tiger Hill, had been named 'India Gate', and the second, another 300 metres to the West, was called 'Helmet'. Approximately one company of Pakistan 12 Northern Light Infantry held the whole feature. 18 Grenadiers along with 8 Sikh, which were already in the area, were tasked to capture Tiger Hill on the night of 3/4 July, 1999. They were provided a team of the High Altitude Warfare School, adequate artillery, engineer and other support. The Air Force too engaged Tiger Hill on 2/3 July 1999 and had several bull's eyes on its missions.[60]

This description from General Malik does not quite begin to explain the extent of the challenges faced and the saga of the recapture of Tiger Hill. Indeed, one might suggest that the story of the recapture of Tiger Hill is one which, while not quite as intense as that for Tololing, was one which showed air support, artillery and small units of infantry operating in close coordination to achieve the desired military outcome.

A battery of FH77s in action against the Pakistani positions high atop a mountain. (Colonel Gurmeet Kanwal/Directorate General of Artillery, Indian Army, via author)

Another FH77 in position, together with stocks of 155mm ammunition. (Colonel Gurmeet Kanwal/Directorate General of Artillery, Indian Army, via author)

For the operation against Tiger Hill, three Indian battalions, all veterans of earlier operations and blooded by some failures, were earmarked – 8 Sikh, 18 Grenadiers and 2 Naga. Air support was provided by IAF Mirage 2000s which conducted a strike with Paveway LGBs on the night of 2-3 July 1999. This strike was particularly effective in neutralizing several bunkers and did assist, perhaps more than earlier air strikes in assisting in the assault as the LGBs were able to disrupt the defences of the infiltrators sufficiently to allow for the Indian Army to conduct an effective operation.[61]

Of the three battalions, the assault would be led by 18 Grenadiers, with 8 Sikh providing fire support. The assault would eventually comprise of two hundred men, and fire base support was provided by the support companies of all three battalions – 81mm mortars, ATGMs, AGS-17s and MMGs. 8 Sikh would also distract the enemy by launching two feint attacks aimed at diverting attention from the efforts of 18 Grenadiers. This, despite intense resistance from the entrenched adversary was to prove quite decisive in enabling the ultimate success of 18 Grenadiers which was neither easy nor assured.

Artillery support was quite lavish with no fewer than 22 batteries of artillery and heavy mortars being allocated to support the attack of 18 Grenadiers. Three field regiments (each of three batteries) – 41, 197 and 315 – three medium regiments (also of three batteries each) – 158, 108 and 139 – two batteries of 1889 Light Regiment, one battery of 244 Heavy Mortar Regiment and one battery of 212 Rocket Regiment. This substantial fire support was coordinated and an effective fire-plan devised by the CO of 41 Field Regiment – which was the artillery unit assigned to 192 Mountain Brigade at the outbreak of hostilities.[62]

Further lessons were learnt since unprepared troops had been rushed-in and had spearheaded assaults against entrenched positions. This time 18 Grenadiers had additional support from the High Altitude Warfare School (HAWS) to assist with mountaineering aspects of the assault.[63] This allowed each assault company of 18 Grenadiers to have an engineer detachment, a section of mules at battalion level plus a platoon each of civilian porters and pioneers to assist in the build-up and deployment for the final assault on Tiger Hill, thus enabling adequate stores of munitions and supplies to be moved into position. 18 Grenadiers moved into its assault positions in small units to avoid large-scale movement and to reduce the chance of detection. One fire base was provided by 8 Sikh with its infantry and battalion support weapons along the south-west slope of the attack. This was in addition to the fire base of 18 Grenadiers with its own battalion and company level support weapons. The routes chosen for the approach to the assault position were the most difficult so as to further deceive the infiltrators and aid the assault against the feature. 18 Grenadiers disposed its forces as follows – four rifle companies and the commando platoon:

- A Company under Major Randhir Singh Rahtore would move along the south-eastern approach to take "Tongue" and then move to the western part of the Collar
- B Company under Major Y. S. Tomar was to serve as the central reserve and to exploit any success of A Company at Tongue
- C Company under Major Joy Dasgupta would coordinate with the Commando Platoon under Lieutenant Balwan Singh and a team from HAWS to take Tiger Hill Top and exploit up the reverse slope

Brigadier Kushal Thakur and his troops of 18 Grenadiers atop Tiger Hill. (Brigadier Kushal Thakur Collection)

A forward observation officer (forward, right), together with his infantry colleagues. (Directorate General of Artillery, Indian Army, via author)

- D Company under Captain Sachin Nimbalkar was to move up the eastern spur to seize "Tooth" and then exploit the eastern part of the Collar.[64]

At 1900hrs, 155mm howitzers being used in the direct firing mode heralded the start of operations, with six such weapons engaging the Tiger Hill Complex. By 1945hrs, the remaining 22 batteries assembled for this task joined in the bombardment. The objectives assigned to 18 Grenadiers were especially targeted, and in combination with air strikes, provided excellent support to the attacking troops who were able to move closer to their objectives.[65]

The fighting for Tiger Hill was extremely intense and lasted from 3 until 8 July 1999. 8 Sikh alone was engaged for 58 hours from 1000hrs on 4 July to 2000hrs on 6 July. The initial assaults by 18 Grenadiers seemed to make good progress with Tiger Hill Top and the feature known as Tooth being reached at 0430hrs on 4 July. However, an intense counterattack pushed both the Commando Platoon and D Company back to Tooth. A and B companies of 18 Grenadiers were pinned down on the north and south approaches while the Commando Platoon and D Company were similarly stopped.[66]

Brigadier Bajwa of 192 Brigade then chose to deploy 8 Sikhs in an offensive role with the objective of interposing a force on the western ridge line so as to cut off the adversary's Lines of Communication as well as enabling 8 Sikh to bring down fire on positions held by the infiltrators on the western face so as to pin them in place and to ensure that they would not be able to disrupt 18 Grenadiers' operations. The task assigned to D Company of 8 Sikhs under Major Ravinder Singh Parmar, in concert with Lieutenant R.K. Sherawat's Commando Platoon was to establish themselves at India Gate. After a bombardment from the company's 84mm Carl Gustavs, which fired 36 HE rounds at hostile fortifications, India Gate was occupied in the early hours of 6 July. An intense series of Pakistani counterattacks started at 0645hrs and reached the edge of the perimeter held by D Company. Of the Pakistani attackers, Captain Karnal Sher of 12 NLI and Major Iqbal of the SSG were killed leading the attacks. However, these attacks were beaten off and the Pakistanis retreated to positions on the feature known as Helmet.[67]

This feature was then assaulted by Major Parmar, Lieutenant Sherawat and twelve men who succeeded in capturing the position. Both officers and eight of the men were wounded. These men were joined by 18 under Subedar Darshan Singh and by a platoon from 18 Grenadiers by 2000hrs on 7 July. The actions of 8 Sikh can be said to be the turning point of the Battle for Tiger Hill. Their capture of Helmet and India Gate enabled 18 Grenadiers to resume their assault, and Pakistani forces were seen to abandon the Tiger Hill Complex and to retreat down the glaciated northern slope. By 0800hrs on 8 July, 18 Grenadiers had occupied all of the Tiger Hill Complex. 18 Grenadiers subsequently moved towards Shviling and Point 4965, securing these two features by 25 July, by which time, hostilities had drawn to a close.[68]

## Pakistani Withdrawal and Clearing Operations

With all tactically important Indian territory now retaken, it remained for India to clear any heights still in Pakistani hands. However, the operation that recaptured Tiger Hill coincided with a concerted push by Pakistan for a face saving way out of the imbroglio. On 4 July, Pakistan effectively agreed to restore the sanctity of the Line of Control. A slow withdrawal of the remaining Pakistani forces began on 11 July and to facilitate the withdrawal, India declared a ceasefire from 17 to 22 July.

However, it became clear that Pakistan's withdrawal was not complete by 22 July and 70 Brigade began operations to clear the heights. These included operations to capture Points 5285, 5300, 5393, Choringpo Sispo, Point 5455 and Point 5410 and the heights opposite the Chrobatla axis. By 0800hrs on 23 July, one company 5 Para had secured the feature known as Conical while another company of the same regiment found itself meshed in a minefield en route to the feature known as Ring Contour. A platoon secured the north flank of the feature known as Saddle, a company of the Indus Wing of Ladakh Scouts secured a foothold on Point 2593, while a company of 17 Garhwal took Point 5285 by first light on 23 July. One company of 1/11 GR took Point 5300 by 1130hrs on 23 July. Counterattacks by Pakistan on both Conical and Saddle were beaten off. By 25 July, 1/11 GR had captured the feature known as Tekri while 5 Para finally captured Ring Contour on the 26th in a two pronged attack. A team of 10 Para SF, attached to 5 Para, took South Saddle on 27 July, following up the success of Ladakh Scouts which had secured Saddle on 26th, effectively neutralizing Point 5360. 22 Grenadiers successfully captured Point 5465 and Churbar Sispo by 22 July, after some difficulties. The final actions of 70 Brigade involved a company of 4/3 GR which secured Point 5165 on 22 July, and last of all Bendingbar Chrup on 3 August.[69]

## Zulu Spur

Meanwhile, 192 Brigade was to embark on the last major operation of the conflict – one which was launched and completed after the Pakistanis purportedly began their withdrawal – to evict the equivalent of four platoons of infiltrators from Zulu Complex. The task was assigned to 3/3 GR and two teams from 9 Para SF supported by 11 batteries of artillery. The operation began on 22 July at 1315hrs where a company sized operation from 3/3 GR secured the Tri Junction feature of Zulu Complex.[70] All eleven batteries of artillery fired upon the features known as Thumb, Zulu Base and Zulu Top, along with

Indian troops atop a recaptured mountain peak posing with a Pakistan Army 120mm mortar. (Albert Grandolini Collection)

Indian troops inspecting firearms and mortars captured from the Pakistani infiltrators. (Photo by Brigadier Kushal Thakur)

An injured soldier from 18 Grenadiers, waiting for evacuation by helicopter. (Photo by Brigadier Kushal Thakur)

Fagot missiles from the 3/3 GR's own firebase in direct fire against the enemy sangars. D Company of 3/3 GR secured Thumb and Zulu Base by 0530hrs on 24 July when the Pakistanis withdrew to Zulu Top.[71]

On 24 July, 9 Para SF began its assault with two teams led by Major Dhaliwal and Captain Sudhir Kumar. Zulu Top was secured by 0630hrs on 25 July. The capture of Zulu Top provoked a platoon sized counterattack by the Pakistanis but this was beaten off after a charge by Captain Kumar and a team of eight men. Reinforcements in the form of two platoons of C Company 3/3 GR arrived by 1000hrs to secure the position and the rest of the Western Spur was secured by B Company of 3/3 GR led by Major Bobo Singh. Despite heavy artillery fire from across the LoC, Zulu Complex was very much secure in Indian hands when hostilities officially ended on 26 July 1999.[72]

## Losses – A Bloody Balance Sheet

Indian losses during the Kargil campaign were heavy. These included 26 officers, 21 JCOs and 452 other ranks killed; 66 officers, 60 JCOs and 1,085 other ranks wounded plus four missing for a total Indian casualty count of 1,714 killed, wounded and missing.[73] Materially, the IAF also lost one MiG-21M, one MiG-27L and one Mi-17, five Indian aircrew being killed in the process.

India's casualties also produced some of its first military heroes. The intense combat to retake the heights assumed almost mythic proportions with the truth of some of the heroic actions of Indian troops being even stranger than fiction and worthy of great admiration. Young officers like Lieutenant Manoj Pandey of 1/11 GR who was killed leading his men to the capture of Khalubar and Captain Vikram Batra of 13 JAK Rifles who was killed leading assaults to recapture Point 5140, became household names. This admiration was not confined to officers with the exploits of Grenadier Yogendra Yadav of 18 Grenadiers in the capture of Tiger Hill and Rifleman (Private) Sanjay Kumar in the capture of Flat Top on Point 4875 also becoming legendary. All of the four named personnel were awarded with India's highest combat gallantry award – the Param Vir Chakra for bravery.[74]

Pakistani losses were somewhat less clear, primarily because it took years for Islamabad to ever admit the involvement of its armed forces. Indian military intelligence estimated them with a total of 772 killed (including 69 officers and 76 SSG personnel), over 1,000 wounded and eight POWs. Troops in contact with the Pakistanis suggest 597 killed, while radio intercepts identified 591 killed. Prisoners included Naik Inayat Ali and Sepoys Hunar Shah, Sher Baz Khan and Mohammad Ayaz from 5 NLI; Sepoy Fazal Aman from 24 Sindh, Sepoys Abdul Hamid and Salik Khan from 33 Frontier Force Regiment and Sepoy Ashraf from 19 Frontier Force Regiment.[75] In addition, a number of diaries and identity documents were captured from Pakistani bodies which established the units from which many of the infiltrators originated. This undoubtedly helped India's narrative that the incursion was the work of Pakistani regulars rather than merely Pakistani supported Mujahidin and served to bolster India's efforts.

Pakistan itself never admitted to the casualties suffered and even now only tangentially accepts that their troops were involved. Pervez Musharraf suggested 357 killed and 665 wounded; Nawaz Sharif's PML-N gives casualties of 3,000 Mujahidin, officers and soldiers of the NLI "rendering sacrifice"; while Pakistan Army named 453 killed in the Batalik-Kargil sector in 1999.[76]

Several Pakistani soldiers were later rewarded with decorations – some posthumously – such as Captain Karnal Sher and Major Iqbal. However, as the Pakistan Army was more than a little reluctant to acknowledge its role in sparking and then encouraging the conflict, many deserving Pakistani soldiers were not accorded due recognition for their sacrifices in a losing conflict. Rather more seriously for Pakistan is the continuing failure to hold senior officers responsible for initiating the conflict and then leaving a brigade sized formation to fend for itself against a determined Indian effort, ultimately successful, to dislodge and repel them. Not surprisingly, a large quantity of arms and ammunition was captured from the infiltrators, either abandoned post-withdrawal or captured in combat. These included:

- four 12.7 mm anti-aircraft guns
- a 14.5mm KPVT heavy machinegun
- 46 heavy machineguns
- 19 grenade/rocket launchers
- 12 82mm and 120mm mortars
- one 23mm anti-aircraft gun
- one 37mm twin barrel anti-aircraft gun
- a FIM-92A gripstock
- three 105mm howitzers (without barrels)
- 198 G-3/AK/M16 and sniper files

The presence of such weapons as howitzers, Stinger MANPADS, 37mm AA guns and 120mm mortars is indicative of the extent to which the infiltrators were lavishly supplied with support weapons.[77]

# 8
# GUNNER'S WAR

While the Kargil conflict was very much an infantryman's war, with Indian infantry clawing its way peak by peak, ridge by ridge, to dislodge the intruders, the conflict was equally a gunner's war with Indian artillery having an impact out of all proportion to the numbers of guns involved.

India deployed some 19 artillery regiments to the Kargil theatre, three of which (141st and 197th Field, and the 108th Medium regiments) were later awarded unit citations for their role in the conflict.[1]

A battery of 105mm Light Field Guns as seen shortly before going into action in the Dras sector. Notable is the 75/24 Indian Mountain Gun in the foreground: this was used in the direct firing role. (Directorate General of Artillery, Indian Army, via author)

Two fully-loaded BM-21 Grad launchers seconds before opening fire. (Colonel Gurmeet Kanwal/Directorate General of Artillery, Indian Army, via author)

The full gamut of Indian artillery regiments was employed and these included light, field, medium, rocket and heavy mortar regiments with some 300 guns, multi barrel rocket launchers and mortars of 120mm and 160mm calibre being deployed in the conflict. As noted earlier, field regiments were equipped with 105mm Indian Field Guns or Light Field Guns; medium regiments were equipped with 130mm M-46 guns and 155mm FH77/B-02 Bofors howitzers. Light regiments operated 120mm mortars, while the sole heavy mortar regiment deployed fielded Tampella 160mm mortars. Some 75/24mm Indian-designed pack howitzers were used in the direct fire role. A regiment with BM-21 122mm rockets was also deployed. This latter unit was to provide exceptional support with its ability to saturate a target with HE in a very short space of time, and just a single battery proving devastatingly effective.

These units were to deliver some 250,000 shells, rockets and mortar bombs during the conflict with an average of 5,000 rounds being fired daily. This rate of fire was merely an average, as during operations a surge of one round per minute per battery was often sustained for 17 days continuously. For the battle to recapture Tiger Hill, some 9,000 artillery rounds were fired at designated targets on the day the iconic objective was retaken.[2] This enabled India to deliver a staggering level of concentrated firepower on Pakistani positions and while there was artillery cover provided by Pakistan's artillery across the Line of Control, the infiltration forces themselves had no effective means to fight back against the range of firepower deployed against them and which completely outclassed

A battery of Indian Field Guns in action during the Kargil War. Notable is the high elevation of their tubes, necessary to hit targets high atop mountain peaks. (Albert Grandolini Collection)

A close-up view of another battery of Indian Field Guns. Several such positions were hit – with remarkable precision – by Pakistani counter-battery fire. (Albert Grandolini Collection)

Clouds of smoke can be seen rising in the background after a shell from Pakistani counter-battery fire narrowly missed a position of FH77 howitzers. (Colonel Gurmeet Kanwal/Directorate General of Artillery, Indian Army, via author)

their own fire-support in respect of range, lethality and also accuracy. This rendered a response by intruder strongpoints almost completely ineffective against Indian artillery regiments or their logistics.

Highly effective counter-battery fire was often experienced by Indian gun positions as Pakistan's army made good use of their US supplied ANTPQ-37 artillery locating radars which outranged India's equivalent systems. When these were combined with Pakistan's own medium and heavy artillery regiments, these were to prove a major threat to Indian artillery gun positions, with the M198 155mm and M115 203mm howitzers being particularly effective. Colonel Goswami was to note that:

> The gun positions came under heavy enemy counter-bombardment from time to time, many a times causing serious casualties. But the gunners there stood fast and continued to respond to the requirements of the Battery.[3]

To cope with this effective counter-battery fire, dummy gun positions were also prepared with guns being locally fabricated out of packing material and lumber. On 13 June one such "quaker-gun" position received one of the heaviest enemy counter-bombardments, and while Pakistani gunners may have been convinced of their impact on targets, there were many instances of the Pakistanis targeting these fake gun positions in lieu of their real counterparts. Significant quantities of ammunition were expended on the part of the Pakistan Army to no discernible effect on the Indian artillery and its ability to support the infantry.[4]

In addition, to further thwart Pakistan's counter-battery efforts, where possible guns were tucked in, hugging the slopes to avoid being spotted by Pakistan's observation post officers. When guns were deployed in this manner, even if the gun positions were found by artillery locating radar, the guns could not be effectively neutralized. It was only when deployed in the open that the Pakistani counter-bombardment had to be faced. The Indian artillery did not possess similar radars with equivalent performance, thus enemy gun positions were fixed through aerial reconnaissance. However, this was a relatively ineffective approach to determining artillery locations for counter-battery efforts on the part of Indian artillery.[5]

India was able to field concentrations of between 100 to 120 guns to fire against single targets, all firing in concert. With medium regiments, the 130mm guns and 155mm howitzers would have brought a heavy weight of ordnance to bear on Pakistani positions, while the light regiments with 120mm mortars, and the 160mm mortars of the single heavy mortar regiment, supplied shorter-range support. While the indirect fire of these guns, augmented by 105mm guns in field regiments providing support to Indian infantry battalions, was to prove very effective and caused significant damage to the intruders, one innovation was the use of the guns in the direct fire role, which

Indian Army's gunners carrying a disassembled 75/24 howitzer up the ridgeline into a direct-firing position. (Directorate General of Artillery, Indian Army, via author)

had hitherto been practiced only in the plains and which had been used with mixed results in the 1965 and 1971 India-Pakistan wars. Initially, 75/24 mountain guns were used in the direct fire role, but the entry of the medium regiments increased the efficacy of such a method of firing. In fact, as the 75/24 gun was increasingly deployed in modest numbers, to compensate for a shortage of fuses for a particular consignment of 105mm shells; fuses were removed from 6,000 rounds of 75mm ammunition for supply to the 105mm regiments. Direct artillery shooting, particularly by the 155mm Bofors, generated a degree of panic among the infiltrators and had a devastating effect as it enabled the rapid destruction of enemy bunkers. Gun accuracy surged and as every round was a hit, a considerable saving in ammunition was achieved.[6]

Alok Deb, who commanded the 197th Field Regiment during the Kargil conflict, and every Indian officer interviewed, spoke highly of the competence and performance of the Pakistan Army artillery. Despite being outnumbered by Indian artillery, Pakistan's artillery was very effective throughout the Kargil operations and delivered accurate counter-battery fire against Indian guns. This was partly due to the use of ANTPQ-37 Fire-Finder radars by the Pakistanis. Fully 50.5% of all casualties brought into the Military Hospital Leh were due to hostile artillery fire. In addition, Pakistani artillery and mortars proved adept at delivering harassing fire, while one particular 5.5-inch gun proved extremely effective in firing illumination shells.[7]

A battery of 130mm M-46 field guns about to open fire. According to Indian reports, these played havoc with Pakistani gun positions and rear installations. (Colonel Gurmeet Kanwal/Directorate General of Artillery, Indian Army, via author)

# 9

# OPERATION SAFED-SAGAR – THE IAF'S CAMPAIGN

The Indian Air Force campaign during the Kargil War warrants special attention as its operations were the first sustained air operations at altitudes exceeding 18,000 feet. Though only a fraction of the IAF was involved in the operations, their achievements were impressive and though three aircraft were lost – one to engine failure and two to MANPADS – the IAF provided much needed support to the Indian Army.

A Cheetah helicopter of the Indian Army Aviation Corps – like this one – underway over the Kargil area was hit by the Pakistani ground fire on 12 May 1999 but managed to return safely to its forward base. (Albert Grandolini Collection)

From as early as 10 May 1999, the Indian Air Force had begun flying reconnaissance sorties to determine the extent and nature of the incursion, this being roughly one week after the presence of intruders was confirmed. Initial reconnaissance operations were conducted by a combination of helicopters, Jaguars equipped with tactical reconnaissance pods and Canberra strategic reconnaissance aircraft. Other than reconnaissance operations, the IAF began a deployment of additional aircraft into the Kashmir Valley. These were brought in sufficient numbers to support any combat tasking that was envisaged.

In addition, as the air defences of the region were largely confined to the defence of air bases and strategic targets, the IAF and the Indian Army's CADA established a rudimentary air defense control arrangement.[1] This included the deployment of additional Light AD regiments to the area with radar directed L70 40mm guns as well as several composite regiments with ZU-23-2 guns with MANPADS of the Igla-1M type. The IAF did deploy its SA-3 Pechora SAMs to defend its bases and vital areas and points in the Kashmir theatre.

The IAF deployed some 150 combat aircraft in the theatre though not all, nor even most, were committed to the actual operations. Some sources suggest that the IAF combat aircraft were deployed in the following numbers:

- Srinagar – 34 (MiG-21, MiG-23BN, MiG-27)
- Awantipur – 28 (MiG-21, MiG-29, Jaguar)
- Udhampur – 12 (MiG-21)
- Pathankot – 30 (MiG-21, MiG-23BN)
- Adampur – 46 (Mirage 2000, MiG-29, Jaguar)[2]

## First Blood

On 12 May, an IAF helicopter was fired at by Pakistani anti-aircraft fire near the most forward-based Pakistani positions overlooking Kargil. Though the helicopter landed with only a damaged rotor, the event caused India's Western Air Command, at the direction of Air Headquarters to go to heightened state of alert and to deploy air defence aircraft on what the IAF terms Operational Readiness Platforms (ORP), known more commonly as Quick Reaction Alert (QRA) at the IAF's northernmost operating locations at Air Force Stations Srinagar and Avantipur. These aircraft were mainly MiG-21s.[3]

On 21 May 1999, however, a major escalation took place when an IAF Canberra PR57 from 106 Squadron on a strategic reconnaissance mission, flown by Wing Commander CH Kulkarni, Squadron Leader A Perumal and Squadron Leader UK Jha, was hit by a Chinese-made Anza infrared surface-to-air missile. The aircraft was able to return, albeit on one engine, to the IAF base at Srinagar, with no loss of life or serious injury: indeed, the aircraft was subsequently repaired.[4]

However, the event caused sufficient concern to the Indian government for it to contemplate something that had hitherto been considered unthinkable – the deployment of air power. The IAF was, however, limited in its ability to function by a very clear instruction that air operations were not to cross the Line of Control. This restriction limited paths of attack, of ingress and egress and almost certainly complicated air operations. On the other hand, the Indian government's decision ensured that hostilities would not escalate into all-out war and that the conflict would be limited. Moreover, India's decision not to cross the Line of Control also meant that the scope for interference by the Pakistan Air Force would be limited as any action on their part would involve operations in Indian airspace.

## Environment and Air Power

Combat aircraft are not optimized to conduct strike operations in mountainous terrain and high altitudes impose power and performance constraints on aircraft. In this regard supersonic combat platforms such as the MiG-21/-23/-27 and the Mirage 2000 had a clear advantage over other types. The Jaguar, despite its excellent weapons delivery system, its excellent overall capability, and its highly effective ordnance and sensors, was decidedly underpowered for effective operations in the Kargil theatre and the type was relegated to reconnaissance missions as a result of this deficiency. However, the high altitude also posed significant challenges in respect of ordnance. In 1999, the IAF had relatively few precision guided munitions and a limited stock of laser-guided bombs. Of the former, priority had to be given to the possibility of a wider war with Pakistan, while in the case of the latter, stocks were decidedly limited.

The performance of munitions is affected due to the massively different condition of the atmosphere at high altitude. There is a substantial difference as compared to sea-level specifications and performance on the part of unguided munitions which will suffer from higher degrees of inaccuracies as compared to manufacturers' data as weapons do not perform as per sea-level specifications. With variations in air temperature and density, which have the effect of altering drag indices, there is a much greater risk of inaccuracy in weapons delivery. Even with computerised weapons aiming systems, unguided bombs are significantly less effective in mountainous terrain, and there is little doubt that the use of 250kg and 500kg

A trio of IAF MiG-23BNs underway in the Himalayan mountains. (Albert Grandolini Collection)

A MiG-23M registered as SM273, fully loaded with a total of six 250kg incendiary bombs, waiting for the next mission during the Kargil War. (Albert Grandolini Collection)

The highly effective Mirage 2000 fleet was inducted only from 30 May.

It should be noted that the IAF was fully aware of the limited capabilities of the MiG-21 fleet in the ground attack role. However, its good power-to-weight ratio and its ability to operate in restricted spaces was of great value in the terrain of the Kargil campaign. The IAF's fleet of MiG-21s, MiG-23BNs, and MiG-27s, was neither equipped with modern attack nor navigation systems and only a handful had been fitted with chaff and flare dispensers. Pilots obtained GPS gadgets on the open market and strapped these to their thighs or held them if a hand was free. In addition to the use of 57mm rockets, the IAFs' MiG fleet was also tasked with dropping 1,000-pound bombs – leftover from the 1965 and 1971 wars – on target points selected by the Indian Army with the intention of triggering avalanches or landslides in order to cut off Pakistani lines of communication and evacuation. The initial strikes had air cover provided by MiG-21s armed with air-to-air missiles, but these were supplemented and later supplanted by MiG-29s. Mil Mi-17s were flown in the Tololing sector and during the period of hostilities, Srinagar airport was closed to civilian traffic. The IAF was only too aware of shortcomings in terms of both its platforms and ordnance to conduct operations in the mountains around Kargil. Less understandable, however, was its early underappreciation of the threat posed by MANPADS in the hands of the Pakistani intruders.

bombs was significantly less effective than they might have been at lower elevations. While near misses could do damage in the plains, in the mountains, however, this is most definitely not the case due to the masking effects of the undulating terrain. Moreover, inaccuracy in the linear dimension would be exaggerated due to the variation in elevation. In contrast, there was a greater level of efficacy with the UB-32 57mm rocket pods which were widely employed by all of the MiGs involved in strike operations. Yet the destructive power of their small warheads in mountainous terrain led to substantially less damage than might be ideal. The use of 250kg unguided bombs from Mirage 2000s was much more effective and this highlighted the requirement for aircraft with effective and accurate and computerized weapons aiming. The requirement for pinpoint accuracy in mountainous terrain is evident but this very terrain and the climatic conditions therein render that accuracy difficult to achieve.

## Operations Commence

The Indian Air Force (IAF) flew its first air support missions on 26 May, operating from the Indian airfields of Srinagar, Avantipur and Adampur. The strike aircraft included MiG-21s – mainly MiG-21Ms – MiG-23BNs, MiG-27s with a few sorties flown by Jaguars principally as reconnaissance aircraft, and Mil Mi-17s as helicopter gunships.

## First Losses

The IAF suffered two unfortunate casualties over the Batalik sector while striking against the major Pakistani logistics hub at Muntho Dalo. On 27 May, a MiG-27 of No.9 squadron crashed due to an engine flame-out apparently caused by the ingestion of gas from a strafing run using its main gun. The pilot, Flight Lieutenant K Nachiketa Rao, was forced to eject and was taken prisoner. A MiG-21M, piloted by Squadron Leader Ajay Ahuja of No. 17 sqn was escorting the MiG-21 and continued to orbit the site trying to provide cover. This MiG-21 was struck by a Stinger MANPAD fired by Captain Waheed of 5 NLI. Squadron Leader Ahuja is thought by the Indian military to have survived the crash but was later killed; allegedly his body bore two point-blank bullet wounds, indicating a post-crash death.[5]

On 28 May, in the Tololing sector, a Mi-17 was shot down – with the loss of all four of the crew – when it was hit by a FIM-92A Stinger MANPAD. The Mi-17, which had a malfunctioning flare dispenser,

1,000lbs bombs installed on a MiG-27M of the IAF, decorated with messages from the ground crews for the enemy on their receiving end. (Albert Grandolini Collection)

A Pakistani soldier with FIM-92A Stinger MANPAD: this proved to be the most dangerous anti-aircraft weapon high in the mountains of the Kargil area. (Albert Grandolini Collection)

was part of a four-ship flight of 129 HU. These helicopters were using 57mm rockets to engage a fortified position and had successfully dodged several Stingers before the third ship of the formation was hit after evading three other missiles. The loss of the Mi-17 and the threat of MANPADS ended the use of the Mi-17 as an attack helicopter, though their use continued as a transport asset. Combat aircraft were compelled to fly at higher altitudes to negate the effects of MANPADS, while additional chaff and flare dispensers were hastily installed on as many aircraft as possible. It is also interesting that the IAF's dedicated attack helicopters – Mi-25 and Mi-35 machines of 104 HU and 125 HU – were not committed to action owing to the poor performance of these aircraft at high altitude.

## Enter the Mirage 2000

The Mirage 2000 was the IAF's most capable multi-role aircraft in 1999. The two squadrons – Nos. 1 & 7 – were tasked with air defence with Super 530D and R.550 Magic 2 missiles. However, the Mirage 2000s were supplied with Thomson-CSF ATLIS II laser designator pods, which were mated to Matra 1,000kg Arcole LGBs, and were earmarked for the destruction of reinforced targets. While undoubtedly deadly, these bombs were extremely expensive. To augment stocks of laser-guided bombs, the IAF decided to combine the standard 450kg bomb to the Paveway II laser-guided bomb kit.

While the IAF had ordered significant numbers of these weapons, they were delivered with a defective part and owing to a post-Pokhran embargo, the IAF could not use these weapons until local technicians manufactured replacement parts to make the weapons compatible with the Mirage 2000. This had other cascading implications as the IAF's technicians and armourers were spread throughout Central Air Command and not all Mirages had the necessary hardpoints for the delivery of air-to-surface ordnance owing to the air defence commitments of the Mirage fleet. In fact, it is possible that of the entire Mirage 2000 fleet, only a dozen aircraft may have been fully operational as strike platforms at that time.[6]

The lopsided commitment of the Mirage 2000 to the air defence task dates from its induction where it was aimed at countering Pakistan's F-16s. Even after the induction of aircraft such as the MiG-29 and the MiG-21 Bison, the Mirage 2000 was a very popular platform with the IAF and was in great demand for its multi-role capability. One critical aspect of the Mirage 2000 deployment was the push to equip the aircraft with old ordnance directed by its excellent attack system. One step that was taken very early in the conflict was the deployment of the aircraft with 250kg bombs of Spanish origin which had been procured for the Ajeet attack aircraft – an Indian development of the Folland Gnat. These modest weapons could be carried in large

The MiG-29 (top) and Mirage 2000 (bottom) proved the most important types in service with the IAF during the Kargil War: the former kept the PAF at bay, thus keeping the skies clear for the later, which – thanks to the quick introduction to service of laser guided bombs – became the most important strike platform. (Albert Grandolini Collection)

As the combination had not been tested, the laser designation time of the Litening pods required manual alteration as the Mirage computer protocol for the said pod was not known. Fuses were not available for old 500kg bombs, so pistol fuses were modified and proved effective. Gwalior air base served as the main base for weapons clearance as old ordnance dating from earlier wars was cleared for carriage on the wing pylons of the Mirage 2000s. The new Litening LDPs were also used for reconnaissance and were extremely effective in pinpointing ammunition and logistics depots for their eventual destruction by the IAF.[8]

numbers by the Mirage 2000, with up to 12 being a routine payload during the Kargil operations. The IAF's use of old ordnance was one of the more remarkable features of the IAF's operations and the fact that such ordnance, dating from the 1965 and 1971 wars still worked was testimony to adequate storage and maintenance being available for such weapons. It should be noted that the IAF was very reluctant to commit the Mirage 2000 fleet to the Kargil strike operations owing to a real fear that the conflict could escalate. Had these aircraft been deployed earlier, IAF sources suggest that the effects of the bombing campaign and the results achieved could have been realized earlier.

### Lack of Laser-Guided Bombs

As already noted, the Mirage 2000s of the IAF were equipped with the ATLIS II/ Bombe Guidée Laser (BGL) Arcole 1,000kg bombs combination. This was less than ideal for use in the Kargil sector. The Atlis II is a French daylight and clear-weather laser/electro-optical targeting pod and the IAF had specifically ordered the combination for targeting recessed Command and Control sites/bunkers and controlling the deep-penetrating highly expensive Arcole LGB. However, the ATLIS pod had problems operating at very high altitudes and were therefore deemed totally unsuitable for deployment in Kargil. As also already noted, the IAF procured a number of the very much cheaper US Paveway II laser-guided bomb kits for use with the Israeli Litening laser designator pods (LDPs) which were to become extremely popular in IAF service – to the present day. However, defective parts could not be replaced thanks to the post-nuclear test US arms embargo and thus requiring IAF remanufacture of the said parts.[7]

### Mirage 2000 in action

The Mirage 2000 initially flew strike operations with unguided bombs, the first of which were the Spanish-made 250kg weapons. Larger bombs, such as British-made 1,000lbs, and newer 450kg bombs were soon made available for use following clearance, and both types of bomb were delivered using the Mirage 2000's onboard CCRP (Computer Controlled Release Point) sighting technique. This required a degree of adjustment to cater for such factors as reduced air density with the attendant variation in ballistic trajectory which inevitably accompanies operations at heights 6,000 to 18,000 feet above sea level. Following the losses on 27 and 28 May, sorties were flown ensuring that the strike packages were successfully kept outside the launch range of MANPADS.

A major success was scored between 16 and 17 June. On 16 June, the main supply depot of the intruders was located at Muntho Dalo in the Batalik sector and on 17 June a strike package of Mirage 2000s destroyed this position, as well as administrative and logistics facilities at Muntho Dhalo, using 450kg bombs with the CCRP technique. This produced devastating results, not just physically but also in terms of adversely affecting the morale of intruders.[9]

Another large logistics camp at Point 4388 in Mashkoh Nallah was spotted using the Litening pod on 23 June and a strike package comprising two Mirage 2000s with unguided bombs hit the site on 24 June. A large number of casualties were apparently caused by this strike but it was not until 10 July that this target was deemed to be completely destroyed. The Mirage 2000 force was used extensively against the heavily defended Tiger Hill. This was attacked throughout June with a combination of LGBs and unguided bombs. Of particular interest is that the IAF used only nine LGBs in the entire conflict – eight delivered by Mirages and one by a Jaguar. This was largely due to the increasingly effective delivery of unguided munitions which proved to be quite adequate to the task.[10]

The IAF flew its first LGB strike on 24 June in a two-seater Mirage 2000, flown by then Wing Commander R Nambiar with then Squadron

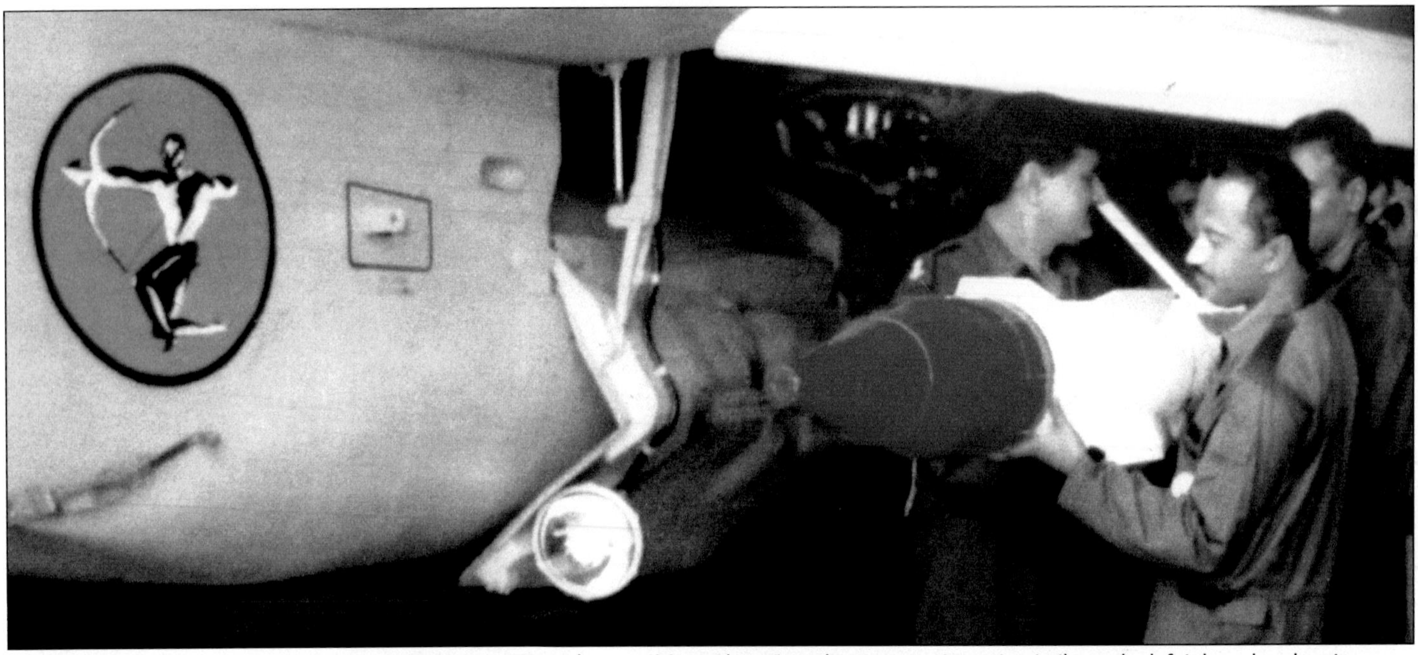

Ground crews loading a Russian-made R-27R (ASCC/NATO-codename 'AA-10 Alamo') medium-range air-to-air missile on the left inboard underwing pylon of a MiG-29 from No. 47 Squadron 'Archers', the insignia of which can be seen to the left. (Albert Grandolini Collection)

Leader DK Patnaik in the rear seat, in the company of another two-seater as back up, and a third carrying no less than the then Chief of Air Staff, ACM AY Tipnis, to observe the strike. A nocturnal LGB mission was flown against Tiger Hill on 28 June 1999 with Squadron Leader Patnaik in the front seat and Wing Commander Nambiar in the rear. This strike was extremely effective and its accuracy was confirmed by the Indian Army. The effect of this particular strike was significant enough for it to be deemed instrumental in paving the way for Indian ground forces to recapture Tiger Hill. It should be noted that all LGBs were delivered by two-seaters, with the rear-seat pilot doubling up as a WSO – this would limit the number of aircraft so equipped to the seven two-seat Mirage 2000s in IAF service at the time.[11]

To say that the Mirage 2000 proved its worth during the Kargil war is an understatement. Its accuracy with unguided munitions was excellent to the extent that a single LGB equipped Mirage 2000 would accompany a two or four ship Mirage formation – each of which carried six to twelve bombs – and deliver its LGB only if the unguided munitions had a sub-optimal effect, or if it spotted a target of opportunity such as a command and control bunker. This enabled the IAF to conserve its limited stock of LGBs while simultaneously getting the maximum benefit from them. It should be noted that in the Mirage 2000 the IAF found a combination of performance, weapons delivery capability, sophistication, and survivability which it had hitherto been unable to find. No other aircraft in the IAF's inventory possessed such a combination, and despite the fact that an advanced strike platform in the form of the Jaguar was readily available, it is telling that the Jaguar saw relatively little service during the Kargil conflict. The MiG-23BN and MiG-27 fleet which bore the brunt of the strike effort and which performed quite well, were still less than optimal compared to the capability and flexibility of the Mirage 2000. The MiG-21, for all its limitation performed creditably but was woefully underequipped for the mountain strike role.

## Strike Missions and Innovation

Following losses to Pakistani MANPADS, all IAF strike missions were flown at an altitude of 10,000 metres, (33,000 feet above sea level), with the aircraft diving when required and then pulling out well out of MANPADs range.[12]

A MiG-29 of the IAF taking-off from Srinagar AB. During the Kargil War, the type played an unglamorous but crucially important role in keeping the PAF firmly on the other side of the LoC. (Albert Grandolini Collection)

It should also be noted that there were operational constraints imposed by the low number of airbases used for operations. This inevitably caused a degree of inefficiency in operations and the number of attack sorties that were flown. Nonetheless, following the initial losses, the IAF was able to fly hundreds of sorties without losing further aircraft. This was combined with dramatically improved effectiveness thanks to the IAF's ability to innovate and adapt new technologies and bombing techniques to improve results.[13]

This improved combat effectiveness was directly attributable to Western Air Command's switch from traditional dive bombing techniques by MiG-23s and MiG-27s, with their attendant low-altitude releases, to a much more accurate method of GPS-aided level bombing from safer and higher altitudes above the effective reach of the infiltrator's MANPADS. At the time of the Kargil conflict only one attack squadron in the IAF – the sole unit being a MiG-23BN squadron which had undergone upgrades – was fitted with GPS systems. The IAF procured hand-held GPS systems on the open market and these, with the target coordinates available, enabled the pilots on approach to deliver their ordnance at the determined distance from the target. The IAF believed that if the coordinates were accurate, the bombing accuracy would be reasonably good. The IAF was also aware that accuracy would be greater at lower altitudes of about 500 feet above the target areas. In order to limit the efficacy of hostile air defences, these sorties were flown at night, which was particularly risky without radar support and with aircraft lacking modern navigation aides. Moreover, the issue of the ordnance used by the MiG-21s, MiG-23BNs and MiG-27s was at least partly resolved by improved weapons delivery techniques. The introduction of the IAF's Mirage 2000H fleet into daily operations substantially improved the destructive impact and accuracy of IAF strike against point targets even with the use of unguided low-drag bombs such as the 450kg bomb and the old Spanish 250kg ordnance. This, as noted above was, thanks to the aircraft's excellent avionics suite that included a continuously computed release point (CCRP) system which improved weapons delivery by compensating for target area wind and enabled vastly improved accuracy. All that a pilot or WSO needed to do was to designate his intended aim point through his cockpit head-up display (HUD) and then depresses an approval button on the aircraft's control stick. This then allowed the computer to release the bomb once all the required delivery parameters were achieved. This approach gave the pilot a high degree of confidence that his weapon would be delivered with adequate accuracy.[14]

The IAF demonstrated additional innovation, especially on its MiG-21s, which despite their lack of sophistication and effective onboard navigation and attack avionics, soldiered on in the close air support role. The IAF used stopwatches and GPS receivers in their cockpits to conduct night interdiction bombing even with the MiG-21. This was a major achievement for the IAF as, despite its limitations, the MiG-21 proved to be a useful close air support asset with unguided rockets and its increased efficacy would have been valued. That the IAF retained ordnance from the 1965 and 1971 wars in its inventory was decidedly puzzling but the ordnance seems to have worked effectively enough. Another innovation by the IAF during the Kargil campaign was the use of unusual mechanisms and devices to conduct surveillance. The IAF lacked sufficient numbers of effective UAVs and its tactical reconnaissance assets needed to be augmented. To this end, the Litening pod with its electro-optical and infra-red imaging, as well as Vicon reconnaissance pods, were used to conduct high-resolution aerial reconnaissance of the airspace over the battlefield.

IAF combat operations continued without interruption for seven weeks except for a brief and ultimately inconsequential delay for bad weather. Without straining its assets, at the height of Operation Safed Sagar, the IAF was generating more than 40 fixed-wing combat sorties a day in both direct and indirect support to XV Corps with the MiG-21, MiG-23BN and MiG-27 squadrons providing direct close air support and the Jaguars and Mirage 2000s providing additional support in delivering precision strikes. In its task, Western Air Command was ably supported by Central Air Command headquartered at Allahabad in Uttar Pradesh. This command was the home of the Mirage 2000 fleet as well as the IAF's No. 102 sqn operating the MiG-25R high-altitude reconnaissance aircraft. These aircraft were deployed in an unusual medium-altitude tactical reconnaissance role to augment the IAF's Jaguars and in recognition of the vulnerability of No.106 Squadron and its Canberra PR.57s.

### Effectiveness

The efficacy of the IAF's operations cannot be seen in isolation from the broader objectives of the Kargil campaign. While the effects of the MiG-21, MiG-23BN and MiG-27 sorties were largely confined to tactical success and their initial operations with 250kg and 500kg bombs were far from effective, the Mirage 2000s scored at least five successful laser-guided bomb hits on forward supply dumps sites and posts. Between the commencement of operations on 26 May and the last day of operations of 12 July 1999, it was evident that the IAF had dramatically improved its bombing accuracy. Even at night, which could have at had a deleterious effect on bombing accuracy, the willingness of the IAF to conduct operations around the clock meant that the Pakistani infiltrators could not retain their posts and were compelled to withdraw.

Moreover, effective Indian reconnaissance of Pakistani artillery positions tasked with supporting the infiltrators rendered them vulnerable to Indian counter-battery fire of ever-increasing efficacy while simultaneously making their own counter-battery efforts less than effective. In all, the IAF flew a total of 550 strike sorties against positions held by the infiltrators as well as bunkers and supply depots. These positions, bunkers, and depots were located through the efforts of about 150 reconnaissance and communications intelligence sorties flown by a variety of IAF platforms. Though the PAF never rose to challenge the IAF, the service dedicated some 500 sorties for air defence and for escorting strike packages and reconnaissance aircraft. In total, IAF fighters and strike aircraft flew 1,730 sorties. In addition, there was a substantial effort on the part of the IAF's helicopter and transport fleet, which between them flew close to 6,000 sorties to supply and sustain India's combat forces in the theatre as well as to provide such much needed services as medical and casualty evacuation. In a real sense, though combat assets attracted the headlines, Operation Safed Sagar and the ultimate Indian victory owed much to the efforts and flexibility of the IAF's transports and helicopters. The air effort delivered by the IAF can be summarized as listed in Table 26, and gives a very clear idea of the roles played by type:

**Table 26: Combat and Support Sorties flown, IAF, Kargil War[15]**

| Type | Number of Sorties | Percentage of Total Effort |
|---|---|---|
| **Fighters** | 1,730 | 22.7% |
| **Helicopters** | 2,474 | 32.4% |
| **Transports** | 3,427 | 44.9% |
| **Total** | 7,631 | 100% |

### Pakistani Air Force during the Kargil War

The PAF did not challenge the IAF over the Kargil theatre of operations. This does not mean that it was inactive or not carefully monitoring the IAF's efforts. One might suggest that the absence of the PAF enabled the IAF to operate freely but it also helped to limit the conflict and showed a degree of mutual awareness that escalating hostilities would be dangerous and as such the PAF's reaction was decidedly proportionate.

A briefing on the "latest situation in Kashmir" at HQ 10 Corps was held on 12 May where, the Corps commander Lt Gen Mehmud Ahmad indicated to PAF representatives that a limited operation had started two days earlier to occupy a number of vacant Indian positions across the LoC overlooking the Dras-Kargil road.[16] When asked about the need for air support, Lieutenant General Ahmad indicated that air support was not envisaged and that the Pakistani ground forces could deal with any IAF aircraft if they intervened and noted that they had deployed Stinger MANPADS at all the occupied positions.[17] Despite words of caution from the PAF regarding the limited engagement envelope of these MANPADS, the Pakistani Army was adamant that the IAF could not detect or identify the Pakistani positions. Moreover, the Army was convinced that the Indian Army would not move artillery from other sectors to increase the firepower available to deal with the intrusions. The Pakistan Air Force was thus not made an integral part of the Kargil planning and was apparently only informed after hostilities had started. In the event, the Pakistani Air Force attempted to improve air surveillance by heli-lifting a radar to the Deosai Plateau and tried to institute an effective combat air patrol cycle which sought to negate the large Indian advantage in BVR air-to-air missiles that then existed. The intention was to conduct an offensive fighter sweep with a view to intercepting and destroying Indian aircraft. At the same time, the PAF chose to ignore a number of shallow Indian incursions during reconnaissance flights.

The PAF F-16s flew out of Kamra and Sargodha but these could not sustain CAPs daily as, owing to US sanctions following Pakistan's nuclear tests, spares were in short supply.[18] The PAF F-16 force was thus reduced to flying random CAPs which themselves ended up being discontinued after only a week, during which times PAF F-16s were locked on to by IAF radars from both Mirage 2000s and MiG-29s. On one occasion Flight Lieutenant Gaurav Chibber, in a MiG-29 escorting a MiG-27 strike package, locked on to two PAF F-16s causing them to abort their intercept. The PAF F-7s and Mirages were deemed to be unsuitable for any effective air combat role in the Kargil theatre and as such the PAF chose to husband its resources in the event that the conflict escalated.

# 10
# DIPLOMATIC ENDGAME

Indian military operations continued from 12 May for seven weeks as New Delhi accepted neither cease-fire requests nor any efforts towards conciliation or negotiations. On the contrary, despite significant difficulties, its armed forces moved inexorably towards evicting the intruders.

As might be expected, the Pakistani government approached the United States of America for assistance in bringing the conflict to an end. Prime Minister Nawaz Sharif became increasingly desperate as realisation dawned at the extent of Pakistan's isolation in respect of the Kargil conflict. Efforts to involve the G8 and UN, after some calls for dialogue, ended with no positive result for Pakistan.[1] This led to Pakistan placing its hopes on the United States. At the same time, India's Prime Minister, Atal Bihari Vajpayee, was absolutely resolute in his view that nothing could be entertained short of a Pakistani withdrawal. To this end, Pakistani Prime Minister Sharif urgently requested American intervention to stop the Indian counterattack. However, Washington was adamant and consistent in its approach that any solution required a Pakistani withdrawal behind the LoC and nothing short of that would suffice.[2]

As the Indian counter-offensive continued, in the last days of June Sharif began to ask to visit President Clinton and to directly plead his case for US intervention. On 2 July Sharif made a call to President Clinton where he appealed for American intervention immediately to stop the fighting and to resolve the Kashmir issue. In contrast, President Clinton was very explicit in his view that he could help only if Pakistan first withdrew to its side of the LoC. The President also consulted with Indian Prime Minister Vajpayee who was adamant that India would not negotiate under the threat of aggression and that Pakistan needed to withdraw across the LoC.[3]

On 3 July 1999, Sharif was even more desperate and told President Clinton he was ready to come immediately to Washington to seek help. The US President repeated his view that Sharif should only come if Pakistan was ready to withdraw and that no help could be forthcoming if Pakistan did not do so. Despite this, Sharif travelled to Washington a day later. In the course of a meeting with Clinton, he attempted to plead the cause of Kashmiri separatism, Pakistan's claim on the territory, and to press for external intervention to "solve" the problem. However, Clinton refused to be persuaded by such arguments and instead insisted on a Pakistani withdrawal. After much debate and consultation, an increasingly desperate Sharif agreed to a draft statement which effectively paved the way for a Pakistani withdrawal. Bruce Riedel, who was present at the meeting and who played a part in the proceedings, concluded:

> After an hour break the President, Sharif and I returned to the discussion. The President put on the table a short statement to be issued to the press drawing from the non-paper Sharif had given us, and the statement we had drafted before the meeting to announce agreement on withdrawal to the LOC. The key sentence read, "the Prime Minister has agreed to take concrete and immediate steps for the restoration of the LOC".
>
> Strobe, Sandy, Rick and I had drafted this key sentence during the break. The statement also called for a ceasefire once the withdrawal was completed and restoration of the Lahore process. Finally, the statement included a reaffirmation of the President's long standing plans to visit South Asia. The President was clear and firm. Sharif had a choice, withdraw behind the LOC and the moral compass would tilt back toward Pakistan or stay and fight a wider and dangerous war with India without American sympathy. Sharif read the statement several times quietly. He asked to talk with his team and we adjourned again.
>
> After a few minutes Sharif returned with good news. The statement was acceptable with one addition. Sharif wanted a sentence added that would say "the President would take personal interest to encourage an expeditious resumption and intensification of the bilateral efforts (i.e. Lahore) once the sanctity of the LOC had been fully restored.
>
> The President handed the sentence to me and asked my opinion. I said we could easily agree to this because the President already supported the Lahore process but we need a clear understanding on how we would portray the LOC issue — we would need to explain to our press that this language meant a Pakistani withdrawal. Clinton agreed and told Sharif that was his intention. Reluctantly, the Prime Minister said yes.
>
> This statement paved the way for an end to hostilities with Pakistani troops withdrawing behind the LoC and India reoccupying all posts hitherto unoccupied by its forces. Indian assets monitored the Pakistani withdrawal and verified the repositioning of the intruding forces to behind the Line of Control.'[4]

## Conclusions

Sharif would not last long after his agreement to the terms in the statement with President Clinton. His government would be toppled in a coup on 12 October 1999 which installed the 'architect of the Kargil adventure' – General Pervez Musharraf – as President of Pakistan. Fortunately, the coup was concluded without bloodshed, but it heightened Pakistan's isolation internationally and further

Indian Minister of Defence, George Fernandes, posing for the press with an RPG-7 rocket propelled grenade captured from Pakistan Army troops during the Kargil War. (Albert Grandolini Collection)

eroded that country's fragile democracy, its civil society and civilian institutions.

Atal Bihari Vajpayee's government was re-elected with a slightly increased majority although the war had little impact on voting preferences. India embarked upon a comprehensive review of its security apparatus and its leading strategic thinker, the late K. Subramanyan, led the Kargil Review Committee which studied the intrusion, was scathing in its analysis and made recommendations to prevent a recurrence. Some of these recommendations were readily implemented while others remain in limbo to date, reflecting India's somewhat haphazard approach to its national security.

The Kargil conflict was South Asia's first post-nuclear war and one which showed the real limits of nuclear deterrence. Both sides lost hundreds of personnel; India's treated as heroes, whilst Pakistan's were forgotten in a losing effort. Pakistan learned that the international community would not diplomatically intervene to a limited Indian response. India's resolve in the face of military adventurism was underestimated by Pakistan to its cost.

This was also India's first "media war" which was extensively covered on national television channels, both public and private, as well as its robust print media: indeed, a new generation of Indian reporters were able to solidify their burgeoning reputations through their coverage.

The conflict showed that conventional war was still possible, albeit limited, in a nuclearized environment. It also demonstrated that military miscalculations and misinterpretations of reactions from an adversary were all too common, and while the conflict was kept within limited proportions – despite the thousands of casualties – there was always the possibility of an expansion of the conflict. Perhaps the final word on the Kargil conflict should be left to retired Lieutenant General Shahid Aziz, former Chief of General Staff of the Pakistan Army: 'It was a failure because we had to hide its objectives and results from our own people and the nation. It had no purpose, no planning and nobody knows even today how many soldiers lost their lives.'[5]

# Bibliography


Ahluwaia, V. K. and Singh, N., (ed.) *Surprise, Strategy and "Vijay": 20 Years of Kargil and Beyond* (New Delhi; Centre for Land Warfare Studies, 2019)

Amarinder, S., *A Ridge Too Far: War in the Kargil Heights 1999* (Patiala; Motibag Palace, 2001)

Badri-Maharaj, S., *The Armageddon Factor: Nuclear Weapons in the India-Pakistan Context* (New Delhi; Lancer, 2000)

Bajpai, K., Chari, P., Cheema, P., Cohen, S., Ganguly, S., (ed.), *Brasstacks and Beyond: Perception and Management of Crisis in South Asia* (New Delhi; Manohar, 1995)

Brar, K. S., *Operation Blue Star: The True Story* (New Delhi; UBSPD, 1993)

Camp, P., 'The Mirage 2000 in Kargil', *Bharat-Rakshak.com*, 16 October 2009

Chengappa R., *Weapons of Peace* (New Delhi; Harper Collins Publishers India, 2000)

Donald, D., Lake, J., *Encyclopaedia of World Military Aircraft, Volume 2* (London; Aerospace Publishing Ltd., 1994)

Gokhale, N. A., *Beyond NJ9842: the Siachen Saga* (New Delhi; Bloomsbury, 2015)

Gunston, B., *The Osprey Encyclopedia of Russian Aircraft, 1875-1995* (London; Osprey, 1995)

Joshi, M., *The Lost Rebellion: Kashmir in the Nineties* (New Delhi; Penguin, 1999)

Karnad, B., *Nuclear Weapons and Indian Security* (New Delhi; Macmillan India Ltd, 2002)

Kampani, G., 'New Delhi's Long Nuclear Journey', *International Security*, Vol. 38, No. 4 (Spring 2014)

Kanwal, G., *Kargil '99: Blood Guts and Firepower* (New Delhi; Lancer, 2000)

Kanwal, G., 'Pakistan's Strategic Blunder at Kargil', *CLAWS Journal*, Summer 2009

Krishna, A., (ed.), *Kargil: The Tables Turned* (New Delhi; Manohar, 2001)

Lambeth, B., 'Airpower at 18,000': The Indian Air Force in the Kargil War', (Washington DC; Carnegie Endowment for International Peace, 2012)

Malik, V. P., *Kargil: From Surprise to Victory* (New Delhi; Harper Collins, 2009)

Malik, V. P., 'The Kargil War: Some Reflections', *CLAWS Journal*, Summer 2009

Nasim, Z., *From Kargil to Coup: Events that Shook Pakistan* (Lahore; Sang-e-Meel, 2018)

*Pakistan Army's Misadventure in Kargil* (New Delhi; Army Liaison Cell, Army Headquarters, 1999)

Perkovich, G., *India's Nuclear Bomb: The Impact on Global Proliferation* (London; University of California Press, 1999)

Prasad, S. N. (ed.), Operations in Jammu & Kashmir, 1947-48 (New Delhi; Natraj, 2005)

Prasad, S. N., Thapliyal, U. P. (ed.), The India-Pakistan War of 1965 (New Delhi; Natraj, 2011)

Prasad, S. N., Thapliyal, U. P. (ed.), The India-Pakistan War of 1971 (New Delhi; Natraj, 2014)

Puri, M., *Kargil: Turning the Tide* (New Delhi; Lancer, 2016)

Qadir, Shaukat, 'An Analysis of the Kargil Conflict 1999', *RUSI Journal*, April 2002

Rikhye, R., Singh, P., Steinemann, P., *Fiza'Ya: Psyche of the Pakistan Air Force* (New Delhi; S. A. S., 1991)

Sawant, G., *Dateline Kargil* (New Delhi; MacMillan, 2000)

Singh, A., *A Ridge Too Far: War in the Kargil Heights* (Patiala, Motibagh Palace, 1999: ASIN B0006E8KKW)

Subramaniam, L. N., 'A Ridge Too Far: Battle for Tololing', *Bharat-Rakshak.com*, 12 October 2006

*The Kargil Review Committee Report: From Surprise to Reckoning* (New Delhi; Sage, 1999)

Thomas, Lt Gen M., 'The RAPID: An Appraisal of India's new look Infantry Division for Warfare in the Plains', *Indian Defence Review*, January 1989

Tufail, K., 'Role of the Pakistan Air Force During the Kargil Conflict', *CLAWS Journal*, Summer 2009

Vinayak, R., 'Tololing Peak: The Battle that probably changed the course of the Kargil War', *India Today*, 5 July 1999

### Asia@War Volumes

Fontanellaz, A., *Paradise Afire, Volume 2: The Sri Lankan War, 1987-1990* (Warwick; Helion & Co., 2019)

Hamid, Maj Gen S. A., *At the Forward Edge of Battle: A History of the Pakistan Armoured Corps, 1938-2016, Volume 1* (Warwick; Helion & Co., 2019)

Hamid, Maj Gen S. A., *At the Forward Edge of Battle: A History of the Pakistan Armoured Corps, 1938-2016, Volume 2* (Warwick; Helion & Co., 2020)

Tufail, Air Cdre K., *Against all Odds: Pakistan Air Force in the 1971 Indo-Pakistan War* (Warwick; Helion & Co., 2020)

# Notes

### Introduction

1 For a detailed account, a good starting point is Prasad (ed.), *Operations in Jammu & Kashmir 1947-48* (details in Bibliography)
2 UN Security Council Resolution 47: The India-Pakistan Question.
3 Ibid.
4 Prasad et al, *The India-Pakistan War of 1965.*
5 Text of Tashkent Declaration (as available at https://mea.gov.in)
6 Prasad et al, *The India-Pakistan War of 1971.*
7 Editorial note: PAF dispute that the 1971 conflict was initiated by their preemptive strikes. See Kaiser Tufail, *Against All Odds* (fuller details in bibliography).
8 Simla Agreement July 2, 1972 (as available at https://mea.gov.in)
9 This will be the subject of a further Asia@War volume.
10 Brar, *Operation Blue Star.*
11 For an account of the early years of the Kashmir insurgency, see Joshi, *The Lost Rebellion.*
12 Gokhale, *Beyond NJ 9842.*
13 Bajpai et al, *Brasstacks and Beyond.*
14 Lahore Declaration February, 1999 ( available at https://mea.gov.in).

### Chapter 1

1 Badri-Maharaj, *The Armageddon Factor*, pp. 149-165.
2 IDR Research Team, 'Some thoughts on the Evolution of Infantry Organization and Tactics', *Indian Defence Review*, July 1991, pp. 51-53.
3 Ibid.
4 ORBAT taken from P. Sawhney, "If Pakistan and India Go to War," *The Asian Age*, November 12–13, 1994.
5 The Parachute Brigade has not been employed as a parachute deployed unit since 1971. but was deployed as a quick-reaction airborne unit during Operation Cactus in the Maldives in 1988.
6 P. Sawhney, "If Pakistan and India Go to War," *The Asian Age*, November 12–13, 1994.
7 Badri-Maharaj, *The Armageddon Factor*, pp. 169–195, (relevant sections are summarised herein).
8 The older tanks had already undergone minor upgrades. For example, both T-55s and Vijayantas received night-vision equipment, and the former had its 100mm gun replaced with the 105mm. Some of the Vljayantas had been given additional applique armour.
9 The L4A4 itself was a slightly modernized and re-chambered version of the Second World War vintage Bren Gun.
10 Thomas, '*The RAPID*', p. 92.
11 The five airborne infantry battalions of the Parachute Regiment were rotated to form a part of the brigade, alternatively serving their field tenures in COIN operations or high-altitude areas. One of the eight special forces battalions served in the brigade on rotation. One of the two field artillery regiments (9 Para Field Regiment and 17 Para Field Regiment) also formed part of the brigade while the other served out its field tenure on rotation. Artillery regiments were equipped with 105mm LFG guns while a number of BMP-2 ICVs were also available for paradropping operations as part of the regiment. 252 AD Battery used the Soviet-made 9K38 Igla-1M (ASCC/NATO-codename 'SA-16 Gimlet') man-portable air defence systems (MANPADs).
12 Indeed, each of the BMPs came with two TDP-1 decontamination kits; however, it remains unknown if the Indian Army maintained and replaced life-expired filters on them, or refurbished and replaced ageing decontamination kits.
13 Badri-Maharaj, *The Armageddon Factor*, pp. 169–195 (relevant sections are summarised herein).
14 Ibid.
15 This deal had been mired in controversy because of Russia's refusal to supply spares, including gun barrels, and doubts over Ukraine's ability to provide spares and support.
16 For a detailed history of the Pakistani Armoured Corps, see Hamid, *At the Forward Edge of Battle* (further details in Bibliography).
17 Maj. S. Bhaduri, 'Weapons Overview: The Artillery Division', *Indian Defence Review: Jan 1992*, p. 114.
18 IISS, *Military Balance: 1996-97*, p. 165.

### Chapter 2

1 This figure is a composite from available sources, one of the best being C. V. Gole 'The IAF in 2001', *Vayu Aerospace*, 1994, p. 42. However, in the early 1990s, two squadrons converted to the MiG-27, including one from MiG-23BNs. Therefore, available MiG-27 squadrons were Nos. 2, 9, 10, 18, 20, 22, 29 & 222. MiG-23BN squadrons were Nos. 31, 220 & 221. Jaguars were operated by Nos. 5, 6, 14, 16 and 27 squadrons.
2 Donald et al, *Encyclopaedia of World Military Aircraft*, p. 305.
3 Rikhye et al, *Fiza'Ya*, pp. 163-164.
4 Gunston, *The Osprey Encyclopedia of Russian Aircraft* & Donald et al, *Encyclopedia of World-Military Aircraft*
5 IISS, *The Military Balance 1996-1997*, p. 166 (London: Oxford University Press, 1996).
6 Rikhye et al, *Fiza'Ya*, pp. 133-134. The squadrons equipped with F-16s were Nos. 9, 11 & 14.
7 Ibid.
8 Donald et al, *Encyclopedia of World Military Aircraft, Volume 2*, p. 331.
9 IISS, *Military Balance 1996-97*, p. 166.
10 Compiled from details in D. Donald & J. Lake, *Encyclopaedia of World Military Aircraft – Volumes 1 &2.*
11 Badri-Maharaj, *The Armageddon Factor*, pp. 199-207.
12 S. P. Baranwal, *Military Yearbook 1990-1991* (Guide, New Delhi: 1991) p. 246. The MOPs were among the most reliable of the early-warning mechanisms available to the Indian Air Force.
13 J. Baranwal, *SP's Military Yearbook 1992-1993* (Guide: New Delhi 1993), p. SS 1-15 & p. 748.
14 Ibid. p. SS 13.
15 Notably, these radars were all long-range surveillance types with ranges in excess of 300km and good performance against targets flying at all altitudes – even those employing electronic countermeasures (ECM).
16 J. Baranwal, *SP's Military Yearbook 1992-1993* (Guide: New Delhi 1993), pp. SS. 1-15 & p. 748.
17 Ibid.
18 Badri-Maharaj, *The Armageddon Factor*, pp. 209-212.
19 Rikye & Steineman, *Fiza'Ya*, p. 95.
20 Ibid.
21 Ibid.
22 Ibid.
23 Ibid.
24 Ibid, p. 100.
25 Source for IAF and PAF ORBATs as of 1999 is Tom Cooper, who compiled the following tables on the basis of reports in contemporary specialised press.
26 Ibid.

### Chapter 3

1 Badri-Maharaj, *The Armageddon Factor* pp. 73-81.
2 'India goes Thermonuclear', http://www-fas-org, p. 2.
3 Ibid.
4 Ibid.
5 Wallace's report was discussed in the *Los Angeles Times*, 16 September 1998. An interesting point was made at the end of the article where an American nuclear weapons scientist indicated that even 15 kilotons could have been a thermonuclear device and said that the seismologists had an inadequate knowledge of nuclear weapons design.
6 The reports about the 1974 test having a yield of only two kilotons surfaced in an article back in 1981, in *The Sunday Observer* (30 August 1981 by Y. Aggarwal). While a few Western experts may cite this, there appears to be a consensus that the 1974 test had a yield of 8-12 kt.
7 D. Albright, The Shots heard round the world, *Bulletin of the Atomic Scientists*: July/August 1998.
8 'BARC scientists defend estimates of n-tests', *Hindu*, September 19 1998.
9 Ibid.
10 Ibid.
11 D. MacKenzie, 'Making Waves', *New Scientist*, 13 June 1998.
12 S. van Moyland & R-Clark, 'The Paper Trail', *Bulletin of the Atomic Scientists*, July/August 1998.
13 Ibid.
14 F. Barnaby, 'Trials provide data for range of weapon yields', *Jane's Defence Weekly*, 7 May 1998, p. 3.
15 Ibid.
16 Ibid.

17 L. Spector Nuclear Ambitions (Westview: Boulder, 1990). p.51; Albright & Hibbs, India's Silent Bomb', *Bulletin of the Atomic Scientists,* September 1992.
18 'South Asian Nuclear-Weapon-Free Zone', *The Arms Control Reporter 1993*, p. 454. B. 176
19 Badri-Maharaj, *The Armageddon Factor,* pp. 95-97.
20 http:/ /www.fas.org/guide/pakistan/nukeindex
21 F. Barnaby, 'Discrepancies claimed in Islamabad's nuclear tests', *Jane's Defence Weekly*, 9 June 1999.
22 Ibid.
23 Ibid.
24 Ibid.
25 Spector, *Nuclear Ambitions*, pp. 114-117
26 A. Haniffa, 'Experts Dubious on Ring Magnet Sales', *India Abroad*, February 23 1996, p. 26.
27 A. Dixit, 'Indian Defence Industry Programmes', *Military Technology*, 12/1994, p. 23.
28 R. Chengappa, 'The Missile Man', *India Today*, April 15 1994, p. 44.
29 Ibid.
30 India Missile Milestones: 1947-2012 (as available at https://www.wisconsinproject.org)
31 Agni-II description as available at https://www.bharat-rakshak.com
32 Chengappa, *Weapons of Peace*, pp. 383-384.
33 Ibid, p. 327.
34 Ibid, pp. 382-384.
35 Ibid, p. 303.
36 G. Kampani, 'New Delhi's Long Nuclear Journey', *International Security*, Vol. 38, No. 4 (Spring 2014), p. 91 and Kargil Review Committee, *From Surprise to Reckoning*, p. 190. The committee reported that estimates of the "number of cores/devices/weapons in Pakistan's possession" varied in different intelligence reports and assessments prepared for the government.
37 G. Kampani, 'New Delhi's Long Nuclear Journey', *International Security*, Vol. 38, No. 4 (Spring 2014), p. 91-92.
38 Ibid, p. 102.
39 Ibid, p. 103.
40 Ibid, pp. 103-104.
41 Chengappa, *Weapons of Peace*, pp. 437-438.
42 *Jane's Defence Weekly*, 15 April 1989, p. 635.
43 *Indian Express*, I February 1997.
44 State Department (USA), *Report to Congress*, January – June 1999. Unclassified Report to Congress on the Acquisition of Technology Relating to Weapons of Mass Destruction and Advanced Conventional Munitions.
45 'Pakistan Fires Medium Range Ballistic Missile, *Defense News,* 28 November 2012.
46 Ibid, pp. 371-372.
47 Perkovich, *India's Nuclear Bomb*, p. 242.
48 Karnad, *Nuclear Weapons and Indian Security*, p. 320.
49 'India capable of building nuke deterrence upto 200 kilotons: Kakodkar', *Deccan Herald,* 24 September 2009.
50 'Pakistan was to deploy nukes against India during Kargil war', *Economic Times of India*, 12 July 2018.

### Chapter 4

1 M. Thomas, "An Analysis of the Threat Perception and Strategy for India," *Indian Defence Review,* January 1990, p. 63.
2 Ibid.
3 S. Bhaduri, 'The Artillery Division – Part III', *Indian Defence Review*, April 1992, p. 118.
4 Thomas, 'An Analysis of the Threat Perception and Strategy for India', p. 63.
5 W. P. S. Sidhu, 'Chinks in the Armour', p. 129 in *India Today,* November 15, 1991.
6 P. Sawhney, 'If Pakistan and India go to War', *The Asian Age,* 12-13 November 1994, p. 13.
7 P. Sawhney, 'Prithvi's Position: India Defends its Missile', *International Defence,* Review July 1997, p. 45.
8 Ibid.
9 M. Thomas, 'An Analysis of the Threat Perception and Strategy', p. 63.
10 Cloughley, 'Pakistan strives to match aims and capabilities', *International Defence Review: March 1995*, p. 73.
11 P. Sawhney, "If Pakistan and India Go to War," *The Asian Age,* November 12–13, 1994, p. 13.
12 Ibid.
13 Ibid.
14 Ibid.
15 IDR Research Team, "Operational Scenario Alpha," *Indian Defence Review,* July 1992, p. 22.
16 Ibid.
17 V.P. Malik, *Lessons from Kargil* (as available at https://web.archive.org/web/20090408082728/http://www.bharat-rakshak.com/MONITOR/ISSUE4-6/malik.html)
18 Shaukat Qadir, 'An Analysis of the Kargil Conflict 1999', *RUSI Journal*, April 2002, p. 26.
19 'Kargil planned before Vajpayee's visit: Musharraf', *Indian Express*, 13 July 2006.
20 'How I Started A War', *Time*, 12 July 1999.
21 V.P. Malik, *Lessons from Kargil.*
22 Gurmeet Kanwal, 'Pakistan's Strategic Blunder at Kargil', *CLAWS Journal*, Summer 2009 pp. 55-56.
23 V.P. Malik, 'Kargil: where defence met diplomacy', *Indian Express*, 25 July 2002.
24 V.P. Malik, 'The Kargil War: Some Reflections', *CLAWS Journal,* Summer 2009, pp. 2-5.
25 That said, Lieutenant-General Javed Nasir, former chief of the Pakistan's Inter Service Intelligence, wrote on 26 June 1999, 'They occupied the vacant Kargil heights as early as January-February this year and kept building stocks and improving defences for the next four months' (see *Islamisation of Pakistan's Military*, published by the Army Liaison Cell, Army Headquarters, New Delhi, p. 16). This in turn indicates not only an earlier intrusion, i.e. an operation put into effect well before the peace efforts of early 1999, but also the level of disconnect between the civil and military leadership of Pakistan.
26 Ravi Rikhye, 'The Northern Light Infantry in the Kargil Operations', ORBAT.com, 25 August 2002.
27 In 1973, the Northern Scouts, Karakoram Scouts and Gilgit Scouts were reorganized as the Northern Light Infantry (NLI) regiment of the Pakistan Army. Almost 85% of NLI troops were from Gilgit and Baltistan and 49% were Shi'a Muslims. The NLI battalions specialised in commando operations, snow warfare and anti-heliborne operations. For details see *Pakistan Army's Misadventure in Kargil* (New Delhi: Army Liaison Cell, Army Headquarters, p. 8.
28 However, some Pakistani sources suggest that this was a 'Pakistan Army only' operation, with minimal or no involvement of any kind of Islamist militants. For example, see 'No Mujahideen: Our Soldiers took part in Kargil: Pak ex-Gen', *The Tribune*, 28 January 2013.
29 Shahid Aziz, 'Putting our children in line of fire', *The Nation*, 6 January 2013.
30 On the contrary, V.P. Malik in *Lessons from Kargil* estimated the initial incursion as involving 1,700 troops from the NLI, while others (like Ashok Mehta, *The Kargil Victory*), suggested that the Islamist militants alone counted about 2,000 combatants, alongside a full brigade of the NLI.
31 Gurmeet Kanwal, 'Pakistan's Strategic Blunder at Kargil', *CLAWS Journal*, Summer 2009, pp. 63-64.
32 As per Indian Army Headquarters estimates, a total of 20 artillery batteries were provided to the NLI battalions for supporting the intrusions. *Pak Army Plan for Intrusions*, (New Delhi: Army Liaison Cell, Army Headquarters) p. 4.
33 Dinesh Kumar, "What it Took and the Run-up to Operation Vijay", *The Times of India, July 19, 1999.*
34 'Saurabh Kalia's parents waging a lone battle to highlight war crimes', *Hindu.com*, 15 June 2012.
35 Gurmeet Kanwal, 'Pakistan's Strategic Blunder at Kargil', *CLAWS Journal*, Summer 2009 p. 57.
36 Ibid.

### Chapter 5

1 'Intelligence failure led to Kargil war: former Lt General', *Economic Times*, 14 January 2019.
2 Kargil Review Committee Executive Summary (available at nuclearweaponsarchive.org)
3 B. Raman, 'Was there an Intelligence Failure?', *Frontline*, Vol.16/Issue 15, 17 July 1999.
4 Ibid.
5 A full transcript of the 'Musharraf Tapes' can be found in Major General Ashok Krishna (ed.), *Kargil: The Tables Turned* (New Delhi, Manohar, 2001), pp. 315-320.
6 Ibid, p. 317.
7 Ibid, p. 319.

### Chapter 6

1 'Indian Army, Kargil War 1999', ORBAT.com
2 Flying units subsequently received battle honours while ground installations and units received theatre honours. Ten flying units received battle honours while five radar/signal units, two air force stations, and one forward base support unit received theatre honours.
3 Based on reporting by bharat-rakshak.com
4 Amarinder Singh, *A Ridge Too Far: War in the Kargil Heights 1999 (*Patiala: Motibagh Palace, 2001), pp. 42-43.

### Chapter 7

1 Ibid, p. 27.
2 Ibid, p. 28.
3 Ibid, 30-31.
4 Ibid, pp. 54-55.
5 Ibid.
6 Ibid.
7 Courtesy Brigadier Gurmeet Kanwal.
8 Amarinder Singh, *A Ridge Too Far: War in the Kargil Heights 1999,* p. 58.
9 Ibid, p. 59.
10 Ibid.
11 Ibid.
12 Ibid, pp. 69-70.
13 Ibid, p. 73.

14 Ibid, p. 57.
15 L.N. Subramaniam, 'A Ridge Too Far: Battle for Tololing', *Bharat-Rakshak.com*, 12 October 2006
16 Ibid.
17 For additional details on the operations in the Dras, Mushkoh and Kaksar Sectors, the author would like to express his gratitude to Brigadier-Genral Gurmeet Kanwal.
18 Ramesh Vinayak, Tololing Peak: The battle that probably changed the course of Kargil war, *India Today,* 5 July 1999.
19 Subramaniam, 'A Ridge Too Far'
20 Vinayak, 'Tololing Peak'
21 Ibid.
22 Ibid.
23 Subramaniam, 'A Ridge Too Far'
24 Singh, *A Ridge Too Far*, p. 229.
25 Ibid pp.120-123.
26 Interview with Brigadier Kushal Thakur, 2 October 2019.
27 Interview with Colonel Balwan Singh, 2 October 2019.
28 Subramaniam, 'A Ridge Too Far'
29 Ibid.
30 Interview with one of the officers involved, provided on condition of anonymity, 3 October 2019.
31 Vinayak, 'Tololing Peak'
32 Ibid.
33 Ibid.
34 Subramaniam, 'A Ridge Too Far'
35 Ibid.
36 Vinayak, 'Tololing Peak'
37 Ibid.
38 Subramaniam, 'A Ridge Too Far'
39 Singh, *A Ridge Too Far,* pp. 77-78.
40 Ibid.
41 Ibid, pp. 80-84.
42 Ibid, p. 94.
43 Ibid.
44 Ibid p. 95.
45 Ibid p. 198.
46 Ibid.
47 Interview with Colonel Lalit Rai, 2 October 2019.
48 Singh, *A Ridge Too Far*, p. 199
49 Ibid.
50 Singh, *A Ridge Too Far*, pp.201-202, & U. Shekhar, e-mail interview, 9 October 2019.
51 Singh, *A Ridge Too Far*, pp. 203-204.
52 Ibid, p. 205.
53 Ibid.
54 Ibid, pp. 206-208.
55 Ibid, pp. 209-211.
56 Singh, *A Ridge Too Far,* p.79.
57 Ibid.
58 Ibid, p. 80
59 Ibid.
60 V.P. Malik, 'The capture of Tiger Hill: A First-Hand Account', *Ministry of External Affairs*, 26 July 2002.
61 Ibid.
62 Singh, *A Ridge Too Far*, pp. 88-89.
63 Ibid.
64 Ibid, pp. 89-90.
65 Ibid.
66 Ibid.
67 Ibid.
68 Ibid.
69 Ibid, pp. 95-96.
70 V.P. Malik, 'Kargil: From Surprise to Victory' (Harper Collins: New Delhi, 2009), p. 185.
71 Ibid, p. 186.
72 Ibid, p. 187.
73 Singh, *A Ridge Too Far,* p. 101 A note here – the term JCO means Junior Commissioned Officer and is a rank unique to the armies of India and Pakistan, dating to the British Indian Army. JCOs have no Western equivalent except perhaps, to an extent, Warrant Officers. The very high officer casualties proportionate to the others reflects a tendency of Indian officers to lead assaults personally even at platoon and section level.
74 Singh, *A Ridge Too Far,* pp. 173-196.
75 Singh, *A Ridge Too Far,* p. 102 & o p. 216.
76 Pranab Dhal Samanta, 'Musharraf now has Pak's Kargil toll: 357', *Indian Express,* 7 October 2006; 'Ill-Conceived planning by Musharraf led to second major military defeat in Kargil: PML-N', *Pakistan Tribune,* 6 August 2006; 'Pak makes it official, names 453 soldiers killed in Kargil War, *Hinudstan Times,* 18 November 2010.
77 Gurmeet Kanwal, 'Pakistan's Strategic Blunder at Kargil', CLAWS Journal, Summer 2009, pp. 63-64.

## Chapter 8

1 'How artillery changed the tide of the Kargil War', *Economic Times,* 13 July 2018.
2 Ishfaq Ul-Hassan, 'Indian Army fired 2.5 lakh Shells to bomb Enemy Positions in Kargil War', *DNA India*, 26 July 2016.
3 Ibid.
4 Ibid.
5 Ibid.
6 Kanwal, *Kargil '99*, pp. 69-70.
7 Alok Deb, 'Artillery in Op-Vijay', in V.K. Ahluwaia and Singh, *Surprise, Strategy and Vijay*, p. 83.

## Chapter9

1 Lambeth, 'Airpower at 18,000', p. 26.
2 Tufail, 'Role of the Pakistan Air Force During the Kargil Conflict', pp. 104-106.
3 P. S. Ahluwalia, 'How Indian Air Force made History with the Kargil War', *Daily 0*, 24 July 2015.
4 R. K. Simha, 'How the IAF Dominated the Skies during Kargil War', *rbth.com*, 26 July 2016.
5 'India loses two Jets', BBC, 27 May 1999.
6 Philip Camp, 'The Mirage 2000 in Kargil', *bharat-rakshak.com*, 16 October 2009.
7 Ibid.
8 Ved Shenag, 'Operation Safed Sagar', *bharat-rakshak.com*, 16 October 2009.
9 Camp, 'The Mirage 2000 in Kargil'
10 Ibid.
11 Ibid.
12 Lambeth, *Airpower at 18,000*, p 26.
13 Ibid.
14 Ibid.
15 Ibid.
16 M Kaiser Tufail "Role of the Pakistan Air Force During the Kargil Conflict" *CLAWS Journal l Summer 2009* pp. 108-110.
17 Ibid.
18 Ibid.

## Chapter 10

1 A. G. Noorani, 'Kargil Diplomacy', *Frontline*, 13 August 1999.
2 B. Riedel, 'American Diplomacy and the 1999 Kargil Sumit at Blair House' (University of Pennsylvania: Centre for the Advanced Study of India, 2002), p. 5.
3 Ibid, p. 6.
4 Ibid pp. 12-13.
5 Khaleeq Kiani, 'Kargil Adventure was a Four-Man Show', *Dawn*, 28 January 2013.